CRIMINAL MINDS

ARTHUR FLEGENHEIMER
ALIASES DUTCH SCHULTZ, ARTHUR SCHUL
GEORGE SCHULTZ, JOSEPH HARMON AN
CHARLES HARMON

Publications International, Ltd.

Let's get social!

 @Publications_International

 @PublicationsInternational

www.pilbooks.com

Table of Contents

Crime and Punishment

Forgeries, jewel heists, bigamy, crimes of passion, serial killings, mob extortion, assassinations, political corruption, counterfeiting, money laundering, con artistry, and more—you'll find crimes of all kind described in these pages. Some are funny, some horrific. Some took place centuries ago yet still pique our interest, while others were headline topics within our lifetime. With eight chapters divided into different themes, you'll find an assortment of crimes, criminals, and other crime-related topics such as investigations and forensic.

Read about:

- How H. H. Holmes brought horror to the World's Fair (page 17)

- The Ohio serial killer case that Eliot Ness couldn't solve (page 32)

- Secrets of "The Body Farm" (page 83)

- The man who married more than 40 women—many of whom he murdered (page 127)

- The time when Charlie Chaplin's coffin was stolen for ransom (page 170)

- The thief who hid diamonds from detection in his soup bowl and was drawn to a perfect string of pearls (page 229)

- The crimes of the real Mr. Ponzi (page 258)

Criminal Minds will inform, entertain, and quite possibly scare you. Dive right in.

H. H. Holmes

Chapter 1

Someone Wicked This Way Comes

Mass Murderers vs. Serial Killers

Serial killers are made of sugar and spice and everything nice, and mass murderers are . . . wait, that's not right. The distinction between the two is actually very simple.

The Mass Murderer

A mass murderer kills four or more people during a short period of time, usually in one location. In most cases, the murderer has a sudden mental collapse and goes on a rampage, progressing from murder to murder without a break. About half the time, these outbreaks end in suicides or fatal standoffs with the police.

Various school shootings over the years have been instances of mass murder, as have been famous cases of postal workers, well, "going postal." A case in which someone murders his or her entire family is a mass murder. Terrorists are lumped into this category as well, but they also make up a group of their own.

The Serial Killer

A serial killer usually murders one person at a time (typically a stranger), with a "cooling off" period between each transgression. Unlike mass murderers, serial killers don't suddenly snap one day—they have an ongoing compulsion (usually with a sexual component) that drives them to kill, often in very specific ways. Serial killers may even maintain jobs and normal relationships while going to great lengths to conceal their killings. They may resist the urge to kill for long periods, but the compulsion ultimately grows too strong to subjugate. After the third victim, an aspiring killer graduates from plain ol' murderer to bona fide serial killer.

The Rest

In between these two groups, we have the spree killer and the serial spree killer. A spree killer commits murder in multiple locations over the course of a few days. This is often part of a general crime wave. For example, an escaped convict may kill multiple people, steal cars, jaywalk, and litter as he tries to escape the police. As with a mass murderer, a spree killer doesn't plan each murder individually.

The serial spree killer, on the other hand, plans and commits each murder separately, serial-killer style. But he or she doesn't take time off between murders or maintain a double life. It's all killing, all the time. One of the best-known examples is the Washington, D.C.-area beltway snipers who killed ten people within three weeks in October 2002.

Of course, if you see any of these types of killer in action, don't worry about remembering the right term when you call the police. They're all equally bad.

The Butcher and the Thief

Meet the two charming fellows who inspired the children's rhyme: "Burke's the Butcher, Hare's the Thief, Knox the boy that buys the beef."

The Cadaver Crunch

In the 1820s, Edinburgh, Scotland, was suffering from a "cadaver crunch." Considering the city was regarded as a center of medical education, the lack of bodies for students to dissect in anatomy classes posed a problem. At the time, the only legal source of corpses for dissection in Britain was executed criminals. Interestingly, at the same time that enrollment in medical schools was rising (as well as the need for cadavers), the number of executions was decreasing. This was due to the repeal of the so-called "Bloody Code," which by 1815 listed more than 200 capital offenses.

The growing need for corpses created a grisly new occupation. "Resurrection Men" dug up the newly buried dead and sold the bodies to medical schools. William Burke and William Hare decided to cut out the middleman: Over the course of a year, they murdered at least 15 people in order to sell their bodies.

A Grisly Business

The pair fell into the cadaver supply business on November 29, 1827. At the time, Hare was running a cheap boarding house in an Edinburgh slum. Burke was his tenant and drinking buddy. When one of Hare's tenants died still owing four pounds, Hare and Burke stole the tenant's corpse from his coffin and sold it to recover the back rent. Dr. Robert Knox, who taught anatomy to 500 students at Edinburgh Medical College, paid more than seven pounds for the body.

Encouraged by the profit, Burke and Hare looked for other bodies to sell to Knox. Their first victim was another tenant at the boarding house, who fell ill a few days later. Burke and Hare "comforted" the sick man with whiskey until he passed out, and then smothered him. The result was a body that looked like it had died of drunkenness, with no obvious marks of foul play.

Over the course of the next year, Burke and Hare lured more victims into the lodging house. They sold the bodies to Knox, who not only accepted them without question, but increased the pair's payment to ten pounds because of the "freshness" of the bodies they provided.

Their initial targets were strangers to Edinburgh, but Burke and Hare soon began to take more risks, murdering local prostitutes and "Daft Jamie," a well-known neighborhood character. People began to talk about the disappearances, and Knox's students began to recognize the bodies brought to them for dissection.

The End of Burke and Hare

Burke and Hare's mercenary killings ended on October 31, 1828, when Burke lured an old Irish woman named Mary Docherty to the house. James and Ann Gray, who were also boarders at the time, met Docherty there. Docherty was invited to spend the night, and arrangements were made for the Grays to board elsewhere. The next morning, the Grays returned and found the old woman's body under the bed. Although they were offered a bribe of ten pounds a week to keep quiet, the Grays ran for the police.

Hare testified against Burke in exchange for immunity. He was released in February 1829 and disappeared from the historical record, though popular legend claims he ended his life a blind beggar on the streets of London. Burke was tried for murder, found guilty, and hanged. Although there was no evidence that Knox had any knowledge of the murders, angry crowds appeared at his lectures and tore his effigy to shreds. He eventually moved to London.

Fittingly, Burke's corpse was turned over to the Edinburgh Medical College for "useful dissection." A bit more oddly, skin from his body was used to bind a small book.

The murders eventually led to the passage of the Anatomy Act of 1832, which provided new legal sources for medical cadavers and eliminated the profit motive that drove Burke and Hare to murder.

More Than a Minor Contribution

How a Civil War surgeon-turned-madman helped shape our understanding of the English language.

An Unlikely Contributor

The *Oxford English Dictionary* (OED) is widely considered the definitive record of the English language. For more than a century, readers have turned to it to understand and pronounce millions of words.

Less well known, however, is the fact that one of its earliest and most important contributors was William Chester Minor, a Civil War surgeon who murdered a man in England, sliced off his own penis, and wrote all his contributions for the world-renowned dictionary while locked inside the padded walls of an insane asylum.

The son of Congregational Church missionaries, Minor was born in Ceylon (now Sri Lanka) in June 1834. At age 14, he was sent to the United States to attend medical school at Yale. After graduation, he enlisted in the U.S. Army, where he served as a physician during some of the Civil War's fiercest skirmishes, including the bloody Battle of the Wilderness in 1864.

The Definition of Madness

Though he had admitted to previously having had "lascivious thoughts" in Ceylon, there is some speculation that exposure to the brutality of war hastened Minor's descent into madness. Whatever the case, he wound up in New York City shortly after the war. While there he developed an unhealthy taste for prostitutes and other assorted "pleasures" found in the city's less savory areas.

By 1868, his erratic behavior landed him in St. Elizabeth's asylum in Washington, D.C. Soon after his release, Minor was relieved of his military commission. He eventually settled overseas in London. If the move to England was intended to halt his increasing insanity, it failed—a year after his relocation, Minor shot and killed George Merrett, whom he suspected of breaking into his home. After a subsequent jury found Minor not guilty by reason of insanity, he was marched off to England's Broadmoor asylum in Berkshire.

A New Hobby

Because of his military pension he was afforded comfortable quarters at Broadmoor, including two rooms, one of which he constructed into a library to house his growing collection of books. Shortly after his "incarceration," a public request was released, asking for volunteers to contribute to the OED. With plenty of free time on his hands and a large collection of books at his disposal, Minor began enthusiastically contributing entries to the fledgling dictionary—a pastime that would take up most of the remainder of his life.

For the next two decades Minor pored through his library, finding quotations for thousands of words in the dictionary by keeping lists of recurring words that matched the current needs of the OED. Minor's lists became so prolific that the editors of the OED eventually just sent Minor their lists of words they needed filled.

Minor's contributions, said to have numbered more than 10,000 entries, were so frequent and numerous that he eventually developed a friendship with the OED's editor, Dr. James Murray, who made the trip to Broadmoor to visit the institutionalized contributor. Murray would later say that Minor's contribution to the OED was so enormous that it "could easily have illustrated the last four centuries [of words] from his quotations alone."

Further Descent

Whatever satisfaction Minor took from his meaningful work on the OED, it did nothing to stop his lunacy, which had grown to such a state that he amputated his own penis in 1902. Still, Murray helped guarantee Minor's release from Broadmoor, which was approved by Home Secretary Winston

Churchill in 1910. Upon his liberation from the asylum, Minor returned to America, where he would remain until his death in 1920.

Jack the Ripper's Eerie Austin Connection

Could America's first serial killer be one of Austin's best-kept and most grisly secrets?

Before Jack the Ripper made his bloody trail through London, Austin experienced a similar murder spree. The Ripper-like murders began on New Year's Eve, 1884. Someone killed Mollie Smith, a servant girl, and put a large hole in her head. Two more women were butchered in similar attacks a few months later.

A Trail of Blood

The killings weren't limited to servants, however. As the Austin murder spree continued, victims became more upscale. Each death was a little more gory. The final murders recorded occurred on Christmas Eve, 1885, almost a full year after they had begun. The victims included Mrs. Eula Phillips, a wealthy woman who—for amusement—worked as a prostitute.

To stop the binge of killing, Austin police began questioning men on the streets after dark. The city erected "moonlight towers" to illuminate the streets. Seventeen of those towers still light downtown Austin and are listed in the National Register of Historic Places. The city's efforts were apparently successful, as the slaughter ended.

The Whitechapel Murders

Jack the Ripper began killing women in London as early as the day after Christmas in 1887. It could be coincidence, but the Ripper's physical description, style of killing, and victims seemed eerily similar to the Austin murders. Possible killers included a man called "the Malay Cook," who left Austin late in January 1886 and was interviewed in London in 1888. According to that interview, he said he'd been robbed by a woman "of bad character." Unless he recovered his money, he planned to murder and mutilate women in London's Whitechapel area.

No one knows if Austin was the training ground for Jack the Ripper, of course, but the possibility is chilling.

The Lizzie Borden Murder Mystery

Most people know the rhyme that begins, "Lizzie Borden took an ax and gave her mother 40 whacks..." In reality, approximately 20 hatchet chops cut down Abby Borden, but no matter the number, Lizzie's stepmother was very much dead on that sultry August morning in 1892. Lizzie's father, Andrew, was killed about an hour later. His life was cut short by about a dozen hatchet chops to the head. No one knows who was guilty of these murders, but Lizzie has always carried the burden of suspicion.

Andrew Borden, an American "Scrooge"

Andrew Jackson Borden had been one of the richest men in Fall River, Massachusetts, with a net worth of nearly half a million dollars. In 1892, that was enormous wealth. Andrew was a shrewd businessman: at the time of his death, he was the president of the Union Savings Bank and director of another bank plus several profitable cotton mills.

Despite his wealth, Andrew was miserly. Though some of his neighbors' homes had running hot water, the three-story Borden home had just two cold-water taps, and there was no water available above the first floor. The Bordens' only latrine was in the cellar, so they generally used chamber pots that were either dumped onto the lawn behind the house or emptied into the cellar toilet. And, although most wealthy people used gas lighting by that point in time, the Bordens lit their house with inexpensive kerosene lamps.

Worst of all, for many years, Andrew was an undertaker who offered some of the lowest prices in town. He worked on the bodies in the basement of the Borden home, and allegedly, he bent the knees of the deceased—and in some cases, cut off their feet—to fit the bodies into smaller, less expensive coffins in order to increase his business.

So, despite the brutality of Andrew's murder, it seems few people mourned his loss. The question wasn't why he was killed, but who did it.

Lizzie vs. William

In 1997, when psychic Jane Doherty visited the murder site, she uncovered several clues about the Lizzie Borden case. Doherty felt that the real murderer was someone named "Willie." There is no real evidence to support this claim, but some say Andrew had an illegitimate son named William, who may have spent time as an inmate in an insane asylum. His constant companion was reportedly his hatchet, which he talked to as though it were a friend. Also, at least one witness reportedly saw William at the Borden house on the day of the murders. William was supposedly there to challenge Andrew about his new will.

Was William the killer? A few years after the murders, William took poison and then hung himself in the woods. Near his swinging body, he'd reportedly left his hatchet on the ground. So with William dead and Lizzie already acquitted, the Borden murder case was put to rest.

Lizzie's Forbidden Romance

One of the most curious explanations for the murder involves the Bordens' servant Bridget Sullivan. Her participation has always raised questions. Like the other members of the Borden household, Bridget had suffered from apparent food poisoning the night before the murders. She claimed to have been ill in the backyard of the Borden home.

During the time Abby was being murdered, Bridget was apparently washing windows in the back of the house. Later, when Andrew was killed, Bridget was resting in her room upstairs. Why didn't she hear two people being butchered?

According to some theories, Lizzie and Bridget had been romantically involved. In this version of the story, their relationship was discovered shortly before the murders. Around this same time, Andrew was reportedly rewriting his will. His wife was now "Mrs. Borden," to Lizzie, not "Mother," as Lizzie had called her stepmother for many years. The reason for the estrangement was never clear.

Lizzie also had a strange relationship with her father and had given him her high school ring, as though he were her sweetheart. He wore the ring on his pinky finger and was buried with it.

Just a day before the murders, Lizzie had been attempting to purchase prussic acid—a deadly poison—and the family came down with "food poisoning" that night. Some speculate that Bridget was Lizzie's accomplice in the murders and helped clean up the blood afterward.

This theory was bolstered when, a few years after the murders, Lizzie became involved with actress Nance O'Neil. For two years, Lizzie and the statuesque actress were inseparable. This prompted Emma Borden, Lizzie's sister, to move out of their shared home.

At the time, the rift between the sisters sparked rumors that either Lizzie or Emma might reveal more about the other's role in the 1892 murders. However, neither of them said anything new about the killings.

Whodunit?

Most people believe that Lizzie was the killer. She was the only one accused of the crime, with good reason. Lizzie appeared to be the only one in the house at the time, other than Bridget. She showed no signs of grief when the murders were discovered. During questioning, Lizzie changed her story several times. The evidence was entirely circumstantial, but it was compelling enough to go to trial.

Ultimately, the jury accepted her attorney's closing argument, that the murders were "morally and physically impossible for this young woman defendant." In other words, Lizzie had to be innocent because she was petite and well bred. In 19th-century New England, that seemed like a logical and persuasive defense. As a consequence, Lizzie went free, and no one else was charged with the crimes.

But Lizzie wasn't the only one with motive, means, and opportunity. The most likely suspects were family members, working alone or with other relatives. Only a few had solid alibis, and—like Lizzie—many changed their stories during police questioning. But there was never enough evidence to officially accuse anyone other than Lizzie.

So whether or not Lizzie Borden truly "took an ax" and killed her parents, she's the one best remembered for the crime.

Lizzie Borden Bed & Breakfast

The Borden house has been sold several times over the years, but today it is a bed-and-breakfast—the main draw, of course, being the building's macabre history. The Victorian residence has been restored to reflect the details of the Borden home at the time of the murders, including the couch on which Andrew lay, his skull hideously smashed.

As a guest, you can stay in one of six rooms, even the one in which Abby was murdered. Then, after a good night's sleep, you'll be treated to a breakfast reminiscent of the one the

Bordens had on their final morning in 1892. That is, if you got to sleep at all. (They say the place is haunted.)

As with all good morbid attractions, the proprietors at the Lizzie Borden B&B don't take themselves too seriously. Before you leave, you can stop by the gift shop and pick up a pair of hatchet earrings, an "I Survived the Night at the Lizzie Borden Bed & Breakfast" T-shirt, or an ax-wielding Lizzie Borden bobblehead doll.

Come into My Parlor

H. H. Holmes has secured a place in history as one of the most horrifyingly prolific killers the world has ever seen.

Born in May 1860 in New Hampshire, Herman Webster Mudgett was a highly intelligent child, but he was constantly in trouble. Charming, handsome, and charismatic, he nonetheless displayed traits of detachment and dispassion from an early age. As a teen, he became abusive to animals—a classic sign of a sociopath.

Fascinated with skeletons and the human body, Mudgett decided to pursue a medical degree. After marrying Clara Lovering, he enrolled in medical school. There, he had access to skeletons and cadavers. He came up with a scheme to fleece insurance companies by taking out policies for family members or friends, using stolen cadavers to fake their deaths, and collecting the insurance money.

When authorities became suspicious, he abandoned Clara and their newborn baby, moving from city to city and taking on various jobs, most likely scheming and manipulating everyone he crossed. In 1886, the charming liar and thief with murderous intentions surfaced in Chicago with a new name: H. H. Holmes. The city would become the site of his deadliest swindle of all.

A "Castle" with a Most Intriguing Floor Plan

If you lived in Chicago in the late 1800s, you were likely consumed with thoughts of the World's Columbian Exposition. Planners hoped it would make America a superstar country and put Chicago on the map as an A-list city. The Great Fire of 1871 had demolished the town, but the fair would bring the city back—and in a big way.

With new people flooding into the city every day looking to nab one of the world's fair jobs, Chicago was experiencing a population boom that made it very easy for people to simply vanish. The handsome and charismatic Holmes recognized this as an opportunity to lure women into his clutches while most people had their focus elsewhere.

He married his second wife, Myrta, in 1887, without ever securing a divorce from Lovering. Holmes quickly shipped Myrta off to live in suburban Wilmette, while he took up residence in Chicago, free to do as he pleased. He secured a position as a pharmacist at a drugstore in Englewood. He worked for the elderly Mrs. Holden, who was happy to have a handsome young doctor to help out at her store. When Mrs. Holden suddenly disappeared, Holmes told people she had moved to California, and he purchased the store.

Next, Holmes purchased a vacant lot across the street from the drugstore and began constructing a house with a floor plan he designed himself. The three-story house at 63rd and Wallace would have more than 60 rooms and 50 doors, secret passageways, gas pipes with nozzles that piped noxious fumes into windowless rooms, chutes that led down to the basement, and an airtight vault.

To add insult to inury, Holmes hired and fired construction crews on a regular basis; it was said that his swindler's streak got him out of paying for most of the materials and labor used to create this "Murder Castle."

Up & Running

Advertised as a lodging for world's fair tourists, the building opened in 1892. Holmes placed ads in the newspaper to rent rooms, but also listed classified ads calling for females interested in working for a start-up company. Of course, there was no start-up company, and Holmes hired the prettiest women or those who could offer him some sort of financial gain. One by one, they inevitably succumbed to his charm. He made false promises to woman after woman, luring them deeper into his confidence. He took advantage of their naïveté to gain their trust and steal their money.

When he was done with a woman, either because she became suspicious of him or because he had gotten what he needed from her, Holmes got rid of her—without remorse or emotion. Sometimes he piped gas into a victim's room to kill her in her sleep; other times he locked her in his airtight vault and listened as she slowly suffocated. Evidence shows he tortured some of them before killing them. After he had brutalized the unfortunate soul, he destroyed the evidence in a vat of acid or a kiln he had built expressly for that purpose, often selling his victims' bones and organs to contacts in the medical field.

The End of "Doctor Death"

After the world's fair ended, creditors put pressure on Holmes, and he knew it was time to flee. Strange as it seems, when Holmes was finally brought to justice, it wasn't initially for homicide; it was for one of his many financial swindles. But as clues about missing women emerged, investigators became suspicious of him for other reasons.

Detective Frank Geyer began to follow the trail of this mysterious man whose identity changed with the weather. Geyer had traced many missing world's fair women back to Holmes's lodging house. He was particularly interested in the whereabouts of three children—Howard, Nellie, and Alice Pietzel. Geyer followed their tracks across the Midwest and into Canada. In Toronto he finally found a house where Holmes had allegedly stayed with several children in tow. Buried in a shallow grave in the backyard, stuffed in a single traveling trunk, he discovered the bodies of the two Pietzel girls. Geyer found the boy's remains several months later in an oven in a home in Indianapolis, Indiana.

When the evidence was brought back to court, Geyer got full clearance to investigate every inch of Holmes's Chicago dwelling. The investigation turned up a lot more than detectives anticipated, and one of America's most chilling stories of murder and crime officially broke.

Inside his heavily guarded cell, Herman Webster Mudgett admitted his crimes. He officially confessed to 27 murders, six attempted murders, and a whole lot of fraud. What he didn't confess to, however, were any feelings of remorse. Holmes was executed by hanging in 1896. He was buried in Holy Cross Cemetery near Philadelphia in a coffin lined with cement, topped with more cement, and buried in a double grave—per his own request. Was he ready to rest eternally after a life of such monstrosity? Or was he afraid that someone would conduct experiments on him as he had done to so many of his hapless victims?

"I was born with the devil in me. I could not help the fact that I was a murderer, no more than the poet can help the inspiration to sing."

—H. H. HOLMES

Chicago Killers

Holmes was far from Chicago's only infamous killer. Some of the most notorious names in American crime were born and bred in the city and its surrounding suburbs.

Not the Superhero Black Widow

I love you—really, I do: Chicagoan Tillie Klimek poisoned her husband, remarried, and then did the same thing three more times, collecting life insurance and claiming that she'd foreseen her husbands' deaths in her dreams. Earning her the monikers "Black Widow" and "Mrs. Bluebeard," Klimek is also suspected of having murdered a handful of her children, cousins, and a boyfriend who didn't take the bait. She was sentenced to life in prison in 1922 and died in 1936.

"Supermen" They Weren't

Richard Loeb and Nathan Leopold grew up in the Kenwood neighborhood. Loeb's father was a Sears, Roebuck & Co. vice president, Leopold's was a wealthy box manufacturer. Loeb was obsessed with crime novels, and Leopold was obsessed with Loeb—and with the idea of Nietzsche's superman, a superior individual who was above the law and could do as he pleased. Leopold believed that a superman could even commit murder. When Loeb conceived of the idea to attempt a perfect crime— one for which they would never be caught—Leopold was his willing accomplice.

In 1924—when Loeb was 18 and Leopold was 19—the two lured Loeb's 14-year-old cousin Bobby Franks into a car and beat the unsuspecting child to death. They attempted to hide the body near Wolf Lake; they did a poor job, however, and a passerby found the body the next day. Investigators then discovered Leopold's glasses in the area where the body was found, and the boys were quickly apprehended.

The trial was a sensation; because the boys had pleaded guilty, the main point of the trial was to determine if the boys would go to prison or be hanged. Defense attorney Clarence Darrow claimed that both boys were mentally unstable because they had been abused by their governesses; using this defense among others, Darrow persuaded the judge to spare the boys' lives, much to prosecutor Robert Crowe's chagrin.

Loeb was killed in prison in 1936. Leopold was a model prisoner and was released in 1958. Even prosecutor Robert Crowe had become convinced of Leopold's reform and considered writing a letter to the parole board on his behalf. Leopold lived most of the rest of his life in Puerto Rico. He died in 1971.

Bobby Franks is buried in Rosehill Cemetery. Some cemetery workers claimed to see a young boy wandering the cemetery at times; when they approached him, he would disappear, however. The workers claimed the ghost did not rest until Leopold's death in 1971.

Keep Your Windows Locked

A raging alcoholic and a sociopath, Richard Speck sneaked into a dorm through an unlocked window and brutally murdered eight nurses in 1966. The systematic killings of the students shocked the nation. The Chicago Police Department sent 60 officers on a hunt for Speck. After listening to the testimony of Corazon Amurao (the sole surviving nurse), the jury at his trial deliberated for only 49 minutes and sentenced him to death. The death penalty was declared unconstitutional in 1972 (while Speck was on death row), and Speck was sentenced to eight consecutive terms of 50 to 150 years each.

Speck's bizarre, cold-blooded persona became the subject of much clinical and popular debate throughout his years in prison. As a child, Speck was abused by his stepfather and suffered several serious falls; he had the IQ of a ten-year-old, and many specialists believe he had undiagnosed brain damage. Speck died of a heart attack in 1991. After no one claimed the body, Speck was cremated, and his ashes were scattered in an undisclosed location.

Beyond Our Reach

A brilliant but tormented mathematician, Ted Kaczynski (aka "the Unabomber") traded his position at Berkeley for a life in Montana, where he read philosophy and became one of the country's most infamous domestic terrorists. Kaczynski, who was raised on Chicago's Southwest Side, was the subject of a massive FBI manhunt after nearly 20 years of mailing bombs to academics and businessmen—as well as attempting to blow up a plane in 1979. The fact that Kaczynski's preferred targets were universities and airlines led FBI agents to dub him the "Unabomber."

Kaczynski has intense suspicions about technological progress and the effect it has on human beings and nature. One prison psychiatrist diagnosed Kaczynski with paranoid schizophrenia in 1998, but others are not convinced. Specialists will likely be studying his case for years to come to determine the root of his psychological distress; conjecture lays blame across the spectrum, from an illness he contracted as an infant to psychological experiments he underwent while he was a Harvard undergrad. Investigators still are not sure how he chose his specific targets. Kaczynski was sentenced to life in prison; he was in a maximum-security lockup in Colorado until his death in 2023. It was reported that he became friends with Timothy McVeigh, who committed the Oklahoma City bombing, until the other man's execution.

"I wonder now, Nathan, whether you think there is a God or not. I wonder whether you think it is pure accident that this disciple of Nietzsche's philosophy dropped his glasses or whether it was an act of Divine Providence to visit upon your miserable carcasses the wrath of God."

—STATE'S ATTORNEY ROBERT CROWE,
IN HIS SUMMATION DURING THE LEOPOLD & LOEB CASE

Murder at the Garden

The world was fascinated when a skirt-chasing Gilded Age architect died atop the landmark he designed.

Concerts by superstars the likes of Jimi Hendrix, Elvis Presley, John Lennon, Michael Jackson, Frank Sinatra, and Barbra Streisand; legendary boxing matches featuring Joe Louis, Rocky Marciano, Sugar Ray Robinson, Joe Frazier, and Muhammad Ali; home games of basketball's New York Knicks and ice hockey's New York Rangers. These are just some of the events that have taken place at Madison Square Garden since the first of its four incarnations was constructed in 1879. Yet, perhaps the most notorious Garden event was the cold-blooded murder of the man who designed the second Garden, located like its predecessor at 26th Street and Madison Avenue.

That man's name was Stanford White, and his 1906 Garden shooting in front of a high-society audience led to the "Trial of the Century." (A somewhat premature title? It would subsequently be shared with court cases starring, among others, Leopold and Loeb, John Scopes, Gloria Vanderbilt, the Nazis at Nuremberg, and O. J. Simpson). Indeed, the aforementioned witnesses were not only elevated in terms of their social status but also in terms of their location, since the crime took place at the venue's rooftop theater during the premiere of the saucy musical Mam'zelle Champagne. Soon, the general public was abuzz with gossip about the sex and jealousy that gave rise to the murder.

Mirrors and a Swing

Stanford White was not only the esteemed architect of numerous neoclassical New York City public buildings and private mansions, he was also a notorious (and married) womanizer who enjoyed assignations at a downtown loft apartment where he had installed a red velvet swing so that his girls could "entertain" him. A standout among them was Evelyn Nesbit, a beautiful artists' model and chorus girl who had met "Stanny" shortly after relocating from Pittsburgh to New York in 1901. At the time, she was 16; he was 47. As Nesbit would later recall, it was during their second rendezvous at the apartment on West 24th Street, where some walls and ceilings were covered in mirrors, that the redhead "entered that room as a virgin," and, she attested, lost consciousness after a glass of champagne and was sexually assaulted. They subsequently had a relationship that lasted several months, though White continued to dally with other women during that time as well.

Thereafter, while White continued treating girls and young women to his swing and mirrors, Nesbit embarked on a relationship with—and was twice impregnated by—young actor John Barrymore. Yet, it was the details of her affair with White that tormented Harry Kendall Thaw, the man whom Nesbit married in 1905. The son of a Pittsburgh coal and railroad tycoon, Thaw was a violent, drug-addicted ne'er-do-well who also had a taste for chorus girls. When he met Nesbit, the stage was set for a tragic showdown.

White's first bad move was to make less-than-complimentary remarks about Thaw to some ladies they both were pursuing. When Thaw learned about these cracks, he wasn't exactly delighted. His annoyance turned to jealous rage when, after he somehow turned on the charm to woo Nesbit, she admitted that she kept declining his proposals of marriage because "Stanny" had taken her virginity. This only made Thaw more determined, and after forcing his marriage proposals—and himself—on the social-climbing Nesbit, the chorus beauty finally relented.

A Pistol in His Pocket
According to Nesbit, she was continually brutalized by Thaw, and his preoccupation with her deflowering at the hands of "The Beast" finally exploded in violence on the night of June 25, 1906. It was on that evening that the Thaws happened to dine

at the Café Martin where White, his son, and a friend were also eating. Like White, the Thaws were planning to attend the play's premiere at the Madison Square Roof Garden, and at some point Harry must have learned about this. After dropping Evelyn off at their hotel so that he could arm himself, he reappeared in a black overcoat (despite the summer heat), whisked his young wife off to the show, and paced nervously up and down between the dinner-theater tables before White arrived at around 10:50 p.m. Thaw continued to hover for the next 15 minutes, until an onstage rendition of a song unfortunately titled "I Could Love a Million Girls" inspired him to approach the seated architect and shoot him three times from point-blank range.

One bullet entered White's left eye, killing him instantly; the other two grazed his shoulders as he fell off his chair. However, since two stage performers had just engaged in a dueling dialogue, most audience members thought the shooting was all part of the fun—until several witnesses screamed. At that point, according to the following day's *Times*, the theater manager leapt onto a table and demanded that the show must go on. Yet, when "the musicians made a feeble effort at gathering their wits" and "the girls who romped on the stage were paralyzed with horror," the manager informed his audience that an accident had occurred and they should leave quietly.

Arrested near the venue's elevators, Thaw asserted that White "deserved it...I can prove it. He ruined my life and then deserted the girl." According to a different witness quoted in the *Times*, Thaw claimed that White had ruined his wife, not his life.

Either way, after the jury at this first "Trial of the Century" was deadlocked, Thaw's plea of insanity at the second resulted in his imprisonment at a state hospital for the criminally insane. Released in 1913 and judged sane in 1915—the year he granted Evelyn a divorce—he was again judged insane and sentenced to an asylum two years later for assaulting and horsewhipping a teenage boy.

An Ongoing Story

The 1955 movie *The Girl in the Red Velvet Swing*, starring Joan Collins as Evelyn Nesbit, Ray Milland as Stanford White, and Farley Granger as Harry Kendall Thaw, recounts the love-triangle murder. An even more fictionalized account was provided in James Cagney's final feature film, Ragtime (1981) with Norman Mailer as White and Elizabeth McGovern as Nesbit.

Following the first two incarnations of the Garden that were constructed at 26th Street and Madison Avenue in 1879 and 1890, Madison Square Garden III opened at 50th Street and Eighth Avenue in 1925. The current version of the indoor arena, located at Eighth Avenue and 33rd Street, opened in 1968.

The Great Plains Butcher

In many cold cases, the victims are known while the killer is a cipher. In the case of Eugene Butler, we know he murdered six people and buried them on his property. Their identities, however, remain unknown.

Born in 1849 in New York, Eugene Butler moved out west to North Dakota in the 1880s. He bought a farm in Niagara, North Dakota, where he lived alone. He was reportedly something of a recluse, minimizing contact with his neighbors. When he visited the nearby town, it was to hire farmhands for busy times.

In 1906, Butler came more prominently to his neighbors attention when he began to visibly suffer from hallucinations and paranoid delusions. He would ride through the countryside at night screaming. Because of this behavior, he was admitted to the North Dakota State Hospital, an asylum for the mentally ill, where he lived relatively quietly until his death in 1913. His neighbors, and staff at the hospital, did not know that in his years at the farm, he had also committed several grisly murders.

It was not until after his death that the bodies of his victims were found, when workmen sent by his relatives to renovate the property discovered a series of skeletons under the cellar. They were young men, probably itinerant farmhands hired by Butler who were not missed when they disappeared. Butler killed them by crushing their skulls; he even built a trap door to more easily dispose of the remains. Money left at the house led some to speculate that Butler became paranoid and thought the men were stealing from him.

None of the victims have ever been identified, and some of the bones were even stolen, probably by people looking for grisly souvenirs of a case that captured the public's imagination.

The Butcher Was a Wienie

So, the mugger is dead, your wife is dead, but you made it out unscathed? Something doesn't quite add up...

In 1920, butcher Carl Wanderer, a veteran of World War I, approached a drifter in a bar and offered him the princely sum of $10 to pretend to rob him. Wanderer explained that he was in the doghouse with his wife, but that if he punched a mugger in front of her, he'd look like a hero. The drifter agreed to the deal.

The next day, as Wanderer and his wife (who was due to deliver the couple's first child the following month) returned home from the movies, the drifter attacked them in the entryway of their apartment building. Wanderer pulled out a gun, shot the drifter to death, then turned and shot his wife to death too. Wanderer told police that his wife had tragically been killed during the ruckus. For a couple of days, Wanderer was hailed as a hero. But the police—and, more importantly, the newspaper reporters—had an uneasy feeling about Wanderer's story. They were especially suspicious of the fact that he and the drifter had exactly the same model of pistol.

Reporters soon discovered that Wanderer had a girlfriend—a 16-year-old who worked across the street from Wanderer's butcher shop. Within weeks, Wanderer's story had fallen apart, and he broke down and confessed to the murders.

Initially put on trial only for the murder of his wife, Wanderer was sentenced to 25 years in prison. The newspapers were outraged that he hadn't been sentenced to hang and published the names and addresses of the jurors so that people could harass them. Eventually, Wanderer was rushed back into court to stand trial for the death of the drifter. This time, he was sentenced to death.

At his hanging, he entertained the reporters by singing a popular song of the day, "Old Pal Why Don't You Answer Me," just before his execution. One reporter said, "He shoulda been a song plugger." Another, however, said, "He should have been hanged just for his voice!" All were thankful Wanderer would sing no more.

Murderess

It was the "trial of the century"—for what may well have been the most poorly executed murder of the time.

It was a terrible thing to wake up to on that March morning in 1927. Nine-year-old Lorraine Snyder found her mother Ruth, her hands and feet bound, begging for help in the hall outside her bedroom. The girl rushed to her neighbors in the New York City suburb, and they called the police.

What the police found was more terrible still. Ruth Snyder's husband Albert lay dead in the bedroom—his skull smashed, wire strung around his neck, and a chloroform-soaked cloth shoved up his nose. His 32-year-old widow told the police that a large Italian man had knocked her out, stolen her jewelry, and assaulted her husband.

But the police found her jewels under a mattress; they also discovered a bloody pillowcase and a bloody, five-pound sash weight in a closet. As if this evidence wasn't damning enough, police located a check Ruth had written to Henry Judd Gray in the amount of $200. Gray's name was found in her little black book—along with the names of 26 other men. To cinch the matter, Lorraine told the cops that "Uncle Judd" had been in the home the previous night. A tie clip with the initials HJG was found on the floor.

A Marriage on the Rocks

Ruth Brown met Albert Snyder—14 years her senior—in 1915. He was an editor of *Motor Boating* magazine, and Ruth was a secretary. She and Albert married and had Lorraine, but their union was flawed from the start. Albert was still enthralled with his former fiancée of ten years ago, who had died; he named his boat after her and displayed her photograph in his and Ruth's home.

In the meantime, Ruth haunted the jazz clubs of Roaring Twenties Manhattan, drinking and dancing 'til the wee hours of the morning without her retiring spouse, whom she had dubbed "the old crab."

In 1925, the unhappy wife went on a blind date and met Judd Gray, a low-key corset salesperson. Soon the duo was meeting for afternoon trysts at the Waldorf Astoria—leaving Lorraine to play in the hotel lobby. Eventually, Ruth arranged for her unsuspecting husband to sign a life insurance policy worth more than $70,000.

The Jig Is Up

At the murder scene, the police questioned Ruth about Gray. "Has he confessed?," she blurted. It wasn't long before she had spilled her guts, though she claimed it was Gray who'd actually strangled Albert.

Meanwhile, 33-year-old Gray—not exactly the sharpest knife in the drawer—was found at a hotel in Syracuse, New York. It didn't take police long to locate him; after leaving Ruth's house, he had actually stopped to ask a police officer when he could catch the next bus to New York City. Gray quickly confessed but claimed it was Ruth who'd strangled Albert. Ruth had mesmerized him, he stated, through alcohol, sex, and threats.

A month after the arrest of the murderous duo, a brief trial ensued. For three weeks, the courtroom was jammed with 1,500 spectators. In attendance were such luminaries as songwriter Irving Berlin and the producers of the Broadway play Chicago. Also on hand was novelist James M. Cain, who drew on the case for his novel *Double Indemnity*, later turned into a film noir classic by director Billy Wilder and writer Raymond Chandler. The media frenzy over the courtroom drama even exceeded coverage of the execution of anarchist-bombers Sacco and Vanzetti. Miming the fevered reporting of city tabloids such as the *Daily News*, the stodgy *New York Times* carried page-one stories on the crime for months.

Guilty!

Ruth and Gray were pronounced guilty after a 100-minute deliberation by an all-male jury. When their appeal failed and their plea for clemency to Governor Al Smith was denied, the deadly pair was driven 30 miles "up the river" to Sing Sing Prison's death row. En route, excited onlookers hung from rooftops to catch a glimpse of the doomed couple.

Robert Elliott, the man slated to execute the pair, professed angst over putting a woman to death; Ruth would be the first female executed since 1899. "It will be something new for me to throw the switch on a woman," he told reporters, "and I don't like the job." The former electrical contractor received threats because of his role as hangman. He asked the warden for a raise to help salve the stress. Yet, Elliott would long continue his grim work, sending a total of 387 convicts to the next world.

The End

On January 12, 1928, at 11 p.m., 20 witnesses—chosen from the 1,500 who'd applied—watched Ruth enter the execution chamber. The Blonde Butcher, as she had been dubbed, was strapped weeping into a wooden chair, a leather cap clamped on her head. "Jesus, have mercy on me," she moaned, "for I have sinned."

In a room close by, Elliott threw a switch, and 2,000 volts surged through Ruth's body. At that instant, a reporter for the *Daily News* triggered a camera hidden in his pants. A garish photo of the murderess's last moment would appear on the paper's front page the next day. The headline read, "DEAD." Minutes later, it was Gray's turn. Although his feet caught fire during the execution, for most witnesses it was Ruth's final moments that were stamped indelibly in their minds.

Ohio's Greatest Unsolved Mystery

From 1935 until 1938, a brutal madman roamed the Flats of Cleveland. The killer—known as the Mad Butcher of Kingsbury Run—is believed to have murdered 12 men and women. Despite a massive manhunt, the murderer was never apprehended.

In 1935, the Depression had hit Cleveland hard, leaving large numbers of people homeless. Shantytowns sprang up on the eastern side of the city in Kingsbury Run—a popular place for transients—near the Erie and Nickel Plate railroads.

It is unclear who the Mad Butcher's first victim was. Recent research suggests it may have been an unidentified woman found floating in Lake Erie—in pieces—on September 5, 1934; she would be known as Jane Doe I but dubbed by some as the "Lady of the Lake." The first official victim was found in the Jackass Hill area of Kingsbury Run on September 23, 1935. The unidentified body, labeled John Doe, had been dead for almost a month. A mere 30 feet away from the body was another victim, Edward Andrassy. Unlike John Doe, Andrassy had only been dead for days, indicating that the spot was a dumping ground. Police began staking out the area.

After a few months passed without another body, police thought the worst was over. Then on January 26, 1936, the partial remains of a new victim, a woman, were found in downtown Cleveland. On February 7, more remains were found at a separate location, and the deceased was identified as Florence Genevieve Polillo. Despite similarities among the three murders, authorities had yet to connect them—serial killers were highly uncommon at the time.

Tattoo Man, Eliot Ness, and More Victims

On June 5, two young boys passing through Kingsbury Run discovered a severed head. The rest of the body was found near the Nickel Plate railroad police station. Despite six distinctive tattoos on the man's body (thus the nickname "Tattoo Man"), he was never identified and became John Doe II.

At this point, Cleveland's newly appointed director of public safety, Eliot Ness (fresh off his Prohibition-era successes), was officially briefed on the case. While Ness and his men hunted down leads, the headless body of another unidentified male was found west of Cleveland on July 22, 1936. It appeared that the man, John Doe III, had been murdered several months earlier. On September 10, the headless body of a sixth victim, John Doe IV, was found in Kingsbury Run.

Ness officially started spearheading the investigation. Determined to bring the killer to justice, Ness's staff fanned out across the city, even going undercover in the Kingsbury Run area. As 1936 drew to a close, no suspects had been named nor new victims discovered. City residents believed that Ness's team had run the killer off. But future events would prove that the killer was back...with a vengeance.

The Body Count Climbs

A woman's mutilated torso washed up on the beach at 156th Street on February 23, 1937. The rest would wash ashore two months later. (Strangely, the body washed up in the same location as the "Lady of the Lake" had three years earlier.)

On June 6, 1937, teenager Russell Lauyer found the decomposed body of a woman inside of a burlap sack under the Lorain-Carnegie Bridge in Cleveland. With the body was a newspaper from June of the previous year, suggesting a timeline for the murder. An investigation indicated the body might belong to one Rose Wallace; this was never confirmed, and the victim is sometimes referred to as Jane Doe II. Pieces of another man's body (the ninth victim) began washing ashore on July 6, just below Kingsbury Run. Cleveland newspapers were having a field day with the case that the "great" Eliot Ness couldn't solve. This fueled Ness, and he promised justice.

Burning of Kingsbury Run

The next nine months were quiet, and the public began to relax. When a woman's severed leg was found in the Cuyahoga River on April 8, 1938, however, people debated its connection to the Butcher. But the rest of Jane Doe III was soon found inside two burlap sacks floating in the river (sans head, of course).

On August 16, 1938, the last two confirmed victims of the Butcher were found together at the East 9th Street Lakeshore Dump. Jane Doe IV had apparently been dead for four to six months prior to discovery, while John Doe VI may have been dead for almost nine months.

Something snapped inside Eliot Ness. On the night of August 18, Ness and dozens of police officials raided the shantytowns in the Flats, ending up in Kingsbury Run. Along the way, they interrogated or arrested anyone they came across, and Ness ordered the shanties burned to the ground. There would be no more confirmed victims of the Mad Butcher of Kingsbury Run.

Who Was the Mad Butcher?

There were two prime suspects in the case, though no one was ever charged. The first was Dr. Francis Sweeney, a surgeon with the knowledge many believed necessary to mutilate the victims the way the killer did. (He was also a cousin of Congressman Martin L. Sweeney, a known political opponent of Ness.)

In August 1938, Dr. Sweeney was interrogated by Ness, two other men, and the inventor of the polygraph machine, Dr. Royal Grossman. By all accounts, Sweeney failed the polygraph test (several times), and Ness believed he had his man, but he was released due to lack of evidence.

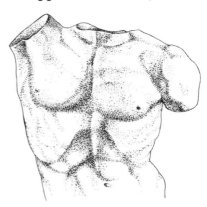

Two days after the interrogation, on August 25, 1938, Sweeney checked himself into the Sandusky Veterans Hospital. He remained institutionalized at various facilities until his death in 1965. Because Sweeney voluntarily checked himself in, he could have left whenever he desired.

The other suspect was Frank Dolezal, who was arrested by private investigators on July 5, 1939, as a suspect in the murder of Florence Polillo, with whom he had lived for a time. While in custody, Dolezal confessed to killing Polillo, although some believe the confession was forced. Either way, Dolezal died under mysterious circumstances while incarcerated at the Cuyahoga County Jail before he could be charged.

As for Eliot Ness, some believe his inability to bring the Butcher to trial weighed on him for the rest of his life. Ness went to his grave without getting a conviction.

To this day, the case remains open.

Backwoods Butcher: Ed Gein

To find the story of one of the most gruesome killers in American history, you don't have to look far from Wisconsin. The terrifying tale of Ed Gein unfolded in the town of Plainfield.

Ed Gein was the son of an overbearing mother who taught him that sex was sinful. When she died in 1945, he was a 39-year-old bachelor living alone in a rundown farmhouse in rural Plainfield.

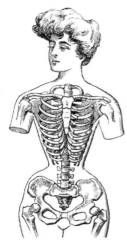

After his mother's death, Gein developed a morbid fascination with the medical atrocities performed by the Nazis during World War II. This fascination led him to dig up female corpses from cemeteries, take them home, and perform his own experiments on them, such as removing the skin from the body and draping it over a tailor's dummy. He was also fascinated with female genitalia, which he would fondle and, on occasion, stuff into women's panties and wear around the house.

He soon tired of decomposing corpses and set out in search of fresher bodies. Most of his victims were women around his mother's age. He went a step too far, however, when he abducted the mother of local sheriff's deputy Frank Worden. Learning that his missing mother had been seen with Gein on the day of her disappearance, Worden went to the Gein house to question the recluse. What he found there defied belief. Human heads sat as prize trophies in the living room along with a belt made from human nipples and a chair completely upholstered in human skin. But for Worden, the worst sight was in the woodshed. Strung up by the feet was the headless body of his mother. Her torso had been slit open, and her heart was found on a plate in the dining room.

Gein confessed but couldn't recall how many people he'd killed. He told detectives that he liked to dress up in the carved-out torsos of his victims and pretend to be his mother. He spent ten years in an insane asylum before he was judged fit to stand trial. He was found guilty, but criminally insane, and died in 1984, at age 77.

The Black Dahlia Murder Mystery

One of the most baffling murder mysteries in U.S. history began innocently enough on the morning of January 15, 1947. Betty Bersinger was walking with her young daughter in the Leimert Park area of Los Angeles, when she spotted something lying in a vacant lot that caused her blood to run cold. She ran to a nearby house and called the police. Officers Wayne Fitzgerald and Frank Perkins arrived on the scene shortly after 11:00 a.m.

A Grisly Discovery

Lying only several feet from the road, in plain sight, was the naked body of a young woman. Her body had numerous cuts and abrasions, including a knife wound from ear to ear that resembled a ghoulish grin. Even more horrific was that her body had been completely severed at the mid-section, and the two halves had been placed as if they were part of some morbid display. That's what disturbed officers the most: The killer appeared to have carefully posed the victim close to the street because he wanted people to find his grotesque handiwork.

Something else that troubled the officers was that even though the body had been brutally violated and desecrated, there was very little blood found at the scene. The only blood evidence recovered was a possible bloody footprint and an empty cement package with a spot of blood on it. In fact, the body was so clean that it appeared to have just been washed.

Shortly before removing the body, officers scoured the area for a possible murder weapon, but none was recovered. A coroner later determined that the cause of death was from hemorrhage and shock due to a concussion of the brain and lacerations of the face, probably from a very large knife.

Positive Identification

After a brief investigation, police were able to identify the deceased as Elizabeth Short, who was born in Hyde Park, Massachusetts, on July 29, 1924. At age 19, Short had moved to California to live with her father, but she moved out and spent the next few years moving back and forth between California, Florida, and Massachusetts. In July 1946, Short returned to California to see Lt. Gordon Fickling, a former boyfriend, who was stationed in Long Beach. For the last six months of her life, Short lived in an assortment of hotels, rooming houses, and private homes. She was last seen a week before her body was found, which made police very interested in finding out where and with whom she spent her final days.

The Black Dahlia Is Born

As police continued their investigation, reporters jumped all over the story and began referring to the unknown killer by names such as "sex-crazed maniac" and even "werewolf." Short herself was also given a nickname: the Black Dahlia. Reporters said it was a name friends had called her as a play on the movie The Blue Dahlia, which had recently been released. However, others contend Short was never called the Black Dahlia while she was alive; it was just something reporters made up for a better story. Either way, it wasn't long before newspapers around the globe were splashing front-page headlines about the horrific murder of the Black Dahlia.

Still Unknown

As time wore on, hundreds of police officers were assigned to the Black Dahlia investigation. They combed the streets, interviewing people and following leads. Although police interviewed thousands of potential suspects—and dozens even confessed to the murder—to this day, no one has ever officially been charged with the crime. More than 70 years and several books and movies after the crime, the Elizabeth Short murder case is still listed as "open." We are no closer to knowing who killed Short or why than when her body was first discovered.

There is one bright note to this story. In February 1947, perhaps as a result of the Black Dahlia case, the state of California became the first state to pass a law requiring all convicted sex offenders to register themselves.

Partners in Murder

Some will tell you that people are just born bad, while others think society is responsible. In the case of 24-year-old Murl Daniels, his turn for the worst came from a chance encounter inside an institution meant to rehabilitate him: the Mansfield Reformatory in Ohio.

In 1948, while serving time at Mansfield Reformatory for a robbery conviction, Murl Daniels was introduced to another inmate, John West, who was incarcerated for stealing an automobile. The two quickly became friends and started discussing all the robberies they could commit together once they were released. According to legend, Daniels and West also made a pact to hunt down and kill all the prison guards and officials they felt had done them wrong.

The Rampage Begins

By July, both Daniels and West had been released. They wasted no time getting started on their new partnership in crime, beginning by holding up Columbus-area bars and taverns. While the two men always carried guns with them, for the first few robberies, they never fired a shot. That all changed when Daniels and West burst into a Columbus tavern owned by Earl Ambrose and shot him to death duringtheir robbery attempt.

Perhaps it was that first taste of blood that set them off. Regardless, after the Ambrose murder, Daniels and West continued their murderous spree and headed north to Mansfield. It is believed the duo's first target was to be a Mansfield guard named Harris, but they didn't know where he lived. They intended to get the address from Harris's supervisor and the superintendent of the prison's farm, John Niebel. Since Niebel also lived on that farm, Daniels and West knew just how to get there.

Cold-Blooded Murder

On the evening of July 21, 1948, Harris and West snuck into the farmhouse and dragged Niebel, his wife, and his 20-year-old daughter from their beds. After forcing the entire family to strip naked, the pair led them out into a field, where all three were shot to death. Daniels and West then fled, abandoning their plan to track down Harris.

The following day, neighbors discovered the bodies of the Niebel family. It didn't take long for authorities to determine that Daniels and West were the men they were looking for. They began the largest manhunt in Ohio history up to that time.

Surprisingly, the killers didn't immediately try to flee Ohio for a more anonymous environment. Rather, they only headed as far north as Cleveland, where they continued their rampage, stealing cars and often shooting and killing the owners in the process. Local newspapers quickly got wind of the pair's crime spree, nicknaming them the Mad Dog Killers.

The End of the Road

When Daniels and West finally decided to get the heck out of Ohio, it was too late. On July 24, the pair were met by a police roadblock as they closed in on the state line. While Daniels was willing to give up quietly, West would not go down without a fight. He opened fire on the officers lining the roadblock and was finally shot dead. Daniels was arrested without incident, thus ending a two-week killing spree that claimed the lives of six innocent victims.

Writing What You Know

In 1994, fans of novelist Anne Perry's Victorian murder mysteries were shocked to learn that the best-selling writer knew her topic a little too well.

Best Friends

It started out innocently enough: Juliet Hulme arrived in New Zealand in 1948, where she met Pauline Parker. Sixteen-year-old Parker and 15-year-old Hulme quickly became best friends, bonding particularly over their shared experience of serious illness and its related isolation. As a young girl, Parker had suffered from osteomyelitis, an infection of the bone marrow that required several painful surgeries. Hulme, meanwhile, had recurring bouts of respiratory ailments, culminating with tuberculosis.

Intelligent and imaginative, the two girls created an increasingly violent fantasy life they called the "Fourth World," which was peopled with fairy-tale princes and Hollywood stars they dubbed the "saints." They wrote constantly, sure their stories were their ticket to the Hollywood of their imagination. At night, the girls would sneak outside to act out stories about the characters they had created.

No Matter What

In 1954, Hulme's parents separated. As her father prepared to return to England, Hulme's parents decided to send Juliet to live with relatives in South Africa. Not only would the climate be better for her health, they reasoned, but also the move would bring an end to a relationship that both girls' parents felt had grown too intense. Ever fantasizing, Hulme and Parker convinced themselves that Parker was also moving to South Africa with Hulme. Not surprisingly, Mrs. Parker refused to allow it. Determined to stay together, the girls decided to kill Parker's mother and flee to America, where they planned to sell their writing and work in the movies that played such an important role in their fantasy life.

On June 22, the girls went on what they described as a farewell outing to Victoria Park with Mrs. Parker. There, they bludgeoned Mrs. Parker to death with half a brick tied in a stocking. The girls expected the woman to die after a single blow so they could blame the death on a fall, but they were horrifyingly wrong—it took 45 blows to kill her. The hysterical girls then ran back to a park kiosk, screaming and covered in blood. The girls' story that Mrs. Parker had slipped and fallen rapidly disintegrated after the police arrived and found the murder weapon in the surrounding woods.

"Incurably Bad"

The trial, with its titillating accusations of lesbianism and insanity, grabbed international headlines, not only because of the brutality of the murder, but also because of the excerpts from Parker's diary that were used as evidence. The diary revealed the intensity of the relationship between the two girls and the fantasy world they inhabited. The diary also made it clear that the murder, flippantly described in its pages as "moider," was premeditated. The entry for June 22 was titled "The Day of the Happy Event."

Parker and Hulme were found guilty following a six-day trial during which the Crown Prosecutor described them as "not incurably insane, but incurably bad." Because they were under 18 and considered juveniles, they could not be given a capital sentence. Instead, they were sentenced to separate prisons for an unspecified term. After five years, they were released on the condition that they never contact each other again.

Hulme returned to England and later took her stepfather's name, Perry. She also changed her first name; as Anne Perry, she went on to write dozens of popular mysteries, many of them falling into the detective fiction and historical murder-mystery genres. Parker, meanwhile, lives in obscurity in an English village.

The murders were fairly forgotten, at least for a time. Years later, Perry's true identity was uncovered as a result of the publicity surrounding the 1994 release of the movie *Heavenly Creatures*, directed by Peter Jackson. The film, starring Kate Winslet as Hulme, focused on the events leading to the murder.

Perry was upset about the film. "It's like having some disfigurement and being stripped naked and set up in the High Street for everybody to walk by and pay their penny and have a look," she told *The New York Times*. "I would like to put my clothes on and go home, please, be like anybody else."

Crime and Punishment

This tale of greed and mass murder ushered in a new era of forensic science.

Love's Labor Lost

Jack Graham's mother, Daisie King, knew her only son was no angel, but she must have hoped he'd change his ways: Barely into his 20s, Graham had little patience for lawful employment, and he'd already been convicted of running illegal booze and check forgery. It's thought that King paid for her son's lawyer and anted up $2,500 in court-ordered restitution on the forgery convictions. By 1953, however, it seemed that Graham was settling down. He married and by 1955 had two children. His mother, a successful businesswoman, bought a house in Colorado for the young couple, built a drive-in restaurant, and installed Graham as its manager.

But the drive-in lost money. Graham blamed his mother's meddling in the management for the loss, but he later admitted he had skimmed receipts. He also confessed to vandalizing the place twice, once by smashing the front window and the second time by rigging a gas explosion to destroy equipment he'd used as security for a personal loan. A new pickup truck Graham bought himself mysteriously stalled on a railway track with predictable results. This too proved to be an attempt at insurance fraud.

Flight to Doom

In the fall of 1955, King wanted to see her daughter in Alaska, and she prepared for her trip there via Portland and Seattle. On November 1, Graham saw her off on United Air Flight 629. Eleven minutes after takeoff, the plane exploded in the sky. Forty-four people died, including King.

Within 24 hours FBI fingerprint experts were at the crash site to help identify bodies. The painstaking task of gathering wreckage from over a three-mile trail of scraps started. By November 7, Civil Aeronautics investigators concluded sabotage was the probable cause of the disaster.

Criminal investigators joined the FBI technical teams. Families of passengers and crew members were interviewed while technicians reassembled the plane's midsection where the explosion likely occurred. In the course of sifting through wreckage, bomb fragments and explosives residue were identified.

Avalanche of Evidence

Inevitably, investigators took an interest in Graham. Not only would he receive a substantial inheritance from his mother's estate, he had also taken out a $37,500 travel insurance policy on her. Moreover, he had a criminal record, and according to witnesses, a history of heated arguments with his mother.

Graham was first interviewed on November 10, and again over the following two days. In a search of his property on November 12, agents discovered a roll of primer cord in a shirt pocket and a copy of the travel insurance policy secreted in a small box. Circumstantial evidence contradicted his statements, including that provided by his wife, half-sister, and acquaintances.

Finally, Graham admitted he'd built a bomb and placed it in his mother's luggage. On November 14, he was arraigned on charges of sabotage. At the time the charge did not carry a death penalty, so he was brought into court on November 17 and charged with first-degree murder.

A Case of Firsts

Notwithstanding the confession, investigators continued to gather forensic evidence, putting together what may have been the most scientifically detailed case in U.S. history up to that date. The case had other firsts as well. It was the first case of mass murder in the United States via airplane explosion. Graham's trial, which began on April 16, 1956, also marked the first time TV cameras were permitted to air a live broadcast of a courtroom trial.

On May 5, 1956, the jury needed only 69 minutes to find Graham guilty. On January 11, 1957, he was executed at Colorado State Penitentiary, remorseless to the end.

Murder in the Heartland

If you ever find yourself in northwestern Kansas looking for the village of Holcomb, don't blink or you'll miss it. It's the kind of place where nothing ever seems to happen. And yet, back in 1959, Holcomb became one of the most notorious locations in the history of American crime.

"Everyone Loved the Clutters..."

In the 1940s, successful businessman Herb Clutter built a house on the outskirts of town and started raising a family with his wife, Bonnie. The Clutters quickly became one of the most popular families in the small village, due largely to their friendly nature. People would be hard-pressed to find someone who had a bad word to say about them.

On the morning of Sunday, November 15, 1959, Clarence Ewalt drove his daughter Nancy to the Clutter house so she could go to church with the family as she did every week. She was a good friend of the Clutters' teenage daughter, who was also named Nancy. Nancy Ewalt knocked on the door several times but got no response. She went around to a side door, looked around and called out, but no one answered. At that point, Mr. Ewalt drove his daughter to the Kidwell house nearby and picked up Susan Kidwell, another friend. Susan tried phoning the Clutters, but no one answered. So the three drove back to the Clutter house. The two girls entered the house through the kitchen door and went to Nancy Clutter's room, where they discovered her dead body.

Unspeakable Acts

Sheriff Robinson was the first officer to respond. He entered the house with another officer and a neighbor, Larry Hendricks. According to Nancy Ewalt, the three men went first to Nancy Clutter's room, where they found the teenager dead of an apparent gunshot wound to the back of the head. She was lying on her bed facing the wall with her hands and ankles bound. Down the hallway in the master bedroom, the body of Bonnie Clutter was discovered. Like her daughter, Bonnie's hands and feet were also bound, and she appeared to have been shot point-blank in the head.

In the basement of the Clutter home, police found the bodies of Herb Clutter and his 15-year-old son, Kenyon. Like his mother and sister, Kenyon had been shot in the head; his body was tied to a sofa.

As atrocious as the other three murders were, Herb Clutter appeared to have suffered the most. Like the others, he had been shot in the head, but there were slash marks on his throat, and his mouth had been taped shut. And although his body was lying on the floor of the basement, there was a rope hanging from the ceiling suggesting that, at some point, he may have been hung from the rope.

Dewey's Task Force

Alvin A. Dewey of the Kansas City Bureau of Investigation (KBI) was put in charge of the investigation. Even though Dewey was a police veteran and had seen his fair share of violent murders, the Clutter murders hit him hard. Herb Clutter was a friend, and their families had attended church together.

At his first press conference after the bodies were discovered, Dewey announced that he was heading up a 19-man task force that would not rest until they found the person or persons responsible for the horrific murders. But he knew it was going to be a tough case. For one, the amount of blood and gore at the scene suggested that revenge might have been the motive.

But the Clutters were upstanding members of the community and loved by all, as evidenced by the nearly 600 mourners who showed up for the family's funeral service. The idea that the murders were the result of a robbery gone bad was also being pursued, but Dewey had his doubts about that, as well. For him, it just didn't fit that the entire Clutter family would have walked in on a robbery and then been killed the way they had. For that reason, Dewey began to believe that there had been more than one killer.

A Secret Clue

There was not a lot of evidence left behind at the crime scene. Not only was the murder weapon missing, but whoever pulled the trigger had taken the time to pick up the spent shells. However, Dewey did have an ace up his sleeve, and it was something not even the press was made aware of. Herb Clutter's body had been found lying on a piece of cardboard. On that cardboard were impressions from a man's boot. Both of the victims found in the basement, Herb and Kenyon Clutter, were barefoot, which meant the boots may have belonged to the killer. It wasn't much to go on, but for Dewey, it was a start. Still, as Christmas 1959 crept closer, the case was starting to come to a standstill. Then, finally, a big break came from an unlikely place: Lansing Prison.

A Break in the Case

The man who would break the case wide open was Lansing Prison inmate Floyd Wells. Earlier in the year, Wells had been sentenced to Lansing for breaking and entering. His cellmate was a man named Richard Hickock. One night, the two men were talking, and Hickock mentioned that even though he was going to be released from prison soon, he had nowhere to go. Wells told him that back in the late 1940s, he had been out looking for work and stumbled across a kind, rich man named Clutter who would often hire people to work around his farm. Once he mentioned Herb Clutter, Hickock seemed obsessed with the man. He wouldn't stop asking Wells to tell him everything he knew about Clutter. How old was he? Was he strong? How many others lived in the house with him?

One night, Hickock calmly stated that when he was released, he and his friend Perry Smith were going to rob the Clutters and murder anyone in the house. Wells said that Hickock even went so far as to explain exactly how he would tie everyone up and shoot them one at a time. Wells further stated that he never believed Hickock was serious until he heard the news that the Clutters had been murdered in exactly the way Hickock had described.

Captures and Confessions

On December 30, after attempting to cash a series of bad checks, Hickock and Smith were arrested in Las Vegas. Among the items seized from the stolen car they were driving was a pair of boots belonging to Hickock. When confronted with the fact that his boots matched the imprint at the crime scene, Hickock broke down and admitted he had been there during the murders. However, he swore that Perry Smith had killed the whole family and that he had tried to stop him.

When Smith was informed that his partner was putting all the blame on him, he decided it was in his best interest to explain his side. Smith gave a very detailed version of how Hickock had devised a plan to steal the contents of a safe in Herb Clutter's home office. The pair had arrived under cover of darkness at approximately 12:30 a.m. Finding no safe in the office, the pair went up into the master bedroom, where they surprised Herb Clutter, who was sleeping alone in bed. When told they had come for the contents of the safe, Herb told them to take whatever they wanted, but he said there was no safe in the house. Not convinced, Smith and Hickock rounded up the family and tied them up, hoping to get one of them to reveal the location of the safe. When that failed, Smith and Hickock prepared to leave. But when Hickock started bragging about how he had been ready to kill the entire family, Smith called his bluff, and an argument ensued. At that point, Smith said he snapped and stabbed Herb Clutter in the throat. Seeing the man in such pain, Smith said he then shot him to end his suffering. Smith then turned the gun on Kenyon. Smith ended his statement by saying that he'd made Hickock shoot and kill the two women.

The Verdict

The murder trial of Richard Hickock and Perry Smith began on March 23, 1960, at Finney County Courthouse. Five days later, the case was handed over to the jury, who needed only 40 minutes to reach their verdict: Both men were guilty of all charges. They recommended that Hickock and Smith be hanged for their crimes.

Sitting in the front row when the verdicts were read was Truman Capote, who had been writing a series of articles about the murders for *The New Yorker*. Those articles would later inspire his best-selling novel *In Cold Blood*.

After several appeals, both men were executed at Lansing Prison, one right after the other, on April 14, 1965. Richard Hickock was the first to be hanged, with Perry Smith going to the same gallows roughly 30 minutes later. Agent Alvin Dewey was present for both executions.

Several years after the murders, in an attempt to heal the community, a stained-glass window at the First Methodist Church in Garden City, Kansas, was posthumously dedicated to the memory of the Clutter family. Despite an initial impulse to bulldoze the Clutter house, it was left standing and today is a private residence.

The Moors Murderers: Britain's Most Hated Couple

A killing spree fascinated and horrified England in the 1960s. Saddleworth Moor had always had an ominous air to it, but tensions suddenly got much, much worse.

Burying a body in highly acidic soil is smart—the flesh decays faster, making it harder for police to tell exactly what happened to the victim. That's what Ian Brady and Myra Hindley were counting on when they buried their victims in an acidic grassy moor.

Normal and Abnormal Childhoods

Myra Hindley was born in 1942 just outside of Manchester. She was a normal, happy girl and even a popular babysitter among families in her neighborhood. At age 15, she left school. Three years later, she secured a job as a typist for a small chemical company. There she met Ian Brady, a 23-year-old stock clerk, and her future partner in life and crime.

Born to a single mother, Brady was given to a nearby family at a young age when his mom, a waitress, could no longer afford to take care of him. In school, he was an angry loner who bullied younger children and tortured animals.

At the chemical company, Hindley became enamored with Brady, an intense young man fascinated with Nazis and capable of reading *Mein Kampf* in German. In her diary, Hindley gushed that she hoped he would love her, although Brady was decidedly distant. It wasn't until a year after they met that he asked her on a date—at the company's Christmas party.

An Off-kilter Romance

Brady's preoccupation with Nazism, torture philosophies, and sadomasochism didn't bother Hindley, and as the couple became closer, they began to photograph themselves in disturbing poses. It became evident that Brady had found a companion to help turn his twisted fantasies into reality: Between 1963 and 1965, the pair murdered five children and buried their bodies in the Saddleworth Moors, leading the gruesome acts to be called the "Moors Murders."

The Murders Begin

Their first victim, 16-year-old Pauline Reade, was on her way to a dance on July 12, 1963, when a young woman offered her a ride. Presumably assuming that it was okay to take a ride from a fellow woman—Myra Hindley—Reade accepted. Along the way, Hindley suddenly pulled the car over to look for a missing glove; Reade helpfully joined Hindley in looking. Meanwhile, Brady had followed the car on his motorcycle. He snuck up behind Reade as she was looking for the glove and smashed her skull with a shovel. Reade's body was later found with her throat slashed so deeply that she was nearly decapitated. Unfortunately, hers wasn't nearly the grisliest death in the Moors Murders.

Four months later, on November 23, 1963, at a small-town market, Hindley asked 12-year-old John Kilbride to escort her home with some packages. He agreed. Brady was hidden in the backseat, and Kilbride became victim number two.

Keith Bennett had turned 12 only four days before June 16, 1964, when he encountered Hindley. Walking to his grandmother's house, he accepted a ride from Hindley, who again claimed to need help finding a glove. This time, instead of waiting in the car, she watched as Brady murdered the boy.

As the murderous couple stalked their fourth victim, their bloodlust swelled. On Boxing Day, an English holiday that falls on December 26, the couple lured ten-year-old Lesley

Ann Downey to their home. Sadly, their youngest victim suffered the most gruesome and memorable fate. The couple took pornographic photos of the gagged child and recorded 16 minutes of audio of Downey crying, screaming, vomiting, and begging for her mother.

Expanding the Circle

But their treacherous ways reached a pinnacle when, perhaps bored with each other, they tried to get Hindley's 17-year-old brother-in-law, David Smith, in on the act. Like Brady, Smith was a hoodlum, not at all liked by Hindley's family. Smith and Brady had previously bonded by bragging about doing bad things, including murder. Until October 6, 1965, however, Smith assumed it was all a joke.

The couple invited Smith to their house, and he waited in the kitchen while Hindley went to fetch Brady. Upon hearing a scream, he ran to the living room to see Brady carrying an ax and what he perceived to be a life-size doll. It wasn't a doll, of course, but 17-year-old Edward Evans. Smith watched as Brady hacked the last bit of life out of the boy. Afraid that he would be next, Smith helped the couple clean up the mess as if nothing had happened. He waited, terrified, until early the next morning and then snuck out and went to the police.

Facing the Consequences

This wretched crime spree shook Great Britain. The trial of Myra Hindley and Ian Brady lasted 14 days, during which dozens of photos were submitted as evidence, including pictures of the couple in torturous sexual poses. Hindley claimed that she was unconscious when most of the photos were taken and that Brady had used them to blackmail her into abetting his crimes. That claim was quickly dismissed, as police investigators who examined the photos testified that she appeared to be fully aware of what was going on and seemed to be enjoying herself.

At the time of the trial, the bodies of Lesley Ann Downey, John Kilbride, and Edward Evans had been discovered, all buried in the moor. Great Britain had just revoked the death penalty, so Ian Brady was sentenced to three sequential life sentences for the murders. Myra Hindley was charged with two of the murders as well as aiding and abetting. She was sentenced to life in prison.

The couple suffered miserably behind bars. After serving nearly 20 years, Brady was declared insane and committed to a mental hospital. Hindley was so viciously attacked that she had to have plastic surgery on her face. In the 1980s, the couple admitted to the murders of Pauline Reade and Keith Bennett and led police to Reade's grave. Hindley claimed remorse and appealed many times for her freedom. She received an open degree from a university, found God in prison, and even enlisted the help of a popular, devout Roman Catholic politician, Lord Longford, in her bid for release. But the high court of England denied her requests. Although she fought for her freedom up until her death in 2002, perhaps Hindley knew deep down that she'd never be free—she even called herself Britain's most hated woman. The BBC agreed and ran the quote, along with her infamous mug shot and jail photos, as her obituary.

Death from on High

When a troubled man exacted revenge from a lofty perch, a stunned nation watched in horror and disbelief. What could cause a man to kill indiscriminately? Why hadn't anyone seen it coming? Could such a thing happen again? Decades later the mystery continues.

In an America strained by an escalating war in Vietnam, the 1966 headline still managed to shock the senses. The "Texas Tower Sniper" had killed his mother and wife before snuffing out the lives of 13 innocents on the University of Texas (UT) campus at Austin. At least the Vietnam conflict offered up motives. Like most wars, battle lines had been drawn, and a steady buildup of threats and tensions had preceded the violence. But here, no such declarations were issued. Bullets came blazing out of the sky for no apparent reason. After the victims breathed their last and the nightmare drew to a close, a stunned populace was left with one burning question: Why?

Undercurrents

Charles Whitman appeared to have enjoyed many of life's advantages. He hailed from a prominent family in Lake Worth, Florida, and from outside appearances the future was Whitman's to make or break. But friction with his abusive father found Whitman seeking escape. After a brutal incident in which he returned home drunk from a party only to be beaten—and nearly drowned in a swimming pool—by his father, the 18-year-old Whitman enlisted in the U.S. Marines. He served for five years, distinguishing himself with a Sharpshooters Badge. After that he attended college at UT. During that period, Whitman also married his girlfriend, Kathy Leissner.

Whitman's life plan appeared to be straightforward. After obtaining a scholarship, he would seek an engineering degree, hoping to follow it up with acceptance at officer's candidate school. But things didn't go as planned.

Opportunity Lost

After leaving the military, Whitman worked toward a variety of goals in and out of school. Unfortunately, the ex-Marine's efforts were fraught with failure, and his frustrations multiplied. In the spring of 1966, Whitman sought the help of UT psychiatrist Dr. Maurice Dean Heatly. In a moment of ominous foretelling, Whitman remarked that he fantasized "going up on the [campus] tower with a deer rifle and shooting people." The doctor, having heard similar threats in the past, was mostly unimpressed. Since Whitman hadn't previously exhibited violent behavior, Heatly took his statement as nothing more than an idle threat.

Surprise Assault

During the wee hours of August 1, 1966, Whitman's demons finally won out, and his killing spree began. For reasons still uncertain, the murderer kicked off his blood quest by first stabbing his mother in her apartment and his wife while she slept; both died from their injuries.

Whitman then made his way to the UT campus and ascended the soon-to-be infamous tower. At his side he had enough provisions, weapons, and ammo to hole up indefinitely. Just before noon, he lifted a high-powered rifle and began shooting. He picked off victims one by one from the observation deck of the 307-foot-tall tower. Whitman's sharpshooting prowess (he once scored 215 points out of a possible 250 in target practice) added to the danger. By the time people finally realized what was happening, quite a few had already been cut down.

Lives Cut Short

As the attacks progressed, Austin police hatched a plan. Officers Ramiro Martinez and Houston McCoy snuck into the tower, surprising Whitman. Both sides exchanged fire. The 96-minute attack ended with two fatal shots to Whitman's head, compliments of McCoy's 12-gauge shotgun. The horror was over. In its ultimate wake lay 16 dead and 31 wounded. An autopsy performed on Whitman revealed a brain tumor that may have caused him to snap.

The authorities later found a note at his home. Its matter-of-fact tone is chilling to this day: "I imagine it appears that I brutaly [sic] kill [sic] both of my loved ones. I was only trying to do a quick thorough job. If my life insurance policy is valid...please pay off all my debts...Donate the rest anonymously to a mental health foundation. Maybe research can prevent further tragedies of this type."

Who Was the Zodiac Killer?

On the evening of December 20, 1968, 17-year-old David Faraday and 16-year-old Betty Lou Jensen headed out on their first date in Benicia, California. Late that night, a passing motorist noticed two lifeless bodies lying next to a car at a "lover's lane" parking spot. It was Faraday and Jensen, who had both been shot to death. The unwitting couple became the first official victims of the Zodiac Killer, who would spend the next six years taunting the police and frightening the public.

Senseless Killings

The murders of Faraday and Jensen stumped investigators. There appeared to be no motive, and forensic data of the time yielded few clues. Why would someone gun down two teenagers who were merely out having fun? No leads developed, and the case quickly grew cold.

Months later, just before midnight on July 4, 1969, another young couple, Michael Mageau and Darlene Ferrin, were in their car at Blue Rock Springs Park in Vallejo, about four miles from where Faraday and Jensen were murdered. As they sat in the car, another car pulled up behind them and the driver exited, approaching their car with a flashlight. The stranger shined the bright light in their faces, and then, without warning, began shooting.

When it was all over, Ferrin was dead; but Mageau, despite being shot three times, somehow survived to speak to what had happened.

About an hour later, at 12:40 a.m. on July 5, a man called the Vallejo Police Department saying he wanted to "report a murder," giving the dispatcher the location of Mageau and Ferrin's car. Using a calm, low voice, he also confessed that he had "killed those kids last year." It was the first contact anyone had with the killer, but it wouldn't be the last.

Clues and Codes

Mageau was able to describe his attacker as a white male with curly brown hair, around 200 pounds, 5 feet 8 inches tall, in his late 20s. It was little to go on, but it was a start. Then, on August 1, three Northern California newspapers, the *Vallejo Times-Herald*, *San Francisco Chronicle*, and *San Francisco Examiner* all received virtually identical handwritten letters that contained crime details that only the killer could know. Each newspaper also received one third of a three-part coded cipher that the writer claimed would reveal his identity. The letters all ended with the same symbol: a circle with a cross through it.

The killer demanded that the ciphers be published on the front pages of each paper, otherwise he threatened to go on another killing spree. But investigators were not convinced that the letters came from the actual killer, so the *Chronicle* published its part of the code on page four, along with a quote from the Vallejo chief of police asking for more proof.

The promised killing spree never materialized, and all three sections of the cipher were published over the next week. Then, on August 7, the *Examiner* received another letter that began with, "Dear Editor This is the Zodiac speaking." The killer now had a nickname which would soon become infamous. In the letter, the Zodiac Killer described details of the crimes known only to police, and taunted them for not yet solving his code, saying that once they did, they "will have me."

The very next day, a high school teacher named Donald Harden and his wife, Bettye, solved the cipher. The disturbing message began with the words "I like killing people because it is so much fun." The Zodiac then said that he was killing people to act as his "slaves" in the afterlife, in a rambling message full of misspellings and typos. Despite the killer's previous taunt, nowhere did the note reveal, or even hint, at the killer's identity.

A Killer Unchecked

On September 27, 1969, the Zodiac Killer struck again. A man wearing a black hood with a circle and cross symbol on his chest attacked college students Bryan Hartnell and Cecelia Shepard as they were picnicking at Lake Berryessa, tying them up and then stabbing them repeatedly. The attacker then drew the circle and cross symbol on Hartnell's car, along with the dates of each murder. Once again, he called the police—this time the Napa County Sheriff's Office—to report his own crime. And once again, the killer left behind a witness, when Hartnell survived the attack. Police were able to lift a palm print from the pay phone where the killer had called the police, but were unable to match it to a perpetrator.

Even with two witnesses, a description of the attacker, fingerprints, and handwritten letters, the identity of the Zodiac Killer remained frustratingly elusive. The last confirmed Zodiac Killer murder occurred on October 11, 1969, when he shot taxi driver Paul Stine in the head and then ripped off part of Stine's bloodstained shirt. The Zodiac Killer then sent another letter to the *Chronicle*, along with a piece of Stine's shirt, in which he mocked police for failing to catch him and threatened to shoot school children on a bus.

More Letters, But No Answers

Over the next few years, the Zodiac Killer kept up a strange correspondence with Bay Area newspapers, hinting at numerous other victims, making bomb threats, and demanding that people begin wearing buttons featuring his circle and cross

symbol. Some of the letters included codes or strange refer-
ences, including a 340-character cipher sent to the *Chronicle*
on November 8, 1969, that has never been solved. He would
often end his letters with a "score" claiming "SFPD = 00
while the Zodiac's "score" continued to climb, suggesting he
continued his killing spree.

The final letter thought to be from the Zodiac Killer was
sent on January 29, 1974; the killer then simply seemed to
disappear. But the investigation into his identity continues
to this day. More than 2,500 suspects have been considered,
including the "Unibomber," Ted Kaczynski, but no one has
ever been arrested. Law enforcement agencies hope that
modern DNA testing may one day yield clues to his identity.
Until then, the closing line of the Zodiac's final letter still
haunts investigators: "Me – 37; SFPD – 0."

The Guru

He is one of the most notorious criminals the country has ever seen. But surprisingly, although Charles Manson spent most of his life in prison, he never actually killed anyone with his own hands; he simply convinced others to do his bidding.

A Troubled Childhood

Charles Manson had it rough right from the start. He was born Charles Milles Maddox on November 12, 1934, in Cincinnati, Ohio, to his 16-year-old mother, Kathleen Maddox. His biological father was nowhere to be found, so his mother married William Eugene Manson just before his birth. But his teenage mother wasn't ready to settle down with a baby and husband, and she often left her young son with various babysitters while she went out to binge drink.

When Manson was five years old, his mother was arrested for assault and robbery, and spent the next three years in prison. Manson was sent to live with an aunt and uncle until his mother's release from prison, then moved with her to West Virginia, where she continued to drink and run into trouble with the law. With such a tumultuous childhood, perhaps it's no surprise that Manson's first serious offense occurred when he was only nine years old. Known for his frequent truancy, the young Manson set his school on fire. This resulted in a stint at a boarding school for delinquent boys, which did nothing to stop his newfound criminal streak.

A Need for Attention

Over the next decade, Manson lived a life of lawlessness, first engaging in petty theft and then moving on to more serious offenses including car thefts and armed robberies. He received his first prison sentence—three years for stealing a car and failing to appear in court—in 1956. Another prison sentence followed in 1960, after Manson attempted to cash a forged check and then later took two women to New Mexico for the purpose of prostitution. While in prison, authorities noted that he had a "tremendous drive to call attention to himself." They would soon discover that their assessment was correct.

When Manson was released from prison in 1967, he moved to San Francisco and rented an apartment with a female acquaintance. Over the next few months, he allowed more and more women to join them, until 19 women were living in the apartment with Manson. The group, often under the influence of LSD and other hallucinogenic drugs, considered him their "guru," and he began teaching his followers disturbing prophecies and implying that he was Jesus.

Dysfunctional "Family"

At he continued to gain followers, Manson moved "the Manson Family" to Spahn Ranch, a Los Angeles movie set that was no longer in use. He continued to prophesy to his followers, telling them that a race war would soon occur in the United States, and Armageddon was imminent. Even more unnerving, Manson began to believe that he himself was the key to unleashing the apocalypse.

Manson's plan was to purposely trigger the prophesied race war by killing white celebrities and pinning their murders on black people. On August 8, 1969, he set his plan in motion. Four of Manson's followers were ordered to go to the house that actress Sharon Tate was renting, and to kill everyone inside. The resulting murders horrified the nation, as did the Manson-ordered murders of Leno and Rosemary LaBianca the next day.

Over the next few months, evidence pointing to many of Manson's Family members mounted, and on December 1, several of his followers were arrested. Manson was already in custody on suspicion of car theft, and the "guru" would never go free again. During the trial, neither Manson nor any of his followers showed remorse for their actions, and on January 25, 1971, Manson was convicted of first-degree murder and sentenced to death. His sentence would later be commuted to life in prison when California abolished the death penalty in 1972. The leader of the murderous Manson Family died on November 19, 2017, at the age of 83, having spent four decades behind bars.

7 Grisly Crimes

Our TV screens are saturated with crime. Every night we witness more bizarre slayings and mayhem than the night before. Makes you wonder how far-fetched those scriptwriters will get. After all, real people don't commit those types of crimes, right? Wrong. In fact, the annals of history are crammed with crimes even more gruesome than anything seen on television. Here are some of the 20th century's wildest crimes.

1. **Ed Kemper:** Ed Kemper had a genius IQ, but his appetite for murder took over at age 15 when he shot his grandparents because he wanted to see what it felt like. Nine years later, he'd done his time for that crime, and during 1972 and 1973, Kemper hit the California highways, picking up pretty students and killing them before taking the corpses back to his apartment, having sex with them, then dissecting them. He killed six women in that manner and then took an ax to his own mother, decapitating and raping her, then using her body as a dartboard. Still not satisfied, he killed one of his mother's friends as well. Upset that his crimes didn't garner the media attention he thought they warranted, Kemper confessed to police. He gleefully went into detail about his penchant for necrophilia and decapitation. He asked to be executed, but because capital punishment was suspended at the time, he got life imprisonment and remains incarcerated in California.

2. **Andrei Chikatilo:** Andrei Chikatilo was Russia's most notorious serial killer. The Rostov Ripper, as he came to be called, began his rampage in 1978 in the city of Shakhty, where he started abducting teenagers and subjecting them to unspeakable torture before raping and murdering them, and, often, cannibalizing their bodies. Authorities gave the crimes little attention, but as the body count grew, police were forced to face the facts—Russia had a serial killer. Chikatilo was actually brought in for questioning when the police found a rope and butcher knife in his bag during a routine search, but he was released and allowed to continue his killing spree. In the end, he got careless and was arrested near the scene of his latest murder. Under interrogation, he confessed to 56 murders. During the trial, he was kept in a cage in the middle of the court, playing up the image of the deranged lunatic. It didn't help his cause, though. He was found guilty and executed with a shot to the back of the head on February 14, 1994.

3. **Cameron Hooker:** With the assistance of his wife, Janice, in May 1977, Cameron Hooker snatched a 20-year-old woman who was hitchhiking to a friend's house in northern California. He locked her in a wooden box that was kept under the bed he shared with Janice, who was well aware of what lay beneath. During the next seven years, Hooker repeatedly tortured, beaten, and sexually assaulted the young woman. Eventually, she was allowed out of the box to do household chores, but she was forced to wear a slave collar. As time went by, Hooker allowed his prisoner more and more freedom, even letting her get a part-time job. Janice's conscience finally got the best of her, and she helped the young woman escape. After seven years of hell, the prisoner simply got on a bus and left. Hooker was convicted and sentenced to 104 years in a box of his own.

4. **Andras Pandy:** Andras Pandy was a Belgian pastor who had eight children by two different wives. Between 1986 and 1989, his former wives and four of the children disappeared. Pandy tried to appease investigators by faking papers to show that they were living in Hungary. He even coerced other children into impersonating the missing ones. Then, under intense questioning, Pandy's daughter Agnes broke down. She told authorities that she had been held by her father as a teenage sex slave and then was forced to join him in killing her family members, including her mother, brothers, stepmother, and stepsister. The bodies were chopped up, dissolved in drain cleaner, and flushed down the drain. Pandy was sentenced to life in prison, while Agnes received 21 years as an accomplice. Until his death in 2013, he still claimed that all of the missing family members are alive and well in Hungary.

5. **Harold Shipman:** The most prolific serial killer in modern history was British doctor Harold Shipman, who murdered up to 400 of his patients between 1970 and 1998. Shipman was a respected member of the community, but in March 1998, a colleague became alarmed at the high death rate among his patients. She went to the local coroner, who in turn went to the police. They investigated, but found nothing out of the ordinary. But when a woman named Kathleen Grundy died a few months later, it was revealed that she had cut her daughter Angela out of her will and, instead, bequeathed £386,000 to Shipman. Suspicious, Angela went to the police, who began another investigation. Kathleen Grundy's body was exhumed and examined, and traces of diamorphine (heroin) were found in her system. Shipman was arrested and charged with murder. When police examined his patient files more closely, they realized that Shipman was overdosing patients with diamor-

phine, then forging their medical records to state that they were in poor health. Shipman was found guilty and sentenced to 15 consecutive life sentences, but he hanged himself in his cell in January 2004.

6. **Fred and Rose West:** In the early 1970s, a pattern developed in which young women were lured to the home of Fred and Rose West in Gloucester, England, subjected to sexual depravities, and then ritually slaughtered in the soundproof basement. The bodies were dismembered and disposed of under the cellar floor. As the number of victims increased, the garden became a secondary burial plot. This became the final resting place of their own daughter, 16-year-old Heather, who was butchered in June 1983.

   Police became increasingly concerned about the whereabouts of Heather. One day they decided to take the family joke that she was "buried under the patio" seriously. When they began excavating the property in June 1994, the number of body parts uncovered shocked the world. With overwhelming evidence stacked against him, Fred West committed suicide while in custody in 1995. Rose received life imprisonment.

7. **John Wayne Gacy:** In the mid-1960s, John Wayne Gacy was, by all outward appearances, a happily married Chicago-area businessman who doted on his two young children. But when Gacy was convicted of sodomy in 1968, he got ten years in jail, and his wife divorced him. Eighteen months later, Gacy was out on parole. He started a construction company, and in his spare time, he volunteered as a clown to entertain sick children. He also began picking up homeless male prostitutes. After taking them home, Gacy would beat, rape, and slaughter his victims before depositing the bodies in the crawl space underneath his house.

In 1978, an investigation into the disappearance of 15-year-old Robert Piest led police to Gacy, following reports that the two had been seen together on the night the boy disappeared. Suspicions were heightened when detectives uncovered Gacy's sodomy conviction, and a warrant was issued to search his home. Detectives found a piece of jewelry belonging to a boy who had disappeared a year before. They returned to the house with excavating equipment and they made a gruesome discovery.

Gacy tried to escape the death penalty with a tale of multiple personalities, but it didn't impress the jury. It took them only two hours to convict him of 33 murders. On May 10, 1994, he was put to death by lethal injection.

The Clean-Cut Killer

One of the most notorious serial killers in history, Ted Bundy confessed to killing 36 women, but the true number may be even higher. His murderous rampage spanned the country, from Seattle to Tallahassee.

A Bright Future

At the time Ted Bundy was born, on November 24, 1946, having a child out of wedlock was often considered shameful. So his single mother, Eleanor Louise Cowell, gave birth to him at a home for unwed mothers in Burlington, Vermont, then allowed her parents to raise him as their son while she was considered his "sister." Cowell never admitted to the identity of Bundy's biological father, but when he was about three years old, she moved with him to Tacoma, Washington, and married his new stepfather, Johnny Bundy.

While Bundy showed some unusual behavior from an early age, such as a fascination with knives, he was also a good student with a seemingly bright future ahead of him. He had a few false starts after high school, bouncing between several universities and working minimum-wage jobs, but Bundy eventually settled at the University of Washington, where he became an honor student who earned a degree in psychology. He even worked at Seattle's Suicide Crisis Hotline Center, where coworkers described him as "empathetic."

A Serial Killer Is Born

Whether that "empathy" was a façade or not, one thing is certain: eventually, it disappeared altogether. Investigators were never able to pinpoint exactly when Bundy went from a promising honor student to a cold-blooded killer, but many believe it was around 1974. In January of that year, he snuck into a University of Washington student's apartment as she slept and viciously bludgeoned her with a metal bedframe. Although she survived, she was in a coma for ten days and sustained permanent physical and mental damage.

Frighteningly, over the next few months, female university students in Washington and Oregon began vanishing. Several witnesses described a man who always seemed to turn up in the area of the disappearances. He was young, had dark hair, drove a tan Volkswagen Beetle, and often had an arm in a sling or a cast on his leg. He would lure women by asking for help carrying books or loading boxes in his car. Police were able to create a composite sketch thanks to witness descriptions, and several people came forward with Bundy's name. His reign of terror might have ended there, but authorities simply thought the young man seemed too "clean cut" to be their perpetrator.

Stopping the Monster

By August 1974, the disappearances in the Pacific Northwest ended, but the same thing began to occur in Utah, Colorado, and Idaho when Bundy started attending the University of Utah Law School. A year later, Utah police caught a break when they stopped a tan Volkswagen Beetle suspiciously cruising a neighborhood early one morning. Inside, Bundy had a veritable "kidnapping kit," complete with ski mask, handcuffs, rope, crowbar, and ice pick. Bundy perfectly fit the description of the offender in a recent kidnapping case, and he was arrested. He was tried, convicted, and sentenced to 15 years in prison for kidnapping, but escaped after only a few months.

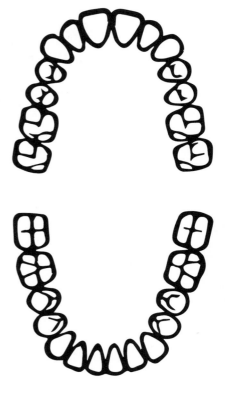

Now on the run, Bundy made his way across the country to Tallahassee, where he broke into a sorority house in the middle of the night, killing two women and leaving two others with terrible injuries. His final victim, a week later, was only 12 years old when she was murdered by Bundy. Police closed in on the serial killer, who had left a trail of evidence and witnesses throughout Florida, and who had no money, no car, and nowhere to run.

Bundy was tried in 1979 and 1980 for several murders and kidnappings, and sentenced to death by electrocution. Before his death, he confessed to dozens of murders and described how he not only killed the women, but would often return to their dead bodies, to bathe them, dress them, and, most disturbingly, engage in necrophilia. In accordance with his will, after he was executed on January 24, 1989, Bundy's ashes were scattered in the Cascade Mountains—the same area where he confessed to killing several women. In death, as in life, Ted Bundy continues to haunt his victims.

Chapter 2

Behind the Crime Scene

Top Ten Crime Scene Traces

Have people learned nothing from TV crime shows? Here's a hint: Just walk through a room, let alone commit a crime, and you'll leave a trace that will detail your every action.

1. **Tool marks:** If you use any sort of physical object to commit your crime—a pickax on a door lock, a ladder to reach a window, a knife or a rag (for any purpose)—it will be traceable. Tools used in any capacity create tiny nicks that can be detected, identified, and tracked by a crime-scene investigator.

2. **Paint:** A simple paint chip left at a crime scene reveals volumes. If it's from the vehicle you used in committing the crime, it indicates the make and model. If paint is found on the tool you used to break into a house, it could place you at the scene. Think it's too hard for investigators to distinguish specific paint colors? There are 40,000 types of paint classified in police databases.

3. **Dust and dirt:** Even if you're a neat-and-tidy sort of criminal, dust and dirt are often missed by the most discerning eye. These particles can reveal where you live and work and if you have a pet (and what kind). If you've trudged through fields or someone's backyard, researchers can use palynology—the science that studies plant spores, insects, seeds, and other microorganisms—to track you down.

4. **Broken glass:** Microscopic glass fragments cling to your clothes and can't be laundered out easily. Crime labs examine tint, thickness, density, and refractive index of the fragments to determine their origins.

5. **Fibers:** The sources include clothing, drapes, wigs, carpets, furniture, blankets, pets, and plants. Using a compound microscope, an analyst can determine if the fibers are manufactured or natural, which often indicates their value as evidence. The more specific the fiber, the easier it will be to identify (consider the differences between fibers from a white cotton T-shirt and those from a multicolored wool sweater). There are more than a thousand known fibers, as well as several thousand dyes, so if an exact match is found, you will be too.

6. **Blood:** A victim's blood tells investigators a lot, but they're also looking for different kinds of blood—including yours if you were injured at the scene—and the patterns of blood distribution. Detectives are well trained in collecting blood evidence to estimate when the crime occurred and who was involved. By the way, don't think it's enough just to clean up any blood, because investigators use special lights that reveal your efforts.

7. **Bodily fluids:** Saliva, urine, vomit, and semen are a crime-scene investigator's dream, providing DNA evidence that will implicate even the most savvy criminal. Saliva is commonly found left behind by a criminal who took time out for a beverage, a snack, or a cigarette.

8. **Fingerprints:** One of the best ways to identify a criminal is through fingerprints left at the scene. But you kept track of what you touched and then wiped everything down, right? It doesn't matter: You still left smeared prints that can be lifted and analyzed. Investigators enter fingerprint evidence into national databases that can point directly to you.

9. **Shoe prints:** If you have feet (and assuming you're not a "barefoot burglar"), you left behind shoe prints. They could be in soil or snow or perhaps on a carpet or across a bare floor. The particular treads on the soles of shoes make them easy to trace, and the bottoms of most shoes have nicks or scratches that make them easy to identify.

10. **Hair:** Humans shed a lot of hair from all parts of their bodies, so bald bandits have no advantage. Hairs as tiny as eyelashes and eyebrows have unique characteristics that reveal a lot about a person, including race, dietary habits, and overall health. And don't forget: While your hair is dropping all over the crime scene, the victim's hair is clinging to your clothing.

The Thief of Police

Some say that the best way to catch a criminal is to think like a criminal. Eugene Francois Vidocq took that idea to heart.

From the Circus to the Army

Born on July 24, 1775, in Arras, France, Eugene Francois Vidocq wasted no time in embracing a life of petty crime. His father owned a bakery and a general store, where he dealt in corn and turned a decent profit, making his family reasonably wealthy and privileged. But that didn't stop a young, teenaged Vidocq from getting into fights and stealing money from his own family's bakery. After several such incidents, his father had him thrown in prison for two weeks, hoping the experience would discourage Vidocq from engaging in crime; unfortunately, the plan didn't work.

Vidocq decided to board a ship to America, stealing a large amount of money to help him get started in his new life. But before he could set off for the new continent, he himself was the victim of a theft, waking up one morning to find his (stolen) money had been, ironically, stolen. Now penniless, Vidocq was forced to join a circus to make ends meet, although he was not a gifted performer. And when he was caught kissing the wife of a puppeteer, his circus career was over.

In 1791 Vidocq joined the army, which turned out to be a much better fit for his talents. Already well-versed in the art of fighting, the teenager gained a reputation for challenging other soldiers to duels, earning the nickname "Reckless." But when he challenged a superior officer to a duel, Vidocq was arrested for insubordination. This didn't sit well with him: he deserted and enlisted in a different army under a false identity.

Master of Escape

In 1793 Vidocq left the army and returned to his hometown of Arras. The next few years were restless and troubled for the young adult. He began to wander around France and Belgium, committing frauds and thefts to support himself. In Lille, France, he fell in love with a woman named Francine Longuet, but she left him for another man. Vidocq attacked and beat him, for which Vidocq was sent to prison.

This began a pattern of arrests, prison, and prison breaks for Vidocq. He became quite adept at slipping away from the authorities who were supposed to be keeping him under lock and key. One time he escaped dressed as a sailor; another time he escaped wearing a nun's habit. He even jumped out a window into a river during one prison break. He spent years on the run, at one point being sentenced to death due to his constant crime sprees.

A U-Turn

By July 1809, Vidocq realized he was up against the proverbial wall. He needed a way out of the crime-filled hole he had dug for himself. So instead of continuing to run from the police, he offered them his services as an informant. The police agreed, and Vidocq began providing information about the many criminals he had worked with over the years. His spying resulted in so many arrests and convictions that in 1811 he officially became a member of the police force. He developed and founded a plainclothes unit of officers called the *Brigade de la Sûreté*, or the Security Brigade, and in 1813, Napoleon Bonaparte declared it a state security force with authority over all of France.

Vidocq resigned from the police force in 1832 and pioneered another idea: He began the first private police agency. Although authorities eventually suppressed the organization, Vidocq's *Bureau des Renseignements* (Office of Information), was the precursor to the modern detective agency.

Vidocq became well-known all over France, where he befriended authors like Victor Hugo, Honore de Balzac, and Alexandre Dumas. His exploits were believed to have inspired some of their stories, including the characters of both the escaped convict Valjean and the policeman Javert in Hugo's *Les Miserables*. Vidocq died on May 11, 1857, at the age of 81, leaving behind a legacy that is a curious mix of criminality and law enforcement.

No Two Fingerprint Readers Are Alike

Even if you're innocent, you may get fingered falsely by a fingerprint. They're not as reliable as people think.

- Until DNA testing came along, fingerprint identification was considered the gold standard of evidence. But it turns out that fingerprint identification is far from foolproof.

- A *Chicago Tribune* investigative study on forensics found that fingerprint analysis is subjective and that even the most experienced examiners make egregious mistakes. *Tribune* reporters reviewed 200 cases of DNA and death row exonerations nationwide over a 20-year period and found that more than 25 percent had been based on flawed forensic testing or testimony.

- Another *Tribune* study examined the "science" of finger-printing. When researchers sifted through the findings culled by an independent proficiency tester, they learned that crime lab examiners often got things wrong. In fact, nearly a quarter of the U.S. labs cited in the study returned false positives.

- Fingerprint identification is far from an exact "science." Analysts look for points of similarity, but there are no universal standards, and no research dictates the number of points that establish a match with certainty. A complete fingerprint is rarely lifted from a crime scene, and yet no research determines how much of a latent (partial) fingerprint is sufficient to create a match.

- A study published in the *Journal of Forensic Sciences* found error rates at or above 2 percent, while another study found the rate could be as low as 0.8 percent or as high as 4 percent. Obviously, there's more than perception and numbers at stake. A false positive at the 2 percent rate would mean that there are approximately 4,800 false convictions or guilty pleas every year.

Leave No Trace?

Movie bad guys are always trying to sand or burn off their fingerprints, but can it really be done?

An Ancient Art

The use of fingerprints as identifiers or signatures dates back thousands of years, when different ancient civilizations used fingerprints on official documents. By the 1300s, someone had already noted, in surviving documents, that all the fingerprints he had seen in his life were unique. Scientists now know that fingerprints emerge during the first trimester of human embryo development and last in the same form for the entire human lifetime. Older people can naturally have very shallow fingerprints that are hard to read, but the shapes of these fingerprints are still the same.

People who work in certain fields are more likely to sand their fingerprints off during their regular daily routines. Construction workers who build with brick, stone, concrete, and other abrasive materials can end up losing their fingerprints. So can people who handle a lot of paper or cardboard. These changes are temporary: since only the topmost layer of skin is abraded, it will come back with the same pattern.

A Modern Problem

In the 21st century, people noticed a new form of fingerprint annihilation. A small number of cancer patients being treated with a chemotherapy drug called capecitabine found that they no longer had fingerprints. In the past, people easily went entire lifetimes without ever noticing their fingerprints, but modern banking and security often require them, and fingerprint technology is now showing up in the protection of personal devices like smartphones and laptops. Patients have been questioned in banks, locked out of their own computers, and stopped in security lines—as if being treated for cancer wasn't hard enough.

Researchers aren't sure whether or not these cancer patients' damaged or obliterated fingerprints will eventually grow back. But how could it be ambiguous like this? The answer is in the makeup of our fingerprints, which grow up into the topmost layer of skin *from* the layer beneath. If you trimmed down your rose bushes for the winter, would you expect tulips the next spring? Without doing major damage to your fingertips, you simply can't get rid of your fingerprints.

The Imperfect Solution

Villains of the past have tried a lot of superficial ways to scrub off their identities. The first known and famous case was a gangster in the 1930s named Handsome Jack, who made cuts to disrupt his fingerprints. His case made a splash in the press, but his mutilated prints were even easier to spot than they had been. Most documented attempts to change fingerprints fall into this category, where the actions taken to obscure the fingerprints create a new, more identifiable, scarred fingerprint.

To truly distort and alter your fingerprints, you would need to disrupt the connection between the two layers of skin where fingerprints root and grow. As of yet, there's no reasonable way to do this. Criminals and other wannabe disappearers may have more luck in the future.

Exposed to Poison

Long a favorite of mystery-novel writers and opportunistic bad guys, poison has an ancient and infamous relationship with people. Some poisons occur naturally and others are manufactured, but all of them spell bad news if you're the unlucky recipient of a dose.

Poison Plants

Deadly Nightshade, aka belladonna: Every part of this perennial herb is poisonous, but the berries are especially dangerous. The poison attacks the nervous system instantly, causing a rapid pulse, hallucinations, convulsions, ataxia, and coma.

Wolfsbane: This deadly plant was used as an arrow poison in ancient China, but its name comes from the Greek word meaning "dart." Wolfsbane takes a while to work, but when it does, it causes extreme anxiety, chest pain, and death from respiratory arrest.

Meadow Saffron: This tough little plant can be boiled and dried, and it still retains all of its poisonous power. As little as seven milligrams of this stuff could cause colic, paralysis, and heart failure.

Hemlock: This plant is probably the best known of the herbaceous poisons: It was used to knock off the Greek philosopher Socrates. Hemlock is poisonous down to the last leaf and will often send you into a coma before it finishes you for good.

Plans of Attack

There are five ways a person can be exposed to poison: ingestion (through the mouth), inhalation (breathed in through the nose or mouth), ocular (in the eyes), dermal (on the skin), and parenteral (from bites or stings).

Helpful Poison Stats

More than half of poison exposures occur in children under the age of six, and most poisonings involve medications and vitamins, household and chemical personal-care products, and plants. Eighty-nine percent of all poisonings occur at home. If you or someone in your house ingests something poisonous, stay calm and call 911 (if the person has collapsed or is not breathing) or your local poison control center (three-quarters of exposures can be treated over the phone with guidance from an expert).

Good Old Arsenic

Mystery novels are filled with stories of characters choosing to off their enemies with arsenic. Colorless and odorless, this close relative of phosphorous exists in a variety of compounds, not all of which are poisonous. Women in

Victorian times used to rub a diluted arsenic compound into their skin to improve their complexions, and some modern medications used to treat cancer actually contain arsenic. When certain arsenic compounds are concentrated, however, they're deadly; arsenic has been blamed for widespread death through groundwater contamination.

The Dubiously Poisoned

Napoleon Bonaparte: Many historians believe that Napoleon died of arsenic poisoning while imprisoned, because significant traces of arsenic were found in his body by forensics experts 200 years after his death. It has been argued, however, that at that time in history, wallpaper and paint often contained arsenic-laced pigments, and that Napoleon was simply exposed to the poison in his everyday surroundings.

Vincent Van Gogh: Emerald green, a color of paint used by Impressionist painters, contained an arsenic-based pigment. Some historians suggest that Van Gogh's neurological problems had a great deal to do with his use of large quantities of emerald green paint.

Food Poisoning

Unfortunately, this is a form of poisoning most of us know something about. When food is spoiled or contaminated, bacteria such as salmonella breed quickly. Because we can't see or taste these bacteria, we chomp happily away and don't realize we're about to become really sick. The Centers for Disease Control and Prevention estimates that in the United States alone, food poisoning causes about 76 million illnesses, 325,000 hospitalizations, and up to 5,000 deaths each year.

Blood Poisoning

This form of poisoning occurs when an infectious agent or its toxin spreads through the bloodstream. People actually have a low level of bacteria in their blood most of the time, but if nasty bacteria are introduced, they can cause sepsis, a life-threatening condition. The bacteria can enter the bloodstream through open wounds or from the bite of a parasite.

Snakebites

Because snakes' venom is injected, snakes themselves are considered "venomous" rather than "poisonous." Still, an estimated 8,000 snakebites occur in the United States every year. Poisonous snakes found in North America include rattlesnakes, copperheads, cottonmouths, and coral snakes. While most of these reptiles won't bite unless provoked, if you are bitten you have to take the antivenom fast. Arthur Conan Doyle's Sherlock Holmes story, "The Adventure of the Speckled Band," famously involves the use of a live snake as a murder weapon.

Skull and Crossbones

When pirates sailed the high seas, they flew a flag emblazoned with a skull-and-crossbones symbol. When seafarers saw this Jolly Roger flag, they knew trouble was on its way. Bottles that contain poisons or other toxic substances often bear this symbol to warn anyone against drinking or even touching the contents with bare hands. Murder mysteries have revolved around a character removing a warning label or switching it to confuse something benign with something poisonous.

Allan Pinkerton—Spying for the Union Cause

The exploits of Allan Pinkerton during the Civil War helped pave the way for the modern Secret Service.

In a letter to President Lincoln dated April 21, 1861, detective Allan Pinkerton offered his services and commented on one of the traits that would make him an icon of law enforcement for generations. "Secrecy is the great lever I propose to operate with," he wrote.

Establishing the Eye

Born in Scotland in 1819, Pinkerton came to the United States in 1842. He originally was a barrel builder by trade, but his skills at observation and deduction led him to a career fighting crime. By age 30, he'd joined the sheriff's office of Cook County, Illinois, and been appointed Chicago's first detective. He later joined attorney Edward Rucker to form the North-Western Police Agency, forerunner of the Pinkerton Agency. As his corporate logo, Pinkerton chose an open eye, perhaps to demonstrate that his agents never slept. Clients began calling him "The Eye." Pinkerton and his operatives were hired to solve the growing number of train robberies, which became more and more of a problem as railroads expanded across the nation. George B. McClellan, president of the Ohio and Mississippi Railroad, took particular notice.

Wartime Duties

In 1861, Pinkerton's agency was hired to protect the Philadelphia, Wilmington, and Baltimore Railroad. In the course of their duties, Pinkerton and his agents learned of a preinaugural plot to kill President-elect Lincoln. The detectives secretly took Lincoln into Washington before he was scheduled to arrive, thwarting the conspirators. Lincoln was inaugurated without incident.

When the war began, Pinkerton was given the duty of protecting the president as a forerunner of today's Secret Service. He was also put in charge of gathering intelligence for the army, now run by his old railroad boss, McClellan. The detective and his operatives infiltrated enemy lines. Using surveillance and undercover work, both new concepts at the time, agents gathered vital information. Pinkerton tried to get details any way he could. His people interviewed escaped slaves and tried to convince literate former slaves to return to the South to spy. He used female spies, and he even infiltrated the Confederacy himself several times using the alias Major E. J. Allen.

Uncertain Information

While much of this was invaluable, his work was tarnished by a seeming inability to identify enemy troop strengths. His reports of enemy troops were detailed, including notes on morale, supplies, movements, and even descriptions of the buttons on uniforms. Yet the numbers of troops he provided were highly suspect.

In October 1861, as McClellan was preparing to fight, Pinkerton reported that Confederate General Joseph Johnston's troops in Virginia were "not less than 150,000 strong." In reality, there were fewer than 50,000. The next year he reported the strength of Confederate General John Magruder at Yorktown, putting troop numbers at about 120,000 when the true number was closer to 17,000.

After the true strength of these forces was discovered, Pinkerton was ridiculed. Some historians believe that Pinkerton was unaware of the faulty information, but others insist he intentionally provided inflated figures to support McClellan's conservative battle plans. The truth will likely never be known, as all of Pinkerton's records of the war were lost in the Great Chicago Fire of 1871.

Return to Civilian Life

After McClellan, one of Pinkerton's staunchest supporters, was relieved of his command by Lincoln, Pinkerton limited his spying activities and shifted his work back toward criminal cases, which included the pursuit of war profiteers. He ultimately returned to Chicago and his agency, working until his death in 1884.

Life on the Body Farm

When Mary Scarborough wrote the lyrics to "Old MacDonald Had a Farm," she probably didn't have a research facility in mind. In fact, one won't find cows, chickens, or pigs that go "oink" at the Body Farm—just scores of rotting human bodies.

E-I-E-I-Oh, Gross

The Body Farm (officially known as the University of Tennessee Forensic Anthropology Facility) was the brainchild of Dr. William Bass, a forensic anthropologist from Kansas. Its purpose, however nauseating, is to help law enforcement agencies learn to estimate how long a person has been dead. After all, determining the time of death is crucial in confirming alibis and establishing timelines for violent crimes.

After 11 years of watching and learning about human decomposition, Bass realized how little was actually known about what happens to the human body after death. With this in mind, he approached the University of Tennessee Medical Center and asked for a small plot of land where he could control what happens to a post-mortem body and study the results. The facility was established in the 1980s.

A Creepy Joint

Just outside of Knoxville, the eerie three-acre wooded plot that Bass claimed for his scientific studies—which is surrounded by a razor wire fence (lest the dead bodies try to escape?)—is where an unspecified number of cadavers in various states of decomposition are kept.

While some hang out completely in the open, others spend their time in shallow graves or entombed in vaults. Others dip their toes and other body parts in ponds. And a few spend eternity inside sealed car trunks.

Body Snatchers

If you're going to start a body farm, it doesn't take a forensic anthropologist to realize that there might be a problem in obtaining bodies. One way is to use bodies that have been donated for medical studies. Another focuses on cadavers that rot away each year at medical examiners offices, with nary a soul to claim them. Enter Bass and his associates. Like "pods" from *Invasion of the Body Snatchers*, these scientists grab every body they can lay their hands on.

Reading the Body

According to Bass, two things occur when a person dies. At the time of death, digestive enzymes begin to feed on the body, "liquefying" the tissues. If flies have access to it, they lay eggs in the body. Eventually, the eggs hatch into larvae that feast on the remaining tissues. By monitoring and noting how much time it takes for maggots to consume the tissues, authorities can estimate how long a person has been dead. Scientists can also compare the types of flies that are indigenous to the area with the types that have invaded the body to determine whether the body has been moved. "People will have alibis for certain periods," says Bass. "If you can determine that the death happened at another time or location, it makes a big difference in the outcome of the court case."

But the farm isn't all tissue decomposition—scientists also learn about the normal wear-and-tear that a human body goes through. For instance, anthropologists look at the teeth of the victim to try to determine their age at the time of death. The skull and pelvic girdles are helpful in determining a person's sex, and scientists can also estimate how tall the person was by measuring the long bones of the legs or even a single finger. Other researchers watch what happens to the five types of fatty acids leaking from the body into the ground. By analyzing the profiles of the acids, scientists can determine the time of death and how long it has been at its current location.

Simulations and Defenses

The prestigious FBI uses the Body Farm as a real-world simulator to help train its agents. Every February, representatives visit the site to dig for bodies that farm hands have prepared as simulated crime scenes. "We have five of them down there for them," explains Bass. "They excavate the burials and look for evidence that we put there."

Stranger Than Fiction

Bass's Body Farm drew the attention of readers when popular crime novelist Patricia Cornwell featured it in her 1994 book, *The Body Farm*. In it, Cornwell describes a research facility that stages human corpses in various states of decay and in a variety of locations—wooded areas, the trunk of a car, underwater, or beneath a pile of leaves—all to determine how bodies decay under different circumstances.

Unfortunately, the real perps are catching on. Some criminals try to confuse investigators by tampering with the bodies and burial sites, spraying the victim with insecticides that prevent insects (such as maggots) from doing their job.

Further Afield

At another facility at the University of New Mexico, scientists have collected over 500 human skeletons and store them as "skeletal archives" to create biological profiles based on what happens to bones over time. And in Germany, the Max Planck Institute for Computer Science has been working on a 3D graphics program based on forensic data to produce more accurate likenesses of the victims. Although many other proposed farms never got off the ground due to community protest, since the inception of Bass's original Body Farm, another farm has been established at Western Carolina University. Ideally, Bass would like to see body farms all over the nation. Since decaying bodies react differently depending on their climate and surroundings, says Bass, "It's important to gather information from other research facilities across the United States."

The Clairvoyant Crime-Buster

Before there were TV shows like Ghost Whisperer *and* Medium, *which make the idea of solving crimes through ESP seem almost commonplace, there was psychic detective Arthur Price Roberts. And his work was accomplished in the early 1900s, when high-tech aids like electronic surveillance and DNA identification were still only far-fetched dreams. Police in those times often used purported psychics to help solve many cases.*

"I See Dead People"

A modest man born in Wales in 1866, Roberts deliberately avoided a formal education because he believed too much learning could stifle his unusual abilities. He moved to Milwaukee, Wisconsin, as a young man where, ironically, the man who never learned to read was nicknamed "Doc."

One of his earliest well-known cases involved a baffling missing person incident in Peshtigo, a small town about 160 miles north of Milwaukee. A man named Duncan McGregor had gone missing in July 1905, leaving no clue as to his whereabouts. The police searched for him for months, and finally his desperate wife decided to go to the psychic detective who had already made a name for himself in Milwaukee. She didn't even have to explain the situation to Roberts; he knew immediately upon meeting her who she was.

Roberts meditated on the vanished husband, then sadly had to tell Mrs. McGregor that he'd been murdered and that his body was in the Peshtigo River, caught near the bottom in a pile of timber. Roberts proved correct in every detail.

Mystery of the Mad Bombers

Roberts solved numerous documented cases. He helped a Chicago man find his brother who had traveled to Albuquerque and had not been heard from for months; Roberts predicted that the brother's body would be found in a certain spot in Devil's Canyon, and it was.

After coming up with new evidence for an 11th hour pardon, Roberts saved a Chicago man named Ignatz Potz, who had been condemned to die for a murder he didn't commit. But his most famous coup came in 1935 when he correctly predicted that the city of Milwaukee would be hit by six large dynamite explosions, losing a town hall, banks, and police stations. People snickered; such mayhem was unheard of in Milwaukee. Roberts made his prediction on October 18 of that year. In little more than a week, the Milwaukee area entered a time of terror.

First, a town hall in the outlying community of Shorewood was blasted, killing two children and wounding many other people. A few weeks later, the mad bombers hit two banks and two police stations. Federal agents descended upon the city, and several local officers were assigned to work solely on solving the bombings. Finally, the police went to Roberts to learn what was coming next. Roberts told them one more blast was in the works, that it would be south of the Menomonee River, and that it would be the final bomb. Police took him at his word and blanketed the area with officers and sharpshooters.

And sure enough, on November 4, a garage in the predicted area blew to smithereens in an explosion that could be heard as far as eight miles away. The two terrorists, young men 18 and 21 years old, had been hard at work in the shed assembling 50 pounds of dynamite when their plan literally backfired. Few people argued with Roberts's abilities after that.

His Final Fortune

Roberts's eeriest prediction, however, may have been that of his own death. In November 1939, he told a group of assembled friends that he would be leaving this world on January 2, 1940. And he did, passing quietly in his own home on that exact date. Many of his most amazing accomplishments will probably never be known because a lot of his work was done secretly for various law enforcement agencies. But "Doc" Roberts had an undeniable gift, and he died secure in the knowledge that he had used it to help others as best he could.

Psychic Detectives

"Doc" Roberts wasn't the only person with a reputation for unusual abilities. When the corpse just can't be found, the murderer remains unknown, and the weapon has been stashed in some secret corner, law enforcement agencies may tap their secret weapons.

"Reading" the Ripper: Robert James Lees

When the psychotic murderer known as Jack the Ripper terrorized London in the 1880s, the detectives of Scotland Yard consulted a psychic named Robert James Lees who said he had glimpsed the killer's face in several visions. Lees also claimed he had correctly forecasted at least three of the well-publicized murders of women. The Ripper wrote a sarcastic note to detectives stating that they would still never catch him. Indeed, the killer proved right in this prediction.

Feeling Their Vibes: Florence Sternfels

As a psychometrist—a psychic who gathers impressions by handling material objects—Florence Sternfels was successful enough to charge a dollar for readings in Edgewater, New Jersey, in the early 20th century. Born in 1891, Sternfels believed that her gift was a natural ability rather than a supernatural one, so she never billed police for her help in solving crimes. Some of her best "hits" included preventing a man from blowing up an army base with dynamite, finding two missing boys alive in Philadelphia, and leading police to the body of a murdered young woman. She worked with police as far away as Europe to solve tough cases but lived quietly in New Jersey until her death in 1965.

The Dutch Grocer's Gift: Gerard Croiset

Born in the Netherlands in 1909, Gerard Croiset nurtured a growing psychic ability from age six. In 1935, he joined a Spiritualist group, began to hone his talents, and within two years had set up shop as a psychic and healer. After a touring lecturer discovered his abilities in 1945, Croiset began assisting law enforcement agencies around the world, traveling as far as Japan and Australia. He specialized in finding missing children but also helped authorities locate lost papers and artifacts. At the same time, Croiset ran a popular clinic for psychic healing that treated both humans and animals. His son, Gerard Croiset, Jr., was also a professional psychic and parapsychologist.

Accidental Psychic: Peter Hurkos

As one of the most famous psychic detectives of the 20th century, Peter Hurkos did his best work by picking up vibes from victims' clothing. Born in the Netherlands in 1911, Hurkos lived an ordinary life as a house painter until a fall required him to undergo brain surgery at age 30. The operation seemed to trigger his latent psychic powers, and he was almost immediately able to mentally retrieve information about people and "read" the history of objects by handling them.

Hurkos assisted in the Boston Strangler investigation in the early 1960s, and in 1969, he was brought in to help solve the grisly murders executed by Charles Manson. He gave police many accurate details including the name Charlie, a description of Manson, and that the murders were ritual slayings.

The TV Screen Mind of Dorothy Allison

New Jersey housewife Dorothy Allison broke into the world of clairvoyant crime solving when she dreamed about a missing local boy as if seeing it on television. In her dream, the five-year-old boy was stuck in some kind of pipe. When she called police, she also described the child's clothing, including the odd fact that he was wearing his shoes on the opposite feet. When Allison underwent hypnosis to learn more details, she added that the boy's surroundings involved a fenced school and a factory. She was proven correct on all accounts when the boy's body was found about two months after he went missing, floating close to a pipe in a pond near a school and a factory with his little shoes still tied onto the wrong feet. Allison, who began having psychic experiences as a child, considered her gift a blessing and never asked for pay. One of her more famous cases was that of missing heiress Patty Hearst in 1974. Although Allison was unable to find her, every prediction she made about the young woman came true, including the fact that she had dyed her hair red.

Like a Bolt Out of the Blue: John Catchings

While at a Texas barbeque on an overcast July 4, 1969, 22-year-old John Catchings was hit by a bolt of lightning. He survived but said the electric blast opened him to his life's calling as a psychic. He then followed in the footsteps of his mother, Bertie, who earned her living giving "readings."

Catchings often helped police solve puzzling cases but he became famous after helping police find a missing, 32-year-old Houston nurse named Gail Lorke. She vanished in late October 1982, after her husband, Steven, claimed she had stayed home from work because she was sick. Because Catchings worked by holding objects that belonged to victims, Lorke's sister, who was suspicious of Steven, went to Catchings with a photo of Gail and her belt. Allegedly, Catchings saw that Lorke had indeed been murdered by her husband and left under a heap of refuse that included parts of an old, wooden fence. He also gave police several other key details. Detectives were able to use the information to get Steven Lorke to confess his crime. Among many other successes, Catchings also helped police find the body of Mike Dickens in 1980 after telling them the young man would be found buried in a creek bed near a shoe and other rubbish, including old tires and boards. Police discovered the body there just as Catchings had described it.

Lock-Picking Know-How

Regardless of what is portrayed in cops-and-robbers flicks, you need at least two tools to pick a lock.

Whether you're a wannabe ruffian or a forgetful homeowner, you should know that it is nearly impossible to pick a lock with only one paper clip, one bobby pin, or one of anything else. Although you can certainly accomplish the task with simple tools, you will need two of them—one to act as a pick and a second one to serve as a tension wrench.

The simple pin-and-tumbler locks on most doors contain a cylinder and several small pins attached to springs. When the door is locked, the cylinder is kept in place by the pins, which protrude into the cylinder. When a matching key is inserted into the lock, the pins are pushed back and the cylinder turns. The key to lock-picking, then, is to push the pins back while simultaneously turning the cylinder. This is why two items are required—a pick to push the pins and a tension wrench to turn the cylinder. Professional locksmiths often use simple lock-picking techniques to avoid damaging the offending lock.

Common household items that can serve as tension wrenches include small screwdrivers and bent paper clips. Items you can use as picks include safety pins, hair fasteners, and paper clips. The determined apprentice may be happy to learn that there is a situation in which one paper clip may suffice in picking a lock: Small, inexpensive padlocks sometimes succumb to large paper clips that are bent in such a way that one end is the pick and the other end is the tension wrench. Even so, the process involves more than just jamming something into the lock and turning the doorknob.

Seasoned lock-pickers rely on their senses of hearing and touch to finish the job successfully. They're anticipating a vibration accompanied by a distinct "click" that means each pin is in alignment.

Mafia Buster!

Joseph Petrosino was one of the first New York cops to take on the Mafia. He was clever, fearless—and effective.

Takin' Names

The name Joseph Petrosino means nothing to most New Yorkers—unless they're police officers, who regard the guy as a legend. In the first decade of the 20th century, Petrosino established himself as one of the toughest, most effective detectives in NYPD history. His beat was Little Italy, and he spent much of his career going toe-to-toe with the Mafia. It was a war that ultimately cost him his life.

Petrosino was brought into the department by Captain Alexander Williams, who had watched Petrosino tangle with local thugs on the city streets. Petrosino didn't meet the police height requirement, but in addition to being tough as nails, he spoke fluent Italian and was familiar with the local culture. Williams quickly realized that Petrosino could be an invaluable asset to the force.

The NYPD put Petrosino to work as a sergeant in 1883. He wasted no time making his presence known within the city's Italian community. Strong and fearless, Petrosino became a brawler when necessary, but he also knew the value of quiet detective work. (Dedication and fearlessness eventually elevated him to the rank of lieutenant.) To gather intelligence, for instance, Petrosino routinely disguised himself as a tunnel "sandhog" laborer, a blind street beggar, and other urban denizens who can slip around unnoticed.

Petrosino solved plenty of crimes during his career, but it was his labor to eliminate the vicious gangs preying on Italian immigrants that made him famous. Italian gangsters started setting up shop in the city around 1900, bringing murder, theft, and extortion with them. Petrosino made it his mission to end their reign of terror.

Unspeakable Violence

Foremost among Petrosino's gangland foes was Vito Cascio Ferro, whom some consider one of the inspirations for Mario Puzo's *The Godfather*. Ferro arrived in New York from Sicily in 1901, already a mob boss to be feared and respected. Petrosino made no secret of his desire to implicate  Ferro in the gruesome murder in which a body had been dismembered and stuffed in a barrel. As Petrosino closed in, Ferro fled to Sicily, vowing his revenge.

Meanwhile, Petrosino continued to battle the various gangs plaguing Little Italy. Kidnapping and murder were on the rise, as was the use of bombs. (In one terrifying incident, Petrosino managed to extinguish a bomb's fuse with his fingers just seconds before the bomb was set to explode.) Determined to stay ahead of the criminals, Petrosino established the nation's first bomb squad, teaching himself and his crew how to dismantle the deadly devices.

In 1908, Vito Ferro again attempted to reach into New York, this time through an intermediary—a murderous Sicilian named Raffaele Palizzolo. At first, clueless city officials embraced Palizzolo, who claimed to want to eliminate the Black Hand, as the Mafia was also called. But Petrosino was skeptical and tailed Palizzolo everywhere. This forced Palizzolo to return to Sicily, much to Ferro's anger.

All the News That's Fit to Blab

Petrosino's boss, Police Commissioner Theodore Bingham, was eager to eliminate New York's Mafia menace once and for all. Early in 1909 he sent Petrosino on a clandestine trip to Italy to meet with law enforcement officials there and gather intelligence. Because the underworld had put a price on his head, Petrosino made the trip disguised as a Jewish merchant named Simone Velletri. Unfortunately, his mission didn't remain a secret for long: While Petrosino was still in transit, the *New York Herald* ran a story that he was on his way to Italy specifically to gather information on Italian gangsters. The source? Bingham, who had stupidly confided in a reporter.

By the time Petrosino arrived in Italy, news of his mission had spread throughout the local underworld. Ferro ordered a hit. On March 12, 1909, two gunmen cut down Petrosino. The detective's funeral was one of the largest in New York history. Police officers and citizens lined the streets as the procession traveled through the city. The journey took five and a half hours—a fitting journey for a man who died for the rule of law.

Chapter 3

The Art (and Artifact) of Crime

Stealing History

Move over, Indiana Jones—the theft of priceless artifacts has been going on for centuries.

It's like something out of a James Bond movie: An international collector pays big bucks to organized criminals to steal priceless antiquities and smuggle them over international borders. National treasures have been purloined for centuries—taken to distant lands to bring prestige and value to museums, treasuries, and private collections.

A Thief In The Night

Sometimes, looters go straight to the source. Since the days of the earliest pharaohs, Egyptian rulers lived in fear of tomb robbers and went to great lengths to protect the possessions they intended to take into the hereafter.

But thieves were not always cloaked peasants who dug into pyramids in the dark of night; sometimes even Egyptian kings entered the graves of their predecessors to "borrow" goodies for use in the afterlife. King Tutankhamen's tomb included a second inner coffin, four miniature coffins, and some gold bands that had been removed from the tomb of his older brother, Smenkare. The tomb of Pharaoh Pinudjem I included "recycled" sarcophagi from the tomb of Thothmosis I, Egypt's ruler from three dynasties earlier. (Perhaps this sort of grave robbing was simply considered "borrowing from Peter to pay Peter," since every Egyptian king was, in theory, a reincarnation of the falcon god Horus.)

More recently, archaeological sites in the western United States have suffered a rash of thefts by shovel-toting bandits intent on digging up Native and Central American artifacts to sell in thriving legitimate and gray-market art and collectibles markets. In 2003, for instance, one Vanderbilt University professor worked with Guatemalan police, villagers, and even local drug lords to track down a stolen 1,200-year-old monument to a Mayan king.

Museums Robbed and Looted

Museum robberies have become a huge problem, especially for institutions that cannot afford state-of-the-art security systems. In 2001, for example, Russia's Culture Ministry stated that, on average, one Russian museum was victimized by theft each month. In Iraq in April 2003, during the chaos of the U.S.-led invasion of Iraq, some 170,000 items were looted or destroyed in the Iraqi National Museum; many of these artifacts subsequently made their way into private hands.

Authorities are slowly stirring themselves to crack down on a burgeoning traffic in stolen artifacts. In 2005, an Italian court sentenced a Roman antiquities dealer to ten years in prison for receiving and exporting stolen artifacts. The dealer's company sold 110 items through the prestigious auction house Sotheby's and sold another 96 artifacts to ten museums around the world before the operation was shut down.

Government Theft

Conquest and colonization have provided other supply sources for collections. The Israelite temple in Jerusalem was looted by invading armies at least twice: by Babylonian King Nebuchadnezzar around 586 B.C., and again by Roman

Emperor Vespasian in A.D. 70. In 480 B.C., when the Persian army sacked Athens, artifacts in the wooden Acropolis temple were carted off to Persepolis as war booty, and during his 1798–99 expedition to Egypt, Napoleon's army uncovered one of the most famous spoils of war, the Rosetta Stone—which was in turn captured by Britain in 1801. Equally famous are the "Elgin Marbles," relief statues from Greece's Parthenon that were brought to London's British Museum in 1816 by the British ambassador to Turkey.

During World War II, the Nazi regime took the pastime of art collecting to a new level. Thousands of priceless paintings, drawings, and sculptures were removed from museums in France and Russia at the behest of senior Nazi leaders. After Europe was liberated in 1945, many works of art were recovered, but others, such as Russia's fabled Amber Room panels, were never recovered at all.

John Myatt, Master Forger

When people hear the word forgery, they usually think of money. But legal currency isn't the only thing that can be faked.

"**M**onet, Monet, Monet. Sometimes I get truly fed up doing Monet. Bloody haystacks." John Myatt's humorous lament sounds curiously Monty Pythonesque, until you realize that he can do Monet— and Chagall, Klee, Le Corbusier, Ben Nicholson, and almost any other painter you can name, great or obscure. Myatt, an artist of some ability, was probably the world's greatest art forger. He took part in an eight-year forgery scam in the 1980s and '90s that shook the foundations of the art world.

Despite what one might expect, art forgery is not a victimless crime. Many of Myatt's paintings—bought in good faith as the work of renowned masters—went for extremely high sums. One "Giacometti" sold at auction in New York for $300,000, and as many as 120 of his counterfeits are still out there, confusing and distressing the art world. But Myatt never set out to break the law.

Initially, Myatt would paint an unknown work in the style of one of the cubist, surrealist, or impressionist masters, and he seriously duplicated both style and subject. For a time, he gave them to friends or sold them as acknowledged fakes. Then he ran afoul of John Drewe.

The Scheme Begins

Drewe was a London-based collector who had bought a dozen of Myatt's fakes over two years. Personable and charming, he ingratiated himself with Myatt by posing as a rich aristocrat. But one day he called and told Myatt that a cubist work the artist had done in the style of Albert Gleizes had just sold at Christies for £25,000 ($40,000)—as a genuine Gleizes. Drewe offered half of that money to Myatt.

The struggling artist was poor and taking care of his two children. The lure of the money was irresistible. So the scheme developed that he would paint a "newly discovered" work by a famous painter and pass it to Drewe, who would sell it and then pay Myatt his cut—usually about 10 percent. It would take Myatt two or three months to turn out a fake, and he was only making about £13,000 a year (roughly $21,000)—hardly worthy of a master criminal.

One of the amazing things about this scam was Myatt's materials. Most art forgers take great pains to duplicate the exact pigments used by the original artists, but Myatt mixed cheap emulsion house paint with a lubricating gel to get the colors he needed. One benefit is that his mix dried faster than oil paints.

The Inside Man

But Drewe was just as much of a master forger, himself. The consummate con man, he inveigled his way into the art world through donations, talking his way into the archives of the Tate Gallery and learning every trick of provenance, the authentication of artwork. He faked letters from experts and, on one occasion, even inserted a phony catalog into the archives with pictures of Myatt's latest fakes as genuine.

As the years went by, Myatt became increasingly worried about getting caught and going to prison, so he told Drewe he wanted out. Drewe refused to let him leave, and Myatt realized that his partner wasn't just in it for the money. He also simply loved conning people.

The Jig Is Up

The scam was not to last, of course. Drewe's ex-wife went to the police with incriminating documents, and when the trail led to Myatt's cottage in Staffordshire, he confessed.

Myatt served four months of a yearlong sentence, and when he came out of prison, Detective Superintendent Jonathan Searle of the Metropolitan Police was waiting for him. Searle suggested that since Myatt was now infamous, many people would love to own a real John Myatt fake. As a result, Myatt and his second wife Rosemary set up a tidy business out of their cottage. His paintings regularly sell for as much as £45,000 ($72,000), and he even has a TV show.

The Museum of Empty Frames

Located in Boston, Massachusetts, the Isabella Stewart Gardner Museum contains paintings, sculptures, tapestries, and other works from Europe, Asia, and America. The museum was named for an American philanthropist and art collector, whose will decreed that her vast collection be permanently displayed to the public. But the museum is not only known for the art that adorns its walls; it is also famous for a brazen unsolved heist.

Isabella Stewart Gardner opened her museum to the public in 1903 and continued to add to her vast collection until her death in 1924. Her will stipulated that no artwork from her collection should ever be sold, and none should be added, and that even the arrangement of the artwork in the museum should remain untouched. In a sense, the museum was frozen in time.

Although Gardner left the museum a $3.6 million endowment, the institution was financially struggling. In 1982, after the FBI uncovered a plot by Boston criminals to rob the museum, the board of trustees decided to use what little funds they had to beef up security.  Motion detectors were added, and closed-circuit cameras were placed around the perimeter of the building. The museum also hired more security guards, although it could only afford to pay slightly above minimum wage.

But even with these improvements, there were still flaws and gaps in the museum's security. For one, there were no cameras located inside the building. Also, the police could only be summoned by pushing a button located at a single security desk. By 1988, independent security consultants had warned the board of trustees that their security measures needed improvement; but due to Gardner's insistence that the museum remain unchanged, no more improvements were made.

A Brazen Heist

In the early morning hours of March 18, 1990, two security officers—23-year-old Rick Abath and 25-year-old Randy Hestand—were on duty in the Gardner Museum. At 1:20 a.m., a buzzer for the outside door rang an intercom at Abath's desk. On the closed-circuit television, Abath could see two men dressed as police officers, who told the guard that they were investigating a disturbance and needed to come in.

Once the "police officers" were inside, they asked Abath to summon Hestand, then lured the pair away from the security desk (the location of the only button to call for help), handcuffed them, and wrapped duct tape around their eyes. The thieves took the two guards down to the basement and handcuffed them to a pipe and workbench, their intention to rob the museum now more than obvious.

In just over an hour, the thieves were able to pack thirteen works of art into their car, making two trips back and forth, pilfering works by Rembrandt, Vermeer, Flinck, Degas, and Manet. They also stole an ancient Chinese vase and a bronze eagle finial. At 2:45 a.m., they left the museum, leaving Abath and Hestand still tied up in the basement. The two guards weren't able to get free until the morning guard shift arrived and called the police.

Empty Frames and a Huge Reward

Right off the bat, the heist puzzled art experts. The objects taken were seemingly random and unconnected. Some of the art was extremely valuable, but others had little worth. What's more, the thieves completely bypassed the third floor of the museum, which housed some of the most valuable paintings in the world. All of this would suggest that the thieves were not hired to execute a specific heist.

Regardless, the items the thieves stole still have an estimated value of between $500 and $600 million. One dealer at Sotheby's even puts the estimate at $1 billion. But to this day, no one knows who pulled off the heist or where they hid the art. Sotheby's, along with Christie's auction house, have posted a reward for the return of the art, which now stands at $10 million.

Because of Gardner's insistence that her museum remain unchanged, empty frames now hang where the stolen art was once displayed. Still frozen in time, the museum patiently awaits their return.

Missing Mona Lisa

Leonardo da Vinci's Mona Lisa, *a painting of an enigmatically smiling noblewoman named Lisa Gherardini, is undoubtedly one of the most famous pieces of art in the world. But surprisingly, it took a brazen theft to make it the popular tourist draw it is today.*

Before She Was Famous

Prior to 1911, the *Mona Lisa* was mostly known only throughout the art world, even though Leonardo da Vinci painted the portrait centuries earlier between 1503 and 1517. Later in life, the artist settled in France, where he worked in the service of King Francis I. Da Vinci and the king became close friends, and after da Vinci's death in 1519, the *Mona Lisa* found a new home with the French king. This may explain why an Italian painting created by an Italian artist eventually wound up in the Louvre, Paris's prestigious art museum.

But even in its home amongst some of the most priceless works of art in the world, the *Mona Lisa* remained a lesser-known piece at the museum. Measuring a modest 30 inches by 21 inches, its small footprint and muted colors weren't exactly calling out for attention. But on August 21, 1911, the inconspicuous little painting suddenly drew big attention when it mysteriously disappeared.

Sudden Notoriety

The poor *Mona Lisa* was so neglected and forgotten at the Louvre, that it took more than a day for her absence to be noticed. The museum's own staff hadn't even observed anything out of the ordinary, and the painting's theft may have been ignored far longer had it not been for an amateur artist who set up his easel to paint the *Mona Lisa*'s gallery and noticed something was amiss. After museum guards did a bit of searching and questioning, it was finally understood that the painting was, indeed, stolen.

Overnight, the *Mona Lisa* became a worldwide sensation, as newspapers around the globe reported on the painting's mysterious disappearance. Rumors began to fly as to the motive of the theft: Some believed the pre-World War I tensions between France and Germany had prompted the Germans to steal the painting out of spite. Others thought the United States was behind it, believing the Americans were attempting to pilfer all of France's best art. Investigators even questioned American banker J. P. Morgan about the theft, theorizing that he may have organized the heist.

Ironically, the empty space where the stolen *Mona Lisa* had hung became more popular than the painting had ever been. The Louvre was overrun with curious visitors, all eager to see the vacant spot that became known as Paris's "mark of shame." And for two years, the spot on the wall remained empty, as investigators hit nothing but dead ends in their search for the stolen painting.

Patriotism or Profit?

Then, one day in November 1913, an art dealer in Florence, Italy, named Alfredo Geri received a letter from a man calling himself "Leonardo." The man claimed to have possession of the *Mona Lisa*, and offered it to Geri at a hefty price. Intrigued but suspicious, Geri called in an expert to authenticate the painting. Once it was discovered to be the real deal, he also contacted the authorities. The man calling himself "Leonardo" turned out to be Vincenzo Peruggia, a former employee at the Louvre, and he was immediately arrested for the theft.

Peruggia claimed "patriotic duty" for his actions, stating that the *Mona Lisa* belonged in Italy, not France. But investigators believed his real motive was much more mundane: money. They theorized that Peruggia intended to sell the painting as soon as he stole it, but he never expected the whirlwind of attention his actions caused. So he was forced to hide the painting for two years while he waited for interest to die down.

Perhaps the most interesting part of the story is how Peruggia pulled off his heist: according to his own confession, he simply took the painting off the wall, removed its frame, wrapped it in a smock, and walked right out the door. Thanks to Peruggia's brazen theft of this modest and ignored artwork, the *Mona Lisa* is now the most visited painting in the world.

Norway's Prize Painting

The eerily otherworldly figure in Edvard Munch's The Scream *is instantly recognizable, not only by art enthusiasts, but by casual observers, as well. But the familiar composition has also caught the eye of thieves on more than one occasion.*

Prolific Inspiration

Many viewers of *The Scream* understandably believe that the strange, almost alien-like figure at the center of the painting is the one emitting the "scream." But according to Munch, it is not the person screaming, but rather the person's surroundings. He described it as "an infinite scream passing through nature," and originally titled the piece *Der Schrei der Natur* (The Scream of Nature). Munch's own anxiety was said to be his source of inspiration for the piece, which has since become a symbol for human unease, fear, and depression.

With such profound and serious inspiration, perhaps it is only natural that Munch created not one, but many versions of the scene. In addition to two paintings, he also created two versions in pastels and approximately 45 lithograph prints. But it is the two paintings, both located in museums in Oslo, Norway, that have attracted the most attention.

A Gold Medal in Theft

The version of *The Scream* that most of us are familiar with is the painting that hangs in Oslo's National Gallery. On February 12, 1994, a visit to a museum was the last thing most people were thinking about. The date did, however, draw all eyes to Norway, as the Winter Olympics opened in Lillehammer. While the world was focused on the opening ceremonies and preparing to watch the showdown between Nancy Kerrigan and Tonya Harding, two men broke through a window at the museum, stole *The Scream* in 50 seconds flat, and left a note reading, "Thousand thanks for the bad security!"

Fortunately, the pilfered painting was found only three months later, at a hotel 40 miles south of Oslo. It took investigators another two years to track down the thieves who had left the cheeky note, and although they were convicted for the crime, they were later released due to legal technicalities.

Art Heist, or Diversion?

The second painted version of *The Scream* hangs in the Munch Museum in Oslo and, like its twin at the National Gallery, was also the target of thieves. But its theft, committed ten years after the first on August 22, 2004, came with an unusual twist. On that day, masked gunmen entered the Munch Museum in broad daylight and stole *The Scream* along with another Munch painting entitled *Madonna*.

After two years of searching, Norwegian police were finally able to recover both paintings, although each had sustained damage. *The Scream*, in particular, seemed to have water stains, and investigators theorized that it had been wrapped in something wet. But why would art thieves treat a painting so carelessly, if they were hoping to sell it or return it for ransom?

Police had a theory: the theft of the painting was not about the painting at all—it was a diversion. Around the same time as *The Scream* theft, a Norwegian police officer had been gunned down during an armed robbery, and the authorities were using all their manpower to track down whoever was responsible. Was *The Scream* stolen in an effort to take the heat off of the culprit in this crime? When a criminal named David Toska was arrested for leading the armed robbery, the Norwegian press reported that his lawyer had, indeed, led the authorities to *The Scream* and *Madonna*.

So it would seem that the theft wasn't about the painting at all, but rather a clever way to move the country's attention away from one crime and onto another. By targeting the most famous painting in Norway—and one of the most famous in the entire world—these art thieves gave police, investigators, and art lovers something to "scream" about.

The Antwerp Job

It was one of the largest robberies in history. Shockingly, more than $100 million in diamonds, gold, silver, and world currencies was stolen from what was thought to be an "impenetrable" vault. And had it not been for a simple panic attack, the thieves may have gotten away with it all.

Diamonds Are Forever

In the 2003 film *The Italian Job*, starring Mark Wahlberg and Charlize Theron, a group of highly skilled thieves pulls off what seems to be an impossible heist. The group of safe-crackers, explosives experts, and computer whizzes manage to expertly pilfer millions of dollars' worth of gold bars, then ride off into the proverbial sunset to begin their new wealthy lives. Of course, those sorts of things only happen in a Hollywood script, right?

Amazingly, sometimes life does imitate art. And that same year, in the early morning hours of February 16, a real-life heist was taking place in the city of Antwerp, Belgium. The city is known for its World Diamond Center, which is home to all of the major diamond mining companies around the globe. In fact, 80 percent of the world's diamonds pass through the Antwerp World Diamond Center at one time or another, making the three-square-block area an obvious target for would-be thieves.

But with such valuable goods in its main vault, the Antwerp World Diamond Center is also equipped with some of the most complicated and state-of-the-art security features found anywhere.

In 2003, these included security cameras, motion detectors, seismic sensors, and magnetic field alarms, as well as a three-ton steel vault door that could only be opened with a four-digit combination.

The Heist of the Century

Enter Leonardo Notarbartolo, an Italian thief who had been honing his skills since the age of six, when he stole $8 from a milkman. Notarbartolo often traveled to Antwerp to pawn off stolen jewelry from his homeland, so he was familiar with the area. And his thieving eye was on the Diamond Center. He knew a robbery in such a secure location would be challenging, but not necessarily impossible.

But Notarbartolo knew he couldn't pull off a heist on his own. So he rounded up a crew with nicknames that sounded like they were straight out of the movies: There was "the Genius," who was an electronics expert; "the Monster," an expert lock-picker, mechanic, and driver; "the King of Keys," one of the best key forgers in the world; and finally, "Speedy," one of Notarbartolo's oldest friends.

After eighteen months of planning, surveillance, and surreptitious filming, the crew finally hit their target on February 16. They expertly picked locks, disabled sensors, rerouted alarms, and, using secret footage they'd taken of a guard opening the vault, dialed in the code. Once inside, the group set to work drilling into 109 safety deposit boxes and emptying the contents into duffel bags. At around 5:30 a.m., they hightailed it out of the area before they were discovered, leaving behind zero clues and a baffling mystery for investigators.

A Big Mistake

But no crime is perfect. While the other three group members hid the loot, Notarbartolo and Speedy drove into the countryside to burn a bag of incriminating evidence. But the gravity of the situation began to weigh on poor Speedy, and instead of burning the evidence, he wound up strewing the garbage around in the mud in a panic and having a bit of a nervous breakdown. Notarbartolo quickly ushered him out of the area in an effort to calm him down, leaving behind videotape, receipts, and envelopes from the Diamond Center. Police were later able to use this evidence to tie the crime back to Notarbartolo and his crafty accomplices.

Notarbartolo was sentenced to ten years in prison, with each of his accomplices— with the exception of "the King of Keys," who was never found—receiving five years. But in one final twist to the story, the expert thief insists that he was set up by a diamond dealer hoping to commit insurance fraud, and that most of the boxes the crew opened were empty. Since most of the reported $100 million stolen has not been recovered, we may never know the truth of what happened in Antwerp.

The Thief of Nova Scotia

Called everything from a "genius" to a "hoarder" to a "psychopath," Canadian John Tillmann was one of the most prolific thieves in the country. But had it not been for a routine traffic stop, the world may have never known his story.

An Early Life of Crime

John Tillmann was born on February 24, 1961, in Halifax, Nova Scotia. Some accounts of his life report that he began stealing by the age of eight, when his grandmother would coerce him into shoplifting from local flea markets. Later in life, he majored in international marketing at Mount Saint Vincent University, and then lived in Moscow for several years, where he learned to speak Russian. Perhaps this was the beginning of Tillmann's fascination with historical artifacts and works of art, but much of his life is shrouded in mystery, so one can only speculate. What is not a mystery is that while in Russia, he met and married university student Katya Anastasia Zhestokova, and soon the couple were living a life of international crime.

Far from shoplifting for his grandmother, Tillmann, with the help of Zhestokova and Zhestokova's brother Vladimir, began traveling throughout Europe, the Middle East, and North and South America, planning and pulling off heists at museums and art houses. Tillmann carefully plotted and organized the thefts. The attractive Zhestokova provided a distraction for any attentive guards, while Vladimir employed his expertise with computer hacking and alarm disabling.

The Letters

Eventually, Tillmann and Zhestokova settled back in Canada, where they continued their life of crime. Tillmann would disguise himself as a maintenance worker, a guard, or a police officer to blend in with his surroundings, then use the sleight of hand skills he'd been perfecting since youth to snatch whatever prize caught his eye. Sometimes he even brought his own mother in on his heists, convincing her to fake chest pains or fainting spells to attract attention while he made off with another treasure. He stole from antique dealers, libraries, museums, and even the Nova Scotia legislature.

Then, late one night, Tillmann and Zhestokova snuck into Dalhousie University in Halifax and hid in a women's bathroom until the night security guard left. Using a duplicate key he had made, Tillmann was able to open a vault in the university's library. After a few hours of searching, the pair made an amazing discovery: two letters—the first written by British Army Officer General James Wolfe, the second written by none other than George Washington. The Washington letter alone was worth at least half a million dollars.

Downfall

Tillmann added the letters to his growing collection of stolen items, but he didn't keep everything he purloined. He became a wealthy man by selling much of his loot on the black market, amassing $2 million worth in property, including a house, a Porsche, and a BMW. It was while he was driving one of his cars in July 2012 that police stopped him for a routine traffic violation. But the stop became anything but routine when officers discovered the stolen Wolfe letter in Tillmann's car. The discovery of this hugely valuable stolen item prompted investigators to search the rest of his property, and they were shocked by what they found.

Over the years, Tillmann and his various accomplices had stolen more than 7,000 items, most of which he'd arranged throughout his house as if it were a museum. There were paintings, photographs, books, furniture, and antiques. Some of the more unusual items included a spear, a brass telescope, a gas mask, and a canoe. Tillmann was so efficient and adept at stealing items that many of his victims weren't even aware that anything was missing until the authorities contacted them.

Tillmann was convicted on 40 counts of theft in 2013 and sentenced to nine years in prison. He was paroled in 2016, but the prolific thief died on December 23, 2018, at the age of 57.

The New Master

How did Dutch artist Han van Meegeren manage to fool a Nazi into buying a forged painting? It took a lot of practice, a little bit of plastic, and the help of a pizza oven.

Beginnings in Architecture

When Han van Meegeren was a child, his father once punished him by forcing him to repeatedly write, "I know nothing. I am nothing. I am capable of nothing." This terrible missive was certainly the antithesis of what a parent should tell a child, and van Meegeren, who was born on October 10, 1889, in Deventer, Netherlands, grew up often feeling inadequate.

Young van Meegeren loved art, but his father forbade him from studying the craft, pushing him towards architecture instead. Van Meegeren attended the Delft University of Technology and excelled at his study of architecture, even designing a boathouse for his rowing club which still stands in Delft today. But his heart wasn't in the vocation, and he never took his final exams. Instead, after marrying and having a son, he moved his family to The Hague, where he studied painting at the Royal Academy of Art.

For many years, van Meegeren made a modest living by teaching, sketching, and painting, and his work was reasonably well respected in the Netherlands. But when he tried expanding his repertoire to include paintings in the style of the old masters, he was criticized for his lack of originality. But far from believing his father's words that he was "capable of nothing," van Meegeren was determined to prove that he was capable of so much more. He vowed to create forged paintings so perfect that no one would suspect they weren't genuine.

Planning and Practice

First, van Meegeren had to decide which artist to emulate. He landed on 17th century artist Jan Vermeer, who is only known to have created about 35 paintings. The life of Vermeer is also less well known than many other painters of the time. This gave van Meegeren two advantages: First, since there were only 35 known Vermeers in the world, it wouldn't be unusual if a previously "lost" painting showed up. And second, van Meegeren could paint whatever he wanted, since no one knew exactly how Vermeer chose his subjects.

But there was another problem: how could van Meegeren make a modern painting look as if it had been around for 300 years? He experimented with many paints, canvases, and aging techniques, but his final method was a bit unusual. Van Meegeren bought a pizza oven, dissolved a small amount of plastic into his paint, and then dried his finished painting in the oven.

The plastic prevented the paint from burning up, and the oven resulted in a perfectly dried, aged appearance.

Fooling the Experts (and the Nazis)

With his newfound technique at the ready, van Meegeren began painting his forged Vermeers. And just as he'd hoped, when art experts saw the paintings, they were convinced they'd stumbled onto "lost" paintings. The fake Vermeers were selling for millions of dollars each, allowing van Meegeren to purchase an exclusive home in Amsterdam, jewelry, and works of art.

Then the Nazis, who looted thousands of pieces of art during World War II, occupied the Netherlands. Hermann Göring, one of the most powerful figures in Nazi Germany, had a huge collection of stolen artwork, and in 1942, he bought one of van Meegeren's "Vermeers," believing it would be the prize work in his collection.

When the war ended and Allied forces discovered Göring's artwork, they found paperwork with the "Vermeer" that mentioned van Meegeren's name. Police soon showed up at the door of his Amsterdam mansion, arresting him for collaborating with the Nazis and plundering Dutch cultural property. Faced with the prospect of prison, van Meegeren confessed that the painting was a fake, and hoped the authorities would be lenient on him for swindling a Nazi.

Van Meegeren was sentenced to only one year in prison, but the artist, who had been in poor health for years, died on December 30, 1947, before he'd even served a day. To his fellow countrymen, van Meegeren died a hero—the artist who was so talented he fooled a Nazi.

The Hitler Diaries Hoax

In 1983, Germany's popular magazine Stern *dropped a bomb: It now had access to Adolf Hitler's secret diaries. Experts soon revealed them as phonies authored by a modern crook, leaving prominent historians and major media looking ridiculous.*

Counterfeit Collectibles

The crook was Konrad Kujau, a man of numerous aliases and lies. He was born in 1938, and after World War II he lived in East Germany. He moved to West Germany in 1957 and began a life of petty crime, specializing in forgery.

A lifetime Hitler fan, Kujau became a noted Nazi memorabilia "collector." Naturally, he manufactured most of his collection, including authentication documents. He built a favorable reputation as a dealer specializing in ostensibly authentic Hitler stuff: signatures, writing, poetry, and art.

The public display of Nazi anything is illegal in Germany, as is Holocaust denial. Even WWII games sold in modern Germany cannot use the swastika. Nazi memorabilia collections remain strictly on the down low. Modern Germans overwhelmingly repudiate Nazism, and those born post-war also dislike association with a horror they didn't perpetrate. It's a painful subject.

Still, every country has closet Hitler admirers, and Germany is no exception. *Stern* journalist Gerd Heidemann was one—he even bought Hermann Göring's old yacht. In 1979, a collector (Kujau under an alias) invited Heidemann to check out his Nazi collection,  including a bound copy of a diary supposedly authored by Hitler. The diary, which covered a period from January to June 1935, had been salvaged from a late-war plane crash in East Germany. The collector also claimed that there were 26 other volumes, each covering a six-month period.

Faulty Fact-Checking

Using his journalistic training, Heidemann went to East Germany and found a backstory that verified a plane crash. Although he didn't dig much deeper, he had a good excuse. At the time, the world thought in terms of East and West Germany. In East Germany, a socialist police state, no one nosed around except where the state approved (which it rarely did). Heidemann and *Stern's* West German homeland was the mainstay of NATO, and the border between East and West Germany bristled with a surprising percentage of the world's military power. *Stern* lacked an easy way to verify anything in East Germany.

So Heidemann basically pitched what he had to *Stern*, and the magazine swung from its heels. Salivating at the "find of a generation," *Stern* authorized Heidemann to offer an advance of $1 million (approximate U.S. equivalent) for the diaries. Kujau played coy, explaining that the other 26 volumes hadn't yet been smuggled out of East Germany. In reality, he needed time to forge them. He finally finished in 1981 and handed over the first volume to Heidemann.

At this point, everyone was too excited to bother with that tedious step called "authentication." *Stern* hadn't even learned Kujau's identity; it was too busy counting its future profit from serialization rights. Anyone who voiced worries about fraud was hushed. Some surprisingly big names entered bids, including *Newsweek, Paris Match,* and the *London Times.*

Stretching the Truth

The diaries themselves purported to reveal a kinder, gentler Hitler, a generally okay guy who wasn't even fully aware of the Holocaust. This Hitler is what modern Nazi sympathizers like to imagine existed, not the weird megalomaniac of actual history. But its improbability also spurred skeptics into gear.

In an attempt to deal with the naysayers, *Stern* got a bit hysterical, insisting that noted British historian Hugh Trevor-Roper had pronounced the diaries authentic. But skeptics faulted the diaries' paper, handwriting, and style. After some controversy, West German authorities ran forensics. The testing proved that the paper, ink, and even glue were of post-WWII manufacture. *Stern* had been bamboozled.

Because *Stern* is to Germany what *Time* and *Newsweek* are to the United States, it had a significant amount of credibility to lose. Several *Stern* editors were soon looking for new jobs. To say that the West German government was "annoyed" is an understatement. After *Stern* fired Heidemann, the police charged him with fraud. Heidemann, in his smartest move in a long time, implicated Kujau. When this news was made public in the media, Kujau went into hiding. In May 1983, he decided to turn himself into the police, who were anxiously waiting to arrest him. After several days of intense questioning, the authorities learned that Kujau was a reflexive, perpetual liar who invented falsehoods to cover his fictions.

The High Price of Greed

Kujau and Heidemann were each sentenced to several years in jail. The judge said *Stern* had "acted with such naiveté and negligence that it was virtually an accomplice in the fraud." The roughly $5 million the magazine ultimately gave Heidemann to pay Kujau was never recovered.

Heidemann's increasingly lavish lifestyle during the forgeries and subsequent investigations suggests that he spent the majority of the money offshore.

After his release, Kujau tried his hand at politics, replica painting, and (again) forgery. He died of complications from cancer in 2000, but his crime is considered one of the most bold and successful hoaxes of the century.

Declassified East German files later showed that Heidemann had been an East German spy, though it's uncertain whether that had anything to do with the hoax. He claims he was actually a double agent working for West German authorities. With his career prospects impaired, he now keeps a low profile.

The Copycat

A well-known proverb asserts that imitation is the sincerest form of flattery. If that's the case, then English art restorer Tom Keating "flattered" scores of artists throughout his lifetime.

Restoring the Masters

Tom Keating was born on March 1, 1917, in London, England. His parents were not well-off, and a young Keating was forced to work odd jobs to supplement his family's income. Eventually he began working with his father as a house painter, an occupation that foreshadowed his future career.

After serving in World War II, Keating was accepted into the art program at Goldsmith's College, University of London. Although his painting instructors were impressed with his technical artistic abilities, they noted that he lacked originality. Keating dropped out after only two years, but his love of painting led him into the world of art restoration.

After college, Keating began working for an art restorer named Fred Roberts. One day, the two restorers were working on a painting by Frank Moss Bennett, and Keating criticized the British painter's work. Roberts challenged Keating to recreate one of Bennett's paintings, but Keating thought he could do even better: he painted an original work in Bennett's style, which he then signed with his own name. When Roberts saw the painting, he was amazed by how authentic the work looked. He covered Keating's name and signed it "F. M. Bennett," then sold it to an art gallery. This was Keating's first taste of the world of art forgery.

Revenge for the Starving Artists

Over the next decade, Keating painted many original pieces and exhibited his work in art galleries, but there was little interest in his paintings. He became frustrated with art dealers, believing them to be greedy and disinterested in working with up-and-coming artists. He accused them of taking money from "naïve collectors" while taking  advantage of "impoverished artists," and thought it was unfair that his fellow artists often went hungry and even died in poverty while the dealers lived lavish lifestyles.

So Keating sought vengeance. Since he believed that he was just as good as Rembrandt, or Degas, or Monet, the artist began creating forgeries to fool the "expert" art dealers. His hope was that by flooding the market with forgeries, he could destabilize the whole system. Keating painted forgeries of 100 master artists, including Renoir, Cezanne, Titian, and his personal favorite, Samuel Palmer.

The forger made sure to leave clues within his paintings that would reveal their true nature, such as small flaws or anachronisms. He also used his knowledge as an art restorer to choose his paints and materials carefully. For instance, he would often place a layer of glycerin underneath the oil paint on a canvas, so when a restorer attempted to clean the work, the glycerin would dissolve and the painting would be ruined.

A Forger Revealed

One day in 1970, auctioneers noticed a curious pattern—a large amount of Samuel Palmer watercolors were suddenly for sale. A statistician and journalist who worked at *The Times* of London, Geraldine Norman, decided to look into the anomaly, sending the paintings to a specialist for inspection. The paintings were deemed to be fakes, and Norman published an article about her findings.

After the article was published, she was approached by the brother of Keating's former lover, Jane Kelly, who revealed Keating as the forger.

Norman published a second article soon after which suggested Keating could be an art forger, and Keating, to his credit, made no excuses. "I do not deny these allegations," he said. "In fact, I openly confess to having done them."

He claimed that around 2,000 of his forgeries had been sold, but he refused to provide a list of them, frustrating investigators.

The forger was arrested and put on trial. However, after a motorcycle accident left him in such poor health he wasn't expected to survive, the charges against him were dropped. But Keating surprised everyone by recovering, amazingly escaping punishment for his crimes. In fact, after his trial, the public became so impressed with his talent that he was given his own television show, *Tom Keating on Painters*, in which he demonstrated classic painting techniques.

Keating died in 1984, but his "genuine forgeries" are still out there, some worth tens of thousands of dollars.

Missing in Mexico

It was one of the world's greatest art heists. Scores of priceless pre-Columbian artifacts were stolen out from under the noses of the guards at Mexico's National Museum of Anthropology on Christmas Eve in 1985. But when authorities caught up to the thieves more than three years later, they were in for a surprise.

A Holiday Heist

Most of us could be forgiven for imbibing a bit too much on Christmas Eve. It is, after all, a festive time of year filled with food, drink, and merriment. But the eight police guards on duty at the National Museum of Anthropology in Mexico City on Christmas Eve, 1985, should have known better. As they began their holiday celebration at the museum, which was sadly lacking in any other security features, thieves snuck into three different exhibition halls and made off with 124 Mayan, Aztec, Mixtec, and Zapotec artifacts.

Although the guards were supposed to make their rounds through each room in the museum at least once every hour, the theft wasn't noticed until Christmas morning, when they changed shifts.

The stolen items included artifacts made of gold, jade, and turquoise, which museum officials estimated were worth "many millions of dollars." The thieves seemed to have targeted artifacts which were small and concealable, yet also extremely valuable, leading investigators to believe that the culprits were professionals. But museum officials were also confused. They believed that the stolen items were much too famous to be sold on the open market, so what motivated the thieves to pull off the immense heist?

Pointing Fingers

After interrogating the eight museum guards and clearing them of the crime, investigators began their search for the perpetrators. One theory posited that a "psychotic millionaire cultist" had arranged the theft, for the sole purpose of having the artifacts in a private collection. But more common theories placed the blame  at the feet of foreign governments, including the KGB and the CIA. The United States, especially, was eyed with suspicion. As Mexican journalist Joel Hernandez Santiago wrote, "It's no secret to anybody that pre-Hispanic pieces stolen from different zones of our country leave Mexico daily, to be taken principally the United States, a country which, lacking its own valuable cultural antecedents, robs or buys others." Ouch.

It took more than three years, until June of 1989, before authorities finally recovered most of the stolen objects from a house in the Mexico City suburb of Satelite. And who were the crafty, devious, "professionals" behind the heist? Their names were Carlos Perches Trevino and Ramon Sardina Garcia, and neither one had ties to a foreign government or a "psychotic millionaire cultist." Rather, they were ordinary men who had dropped out of college and decided to focus on something other than school. Mainly, breaking into the National Museum of Anthropology.

Not-So-Well-Laid Plans

Trevino and Garcia spent six months planning the heist, visiting the museum more than fifty times and making note of details. They photographed the exhibition halls and artifacts, studied the schedules of the security guards, and made sketches of their plans. On the night of the theft, the duo hopped a fence, crawled through the air conditioning ducts, and made their way to the museum's Maya Room, where they spent 30 minutes loading up a canvas bag with items they could easily transport back through the air ducts.

Once they had the loot, the two amateur art thieves were unsure what to do with it. The canvas bag full of priceless artifacts sat on a shelf in Trevino's closet for a year, until he moved to the resort town of Acapulco. There, he made a fatal error: he tried to trade some of the items to a drug trafficker named Salvador Gutierrez in exchange for cocaine. When Gutierrez showed little interest, Trevino took the stash of artifacts back to Mexico City.

But when Gutierrez was arrested on drug charges in 1989, he ratted out Trevino, and authorities closed in. He and Garcia were charged with theft and damage to national treasures, and Trevino was hit with the extra charge of cocaine trafficking and possession due to his dealings with Gutierrez. Far from being professionals, these two would-be art thieves would've been much better off had they stayed in school.

Chapter 4

Murderous Marriages: Weddings Gone Wrong

Wedding Police Blotter

In these real-life examples of weddings-gone-wild, there's plenty of fodder for front page headlines. When police arrived at these nuptials, they encountered all sorts of disturbances, from fistfights to shouting matches.

Outspoken Ex-Girlfriend: When Marie Salomon attended the Bridgeport, Connecticut, wedding ceremony of her ex-boyfriend, the minister uttered the weighted phrase: "Speak now or forever hold your peace." Salomon stood and yelled her objections in the middle of the ceremony. Eventually, police were called to the scene, and Salomon was charged with breaching the peace and trespassing.

Crowbar Crasher: If you think that was bad…when Lisa Coker showed up at her ex-boyfriend's wedding reception, she didn't come empty-handed. Coker brought a crowbar and a razor blade to the Tampa, Florida, affair. After fighting with the mother of the groom, who then required 16 stitches, Coker was arrested.

Groom vs. Fashion Police: John Lucas, age 53, was arrested during his own wedding reception when a police officer working the event attempted to enforce the venue's dress code. According to police, Lucas's nephew appeared at the Kenner,

Louisiana, reception dressed in sagging pants. (The nephew denied the charge to newspapers.) A police officer told the teenager to pull up his pants, and he refused. The situation escalated quickly, and when the groom and his brother defended the 19-year-old, the police all three men for disturbing the peace.

Attack of the Bride's Sister: Annmarie Bricker wasn't invited to her sister's Hebron, Indiana, wedding reception, but she went anyway. Bricker wanted to talk out a few family problems, and by the time police arrived, the 23-year-old had wrestled the bride to the ground and pulled out clumps of the woman's hair. Bricker was arrested on a misdemeanor battery charge and later resigned from her job as a 911 dispatcher.

Newlyweds Cash In: Brian Dykes and Mindy McGhee wed at a quaint chapel in Sevierville, Tennessee, then promptly robbed the place. After the wedding, the couple waited until the cover of darkness and then stole a cash-filled lockbox from the chapel. They were later found at a local restaurant where they confessed to the $500 theft and were jailed on $10,000 bonds.

Right in the Kisser: How can a prenuptial party go wrong? When the groom kisses the bride's friend, for starters. Apparently, the bride's 12-year-old son reported that her fiancé smooched one of the female attendees. The bride-to-be tackled the groom, punched him in the face, threw his watch in the bushes, and broke his glasses. The Poulsbo, Washington, woman was jailed on assault charges.

Bride and Groom Brawl: Pittsburgh, Pennsylvania, newlyweds David and Christa Wielechowski spent the night in jail after duking it out in a hotel hallway. The couple insisted they were joking when the groom kicked his vociferous bride squarely in the rear. When hotel guests came to the bride's rescue and restrained the groom, the bride attacked them. The brawl then moved into an elevator and to the hotel lobby, drawing more guests to the fracas. The groom—a local dentist—was booked into the county jail with a black eye and only one shoe. His bride, still wearing her wedding gown, was in a separate holding cell.

Makin' It Rain: In Tampa, Florida, in 2009, groom Markeith Brown finished off his wedding reception by tossing dollar bills onto the dance floor while the younger guests snatched them up. Apparently, this didn't go over so well with one of the other guests, who made that fact known. An all-out brawl followed: More guests got involved; non-guest reinforcements were called in; a policeman got punched; and the groom's grandma ended up with hands around her throat. Fortunately, the groom managed to avoid arrest, and he and his bride (who was none too happy about the whole thing) were able to go on their (hopefully uneventful) honeymoon cruise.

Brazen Bigamists

Some people really like the institution of marriage. In fact, some like it so much they get married again and again. Most of them get divorced between weddings— but a few went another route.

Bigamy is a felony in 37 states, carrying a sentence of up to ten years in prison. The problem? Prosecutions are not that common, and many times, offenders come away with a slap on the wrist.

Making (Serial) Marriages Work

Anthony Glenn Owens was a man of God, pious and devoted to his church. At least that's what one Texas woman thought when he proposed to her in 2002. He even traveled all the way to Mississippi to ask her father for permission for her hand. Maybe her dad would have said no if he'd known what the new bride discovered. Owens was already married—to seven other women. Apparently he didn't believe in divorce.

After the couple established a new life and a church in Georgia, a female pastor told the woman that she'd seen Owens with seven other women over the years. She said he had cheated on them and stolen from them. The newest Mrs. Owens began to investigate her husband's past. She found several marriages and no divorces. So she took her findings to the police. Four of the wives came forward, claiming that Owens had used them and left them broke.

Owens was sentenced to two years in prison and four more years of probation. His defense? He never meant to hurt anyone, and as a man of God, he was misled by teachings of the Mormon faith (although he was not Mormon himself). He was released in 2005 but was back in jail by 2007 for parole violations. What did he do with his free time in those 18 months of freedom? He proposed to four more women.

When You Love Love Too Much

Ed Hicks is another man who just can't get enough of a good thing. In fact, his profile on an Internet dating site claimed he was "in love with love." When the law caught up to him in 2005, he was married to two women and had been married to at least five others. In three cases, he didn't bother with divorce between the ceremonies. Unlike the devious Owens, who stole from his many wives before moving on, Hicks appeared to be a sweet-talking romantic who is handy around the house. In short, the wives liked the guy. "He could be a real nice husband," explained Sharon Hicks Pratt, wife number two. "But he had to have more than just one woman."

What was once a problem for the women turned into a problem for Hicks when the ladies began to find out, and the dominoes began to fall. The last three wives even formed an unofficial support group—and are committed to warning future wives about his secret past. Even after his arrest, Hicks began an online relationship with at least four other women. The wives must know his type by now, because three of those "pen pals" were fictional women created by wife number six to see if he'd take the bait. He did.

Equality of the Sexes

Lest you get the idea that women are constant victims, and only men can cheat in the name of love, consider the case of Kyle McConnell (a woman) from Roseville, Michigan. She was charged with felony bigamy and sentenced to 22 months to ten years in prison.

The popular McConnell had a talent for finding lonely men, marrying them, and stealing their money, according to sheriff's Detective Tim Donnellon. Apparently, her pattern was to drain their bank accounts and move on to the next guy by the time the current husband found out.

It worked pretty well, too. All in all, she managed to marry about 15 men. Isn't love grand?

Bluebeard in the Flesh

"All of the women for Johann go crazy!"

In 1905, when the police finally caught up with Johann Hoch, he had already proposed to what would have been his 45th wife. His habit was to meet a lonely middle-aged woman, propose, marry her, and take her money in the space of about a week. Depending on Johann's mood, about a third of the women were murdered; the others were simply abandoned.

Hoch was born John Schmidt in 1855 in the Grand Duchy of Hesse in what is now Germany. He allegedly married one wife while still living in Europe, and they immigrated to the United States around 1890. There, he began using a pseudonym and marrying—and burying—more women. He went by numerous aliases over the years, including Jacob Erdoff, C.A. Calford, Jacob Huff, Joseph Hoch, Dr. G.L. Hart, Jacob Hock, Adolf Hoch, Fred Doess, Martin Dose,

Henry Hartman, Henry Bartells, H. Ireck, John Healey, William Frederick Bessing, and Count Otto van Kurn.

Along with changing his name, he changed his location. Hoch moved from place to place, including but not limited to Chicago, San Francisco, Baltimore, Ohio, Indiana, and several cities in New York state.

Hoch's method of murder was slipping his new bride some arsenic, which was a perfect crime in those days. Arsenic was used in embalming fluid, so the minute an undertaker came into the house, convicting someone of arsenic poisoning was basically impossible.

When the story came to light, the press was fascinated—how could an ugly man who spoke like a comedian with a German accent convince so many women to marry him? Why, his last Chicago wife (his 44th overall) had agreed to marry him while her sister (wife #43) was lying dead on her bed! The *Herald American*, which could be counted on to print the wildest rumors in town, claimed that Hoch used hypnosis on the women and that he had learned all he knew about murdering from the infamous H. H. Holmes.

Hoch's power over women made it seem as though he must have had access to some sort of magic spell. As his trial continued, wife #44, the woman who had first reported him to authorities, came to his cell daily to bring him money and beg him to forgive her. He received numerous letters containing marriage proposals while in prison. Any marriage would have been a short one—Johann was hanged in 1906 and buried in a potter's field.

Legend has it that as Hoch was about to be hanged, he said to the guards, "I don't look like a monster now, do I?" After the deed was done, one of the guards replied, "Well, not anymore."

Testimony from the Other Side

When Zona Heaster Shue of Greenbrier County, West Virginia, died suddenly at age 23, her doctor attributed her passing to natural causes. But when Zona's mother encountered her ghost, a shocking tale of murder was revealed. Would testimony from the Other Side help to nab Zona's killer?

Gone Too Soon

On January 23, 1897, a boy who was doing chores at the Shue home discovered Zona's limp body lying at the bottom of the stairs. He ran to tell her husband—Edward Stribbling "Trout" Shue—and then he summoned a doctor. When Dr. George W. Knapp arrived, Shue escorted him to the bedroom where he'd moved Zona's lifeless body. Although Shue had already dressed Zona for burial, Knapp examined her body. As the doctor went about his duties, Shue became noticeably distressed, so Knapp cut the examination short. Suspecting natural causes as the reason for Zona's passing and not wishing to upset her husband any further, Knapp reported her cause of death as "everlasting faint" but later changed the finding to "childbirth." Although Zona hadn't told anyone that she was pregnant, the doctor surmised that complications from a pregnancy must have been the culprit because he'd recently treated her for "female trouble." During his hasty examination, Knapp noticed a few bruises on Zona's neck but quickly passed them off as unrelated.

Whirlwind Courtship

Little is known about her life, but it is believed that Zona Heaster was born in Greenbrier County, West Virginia, around 1873. In October 1896, she met Shue, a drifter who had recently moved to the area to work as a blacksmith.

Only months after they met, Zona Heaster and Edward Shue married. But for reasons that she couldn't quite explain, Zona's mother—Mary Jane Heaster—had taken an instant disliking to her son-in-law. Despite her concerns, the newlyweds seemed to get along until that tragic day when Zona was found dead. In an instant, Mary Jane's world was turned upside down. She grieved, as would any mother who must bury a child, but she sharply disagreed with Dr. Knapp's determination of her daughter's cause of death. In her mind, there was only one way that her daughter could have died at such a young age: Shue had killed her and had covered it up.

It All Comes Out in the Wash

At Zona's wake, those who came to pay their respects noticed Shue's erratic behavior. He continued to openly mourn his wife's passing, but something seemed odd about the way he grieved. His mood alternated between extreme sadness and sudden manic energy. He tended to his wife's body like a man possessed, allowing no one to get close to it. He also tied a large scarf around his wife's neck for no apparent reason, and even stranger, he placed a pillow on one side of Zona's head and a rolled-up cloth on the other; he told puzzled onlookers that they would help her "rest easier." And when Zona's body was moved to the cemetery for burial, several people noticed a strange looseness to her neck as they transported her. Not surprisingly, people began to talk.

Mary Jane Heaster did not have to be convinced that Shue was acting suspiciously about Zona's death. She had always hated him and wished that her daughter had never married him. She had a sneaking suspicion that something wasn't right, but she didn't know how to prove it. After the funeral, Mary Jane Heaster washed the sheet that had lined her daughter's coffin. To her horror, the water inside the basin turned red. Then, even more shockingly, the sheet turned pink and the water again turned clear. Mary Jane was convinced that this was a sign, so she began praying that her daughter would come to her to reveal the truth. A few weeks later, her prayers were answered.

Ghostly Visions

According to Mary Jane, Zona's apparition came to her over the course of four nights. It described how abusive Shue had been throughout their marriage and stated that he was responsible for her death. The tragedy occurred because Shue thought that Zona hadn't cooked meat for supper; he went into a rage, strangled her, and broke her neck. To demonstrate the brutality of Shue's attack, Zona's ghost rotated her head completely around. This horrified Mary Jane, but it also brought her some relief; her beloved daughter had returned from the grave to seek the justice that she deserved. Armed with the unbridled power of a mother's love, Mary Jane was determined to avenge her daughter's death.

Please Believe Me!

Mary Jane immediately told local prosecutor John Alfred Preston of her ghostly visit, and begged him to investigate. Whether or not he took Mary Jane at her word is open to debate, but Preston did agree to interview Knapp and others associated with the case.

After learning that Dr. Knapp's examination had been cursory at best, Preston and Knapp agreed that an autopsy would help to clear things up, so Zona's body was exhumed. A local newspaper reported that Edward Shue "vigorously complained" about the exhumation but was forced to witness the proceedings. When Dr. Knapp proclaimed that Zona's neck was indeed broken, Shue was arrested and charged with his wife's murder.

While Shue awaited trial, tales of his unsavory past started coming to light. It was revealed that he'd been married twice before. His first marriage (to Allie Estelline Cutlip) had ended in divorce in 1889, while Shue was incarcerated for horse theft. In their divorce decree, Cutlip claimed that Shue had frequently beaten her. In 1894, Shue married Lucy Ann Tritt; however, the union was short-lived—Tritt died just eight months into their marriage under "mysterious" circumstances. In the autumn of 1896, Shue moved to Greenbrier County, where he met Zona Heaster. Was there a pattern of violence with this lethal lothario?

Trial

Shue's trial began on June 22, 1897. Both the prosecution and the defense did their best to discredit each other. For every witness who spoke of Shue's ill temper, another likened him to an altar boy. After Shue took the stand, many agreed that he handled himself skillfully. Then it was Mary Jane Heaster's turn. When questioned by the prosecution, her ghostly encounter with her daughter was not mentioned. But when she was cross-examined by Shue's attorney, Mary Jane recalled in great detail how Zona's spirit had fingered Shue as her abuser and killer. The defense characterized Mary Jane's "visions" as little more than a grieving mother's ravings, assuming that the jury would agree. They were wrong. When the trial concluded, the jury quickly rendered a guilty verdict. Not only had they believed Mary Jane's supernatural tale, they fell just short of delivering the necessary votes to hang Shue for his evil deeds; instead, he was sentenced to life in prison. And as it turned out, that wouldn't be very long.

Epilogue

In July 1897, Shue was transferred to the West Virginia Penitentiary in Moundsville, where he lived out the rest of his days. The convicted murderer died on March 13, 1900, of an epidemic that was sweeping the prison. But his name lives on, as does the ghostly legend of Zona Heaster Shue. A historical marker located beside Route 60 in Greenbrier County reads: "Interred in nearby cemetery is Zona Heaster Shue. Her death in 1897 was presumed natural until her spirit appeared to her mother to describe how she was killed by her husband Edward. Autopsy on the exhumed body verified the apparition's account. Edward, found guilty of murder, was sentenced to the state prison. Only known case in which testimony from ghost helped convict a murderer."

The Woodchipper Murder

It's rare for a murderer to be convicted without a body to help prove guilt. But the murder of Helle Crafts, whose body was not recovered, not only ended with a conviction, but inspired a chilling scene in a Hollywood movie.

Sudden Disappearance

It was a match that seemed made in heaven. Danish-born flight attendant Helle Nielsen married airline pilot Richard Crafts in 1979, and the couple settled in Newtown, Connecticut, with their three children. But their happy married life didn't last long. Within seven years of marrying, Helle discovered that her husband was having affairs and hired a private investigator to expose the infidelity. She also contacted a divorce lawyer. It was clear that the scorned woman was planning to leave her husband and start a new life.

On the snowy night of November 18, 1986, after working on a long international flight, Helle was dropped off at her home but one of her friends. That was the last time anyone—except Richard—saw her. Over the next few weeks, he told several stories that attempted to explain her whereabouts, telling some people that she was visiting her parents in Denmark, while telling others that she was on vacation with a friend in the Canary Islands. He even told some of her friends that she had simply left with no warning, and he had no idea where she was.

Evidence of Foul Play

Helle's friends were understandably suspicious. She was finally reported missing on December 1, but it took weeks for authorities to look at the case with more detail. By Christmas, they had a warrant to search the Crafts' house. While Richard and his kids were vacationing in Florida for the holiday, police went through the house with a fine-tooth comb, searching for evidence. What they discovered was disturbing: pieces of carpet had been removed from the bedroom floor and there was a blood smear on the bed. But perhaps most damning were Richard's credit card records, which showed that around the time of Helle's disappearance, he had bought a freezer and new bedding, and rented a woodchipper.

As the circumstantial evidence mounted, a local man named Joseph Hine came forward with some new information. Hine drove a snowplow in the winter, and on the night that Helle disappeared he was plowing the road and noticed a rental truck with an attached woodchipper parked next to an area lake. Investigators also discovered a receipt for a chainsaw, which could not be found in the house. Armed with the new information, authorities began searching in and around the lake, where they discovered small amounts of human tissue, a tooth crown, a fingernail, bone chips, blond hairs, and blood that matched the same type as Helle's. The chainsaw was found in the lake, where it was still covered in hair and blood that matched Helle's DNA.

Murder and a Movie

While investigators were certain that Richard had killed his wife, they could not charge him with the crime until she was officially recorded as dead. This is difficult to do without the identification of a body, but a forensic dentist 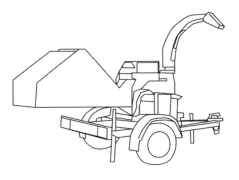 was able to positively identify the tooth crown as belonging to Helle, and a death certificate was issued. Richard was immediately arrested. Authorities theorized that he struck Helle in the head in their bedroom, causing blood stains on the carpet and bedding, which he disposed of. He then froze her body in the freezer, cut her apart with the chainsaw, and ran the pieces through the woodchipper, believing he'd committed the perfect murder.

After a trial that ended with a hung jury, a second trial found Richard guilty on November 21, 1989, and he was sentenced to 50 years in prison. Richard's own sister, who took custody of his children, urged the judge to impose the maximum sentence, citing the fact that he never showed remorse. The horrific nature of his crime eventually caught the attention of film directors Joel and Ethan Coen, who used it as inspiration for the famous "woodchipper" scene in their 1996 film *Fargo*.

Operation Royal Charm: A Wedding Bust

Undercover FBI agents spent several years watching their targets, members of an international counterfeiting and smuggling ring, and developing a relationship with them. Then the ultimate wedding sting operation just fell into place.

Nice Day for a Fake Wedding

Two of the agents, who had gained the trust of the criminals, posed as bride and groom, with a fake wedding that was months in the making. A date was set, and invitations were sent out. The wedding was planned for 2 p.m. on a Sunday afternoon in August 2005, just off the coast of New Jersey. A luxury yacht named *Operation Royal Charm* was docked outside of Atlantic City, and guests started arriving from far and wide. No detail was forgotten; guests and the bridal party were decked out in wedding finery befitting the high rollers that they were. There were even wedding presents, including a pair of Presidential Rolex watches.

But when the guests boarded a boat that they thought would take them out to the yacht, they got a bit of a surprise. There was no wedding! And instead of a cruise on a luxury boat, eight wedding guests got caught in an FBI sting that led to the arrest of about 60 other residents of Asia and the United States, all involved in a variety of international trafficking crimes.

Quite the Wedding Gifts

Authorities seized $4.4 million in counterfeit $100 bills, $42 million worth of counterfeit cigarettes, $700,000 worth of fake U.S. postage stamps and blue jeans, and very real quantities of Viagra, ecstasy, and methamphetamine. The criminals were also charged with conspiracy to ship $1 million of automatic rifles, silenced pistols, submachine guns, and rocket launchers—none of which were delivered.

Bad Brides

These ladies may have gone a little over the top on their wedding days. And we don't mean with the decorations...

Married Mugshot

In March of 2009, newlyweds Jade and Billy Puckett left their wedding reception, only to be caught in a "March Madness" DUI sting that was being conducted by deputies in Harris County, Texas. When Billy was charged with driving under the influence, Jade became belligerent and was charged with public intoxication. But it didn't end there! Jade claimed she was not allowed to change clothing and was humiliated when an unidentified male in the courtroom took photos of her in her wedding dress—photos that wound up on the Internet. She filed a complaint with the Harris County Precinct 8 Constable's office just days after her arrest.

Bridezilla Indeed!

Mark Allerton and Teresa Brown were friends for 16 years before they got hitched in a 2007 fairy-tale wedding at a castle in Aberdeen, Scotland. The castle is used in the popular British soap opera *Monarch of the Glen*, but the fight Mark and Teresa got into after the ceremony was even more dramatic than the show. According to police, Teresa attacked Mark with one of her stiletto heels, leaving him with a bleeding puncture wound on his head. Teresa spent two days in jail, but Mark stood by her, saying they had no plans to split. The bride said her freakout was caused by a reaction to an antidepressant. Note: Might want to adjust those meds before the wedding.

Breaking up the Band

Elmo Fernadez and his wife Fabiana had been married in a civil ceremony long before, but in 2008, they decided to renew their vows in a religious ceremony in Port Chester, New York. Everything was going swimmingly until the reception, when the band explained that they could only play music when the DJ was not playing. Fabiana didn't care for that excuse and went on a rampage, knocking over a set of $600 conga drums and destroying other equipment valued at $350. Girlfriend just wanted her money's worth! The cops hauled in Fabiana, her husband, and her daughter that night.

Celebrity Wedding Ruckus

In 2007, groom Carlos Barron and bride Tara Hensley were arrested on their wedding night after partying at a Huntington, South Carolina, nightclub called Envy. Police said they had no choice but to arrest the couple and three other members of the wedding party after they received a report of shots fired, and the crowd refused to disperse. But when it was revealed that one of the arrestees was Cincinnati Bengals running back Quincy Wilson, the boys in blue had a little more explaining to do.

Two Birds with One Threat

Diane Carnes did something not-too-bright on the day before her March 2008 wedding. It seems Diane thought it would be convenient to schedule her wedding at the Scotts Bluff County, Nebraska, courthouse while she was already there taking care of a pesky suspended license violation problem. Her license had been revoked after a DUI, but she got caught driving again. At her trial, Diane threatened one of the jurors, but no matter—she scheduled her wedding for the next day and went on home. The thing is, threatening a juror is a little bit illegal, so when Diane showed up the next day for her wedding, she was arrested. What a way to start a new, married life!

Real-life Wedding Crashers

Sure, 2005's Wedding Crashers, *starring Owen Wilson and Vince Vaughn, was a hit. In real life, however, the premise is not quite as funny.*

Crash Like No Other

In September 2007, a reception hall in quiet Idaho Falls, Idaho, was home to one of the most audacious attempts to crash a wedding ever recorded. Throughout the evening, one of the female guests dined, danced, and snatched a bite of wedding cake before the bride and groom even had a chance to cut the first piece. The woman signed the guest book, chatted with the wedding party, posed for photographs, and helped decorate the couple's getaway car.

But, as newlyweds Sciara and Charles Dougherty would later discover, Kimberly Cooper was not on the guest list. Cooper, with her 12-year-old daughter in tow, stole hundreds of dollars in wedding gifts. When police discovered several wedding presents and gift cards from the wedding in Cooper's home, she blamed her daughter for the crime.

Cooper was also accused of crashing another wedding, just hours after the Doughertys' reception ended. Newlyweds Courtney and Josh Van Tress became suspicious after gift cards went missing, and no one seemed to be able to explain Cooper's presence as a "mystery guest." When the couple saw Cooper the next day during a chance encounter at a local Target store, they confronted her—as she was busy paying for purchases with gift cards from their wedding.

Dress the Part... or Not

Unfortunately, there are a number of accounts of wedding crashers helping themselves to more than prime rib and cake. In August 2007, Anthony and Jennifer Smith of Garden Grove, California, returned from their honeymoon to discover a guest stole money-filled envelopes from their cache of wedding gifts.

The well-dressed guest wore blue and burgundy clothing—just like the rest of the wedding party—and made off with about $1,500 in cash.

But not every crasher blends in as seamlessly. In September 2009, police in Seymour, Indiana, reported that a man wearing a baseball cap and T-shirt appeared uninvited at Aaron and Margaret Thompson Brown's wedding, where he swiped a large wire birdcage. That doesn't sound so bad, unless you know that the birdcage was meant to feather the newlywed's nest. It was filled with checks, gift cards, and cash worth about $5,000.

Lawrencia Bembenek: Run, Bambi, Run!

"Bambi." Laurie Bembenek would be the first to tell you she hates that nickname. It's all part of the image portrayed by the prosecution when she was on trial for murder. They suggested that she was a materialistic second wife—and a cold-blooded, calculating murderer.

A Murder in Beer City

Milwaukee isn't typically known as a hotbed of crime. Maybe that's why Lawrencia Bembenek's case garnered such a following—from the murder to her conviction, to her escape and ultimate release. It all began on May 28, 1981, when Christine Schultz was found murdered in bed in her Milwaukee home. The victim was the ex-wife of Fred Schultz, a detective for the Milwaukee Police Department. Laurie was his second wife—and the only one with motive, means, and opportunity to commit the crime, according to the district attorney.

Although all of the evidence was circumstantial, it still mounted against Bembenek. Fred Schultz had an alibi for the time of the murder, while Laurie did not. There was no sign of a break-in at the Schultz home, but Laurie had access to Fred's key. Even more incriminating, she had access to Fred's off-duty revolver.

As a former police officer, she knew how to use the gun. And finally, a wig with fibers similar to those found at the crime scene was found in the plumbing system of Laurie's apartment building.

The case drew national attention. It had all the hallmarks of a steamy crime drama—a love triangle gone wrong, a second wife fighting for what should have been hers, and a former Playboy bunny and model turned vindictive.

Presumed Guilty

With no alibi, Bembenek's best defense was the eyewitness testimony of her 11-year-old stepson, who said the murderer was a heavyset, wig-wearing man with broad shoulders. There was also the matter of possible police retribution. Laurie had been fired from her position on the police force. The police said it was for possession of marijuana while she said she had stood up to sexual harassment.

None of that seemed to matter. The jury had heard enough. Laurie Bembenek was found guilty in March 1982 and sentenced to life in prison at the Taycheedah Correctional Institution.

For years she maintained her innocence but was unable to get her conviction overturned. She eventually met and became engaged to Nick Gugliatto, the brother of a fellow inmate. In July 1990, she escaped with Gugliatto's help and they ran to Thunder Bay, Ontario, Canada, where they lived secret lives for three months. At that point, the couple was featured on an episode of *America's Most Wanted*, and people recognized them, leading to a quick arrest. Back in Wisconsin, Laurie pleaded no contest to second-degree murder and was sentenced to time served. She was free.

Life After Prison

Since that time, more evidence has been found that exonerates Laurie. For starters, there was semen at the scene, making it likely that Christine was raped and the murderer was male. Also, the bullets recovered didn't match the service revolver Laurie was thought to have used. Finally, her husband had prior contact with a criminal who later told friends that he committed the crime.

Since her release, Laurie has found it hard to adjust to the outside world. She's had problems with drugs and alcohol and has had difficulty finding work. Scheduled to appear on the *Dr. Phil Show* in 2002, she felt claustrophobic in her hotel room and jumped from a window. Her leg was injured so badly that it had to be amputated.

Laurie has written a book and been the subject of a made-for-TV movie. But despite the infamy, Laurie's most fervent desire is still elusive—that her conviction be overturned.

The Ghost of the Sausage Vat Murder

The story of Louisa Luetgert, the murdered wife of "Sausage King" Adolph Luetgert, is a gruesome tale of betrayal, death, and a lingering specter. It is also one of the greatest stories in Chicago lore. According to legend, each year on the anniversary of her death, Louisa appears on the corner of Hermitage Avenue where it once crossed Diversey Parkway. But her ghost not only haunts her old neighborhood; allegedly, she also coaxed her treacherous husband into an early grave.

Land of Opportunity

Adolph Luetgert was born in Germany and came to America after the Civil War. He arrived in Chicago around 1865 and worked in tanneries for several years before opening his first business—a liquor store—in 1872. Luetgert married his first wife, Caroline Roepke, that same year. She gave birth to two boys, only one of whom survived childhood. Just two months after Caroline died in November 1877, Luetgert quickly remarried a much younger woman, Louisa Bicknese, and moved to the northwest side of the city. As a gift, he gave her an unusual gold ring that had her initials inscribed inside the band. Little did Luetgert know that this ring would prove to be his downfall.

Trouble for the "Sausage King"

In 1892, Luetgert built a sausage factory at the southwest corner of Hermitage and Diversey. But just a year later, sausage sales declined due to an economic depression. Luetgert had put his life's savings into the factory, along with plenty of borrowed money, so when his business suffered, creditors started coming after him.

Instead of trying to reorganize his finances, however, Luetgert answered a newspaper ad posted by an English millionaire who made a deal with him to buy out the majority of the sausage business. The Englishman proved to be a conman, and Luetgert ended up losing even more money in the deal. Luetgert eventually laid off many of his workers, but a few remained as he attempted to keep the factory out of the hands of creditors for as long as possible.

Luetgert's business losses took a terrible toll on his marriage. Friends and neighbors frequently heard the Luetgerts arguing, and things became so bad that Luetgert eventually started sleeping in his office at the factory. He carried on with several mistresses and even became involved with a household servant who was related to his wife. When Louisa found out about his involvement with her relative, she became enraged.

Luetgert soon gave the neighbors even more to gossip about. One night, during another shouting match with Louisa, he allegedly took his wife by the throat and began choking her. After noticing alarmed neighbors watching him through the parlor window, Luetgert reportedly calmed down and released his wife before she collapsed. A few days later, Luetgert was seen chasing his wife down the street, shouting at her and waving a revolver.

Vanishing Louisa

Louisa disappeared on May 1, 1897. When questioned about it days later, Luetgert stated that Louisa had left him and was possibly staying with her sister or another man. When Louisa's brother, Dietrich Bicknese, asked Luetgert why he had not informed the police of Louisa's disappearance, the sausage maker told him that he'd hired a private investigator to find her because he didn't trust the police.

When Bicknese informed the police of his sister's disappearance, Captain Herman Schuettler and his men began to search for Louisa. They questioned neighbors and relatives, who detailed the couple's violent arguments. Schuettler summoned Luetgert to the precinct house on a couple of occasions and each time pressed him about his wife's disappearance. Luetgert stated that he did not report Louisa's disappearance because he could not afford the disgrace and scandal.

During the investigation, a young German girl named Emma Schimke told police that she had passed by the factory with her sister at about 10:30 p.m. on May 1 and remembered seeing Luetgert leading his wife down the alleyway behind the factory.

Police also questioned employees of the sausage factory. Frank Bialk, a night watchman at the plant, told police that when he arrived for work on May 1, he found a fire going in one of the boilers. He said Luetgert asked him to keep the fire going and then sent him on a couple of trivial errands while Luetgert stayed in the basement. When Bialk returned to the factory, he went back to the boiler fire and heard Luetgert finishing his work at around 3:00 a.m.

Later that morning, Bialk saw a sticky, gluelike substance on the floor near the vat. He noticed that it seemed to contain bits of bone, but he thought nothing of it. After all, Luetgert used all sorts of waste meats to make his sausage, so he assumed that's what it was.

On May 3, Luetgert asked another employee, Frank Odorofsky, to clean the basement and told him to keep quiet about it. Odorofsky put the slimy substance into a barrel and scattered it near the railroad tracks as Luetgert had requested.

A Gruesome Discovery

On May 15, the police search was narrowed to the factory basement and a vat that was two-thirds full of a brownish, brackish liquid. Using gunnysacks as filters, officers drained the greasy paste from the vat and began poking through the residue with sticks. Officer Walter Dean found several bone fragments and two gold rings—one a heavy gold band engraved with the initials "L. L."

Luetgert, proclaiming his innocence, was questioned again shortly after the search and was subsequently arrested for the murder of his wife several days later. Despite the fact that Louisa's body was never found and there was no real evidence to link her husband to the crime, the police and prosecutors believed they had a solid case against Luetgert. He was indicted for Louisa's murder, and the details of the crime shocked the city. Even though he had been charged with boiling Louisa's body, rumors circulated that she had actually been ground up into sausage that was sold to local butcher shops and restaurants. Not surprisingly, sausage sales dropped dramatically in Chicago in 1897.

Hounded to the Grave?

Luetgert's trial ended in a hung jury on October 21. The judge threw out the case, and prosecutors had to try the whole thing again. A second trial was held in 1898, and this time Luetgert was convicted and sentenced to a life term at Joliet Prison.

While in prison, Luetgert continued to maintain his innocence and was placed in charge of meats in the cold-storage warehouse. Officials described him as a model prisoner. But by 1899, Luetgert began to speak less and less and often quarreled with other convicts.

He soon became a shadow of his former, blustering self, fighting for no reason and often babbling incoherently in his cell at night. But was he talking to himself or to someone else?

Legend has it that Luetgert claimed Louisa haunted him in his jail cell, intent on having revenge for her murder. Was she really haunting him, or was the ghost just a figment of his rapidly deteriorating mind? Based on the fact that neighbors also reported seeing Louisa's ghost, one has to wonder if she did indeed drive Luetgert insane.

Luetgert died in 1900, likely from heart trouble. The coroner who conducted the autopsy also reported that his liver was greatly enlarged and in such a condition of degeneration that "mental strain would have caused his death at any time."

Perhaps Louisa really did visit him after all.

The Ghost of Louisa Luetgert

Regardless of who killed Louisa, her spirit reportedly did not rest in peace. Soon after Luetgert was sent to prison, neighbors swore they saw Louisa's ghost inside her former home, wearing a white dress and leaning against the fireplace mantel.

The sausage factory stood empty for years, looming over the neighborhood as a grim reminder of the horrors that had taken place there. Eventually, the Library Bureau Company purchased the factory for a workshop and storehouse for library furniture and office supplies. During renovations, they discarded the infamous vats in the basement.

On June 26, 1904, the old factory caught on fire. Despite the damage done to the building's interior, the Library Bureau reopened its facilities in the former sausage factory. In 1907, a contracting mason purchased the old Luetgert house and moved it from behind the factory to another lot in the neighborhood, hoping to dispel the grim memories—and ghost—attached to it.

Hermitage Avenue no longer intersects with Diversey, and by the 1990s, the crumbling factory stood empty. But in the late '90s, around the 100th anniversary of Louisa's death, the former sausage factory was converted into condominiums and a brand-new neighborhood sprang up to replace the aging homes that remained from the days of the Luetgerts. Fashionable brick homes and apartments appeared around the old factory, and rundown taverns were replaced with coffee shops.

But one thing has not changed. Legend has it that each year on May 1, the anniversary of her death, the ghost of Louisa can still be spotted walking down Hermitage Avenue near the old sausage factory, reliving her final moments on this earth.

Chapter 5

Star-Studded Crimes

When Celebs Go Bad!

Back in the day, celebrities were publicly pilloried for their bad behavior. Sometimes, anyway. As you'll read later in this chapter, a little bit of scandal could ruin some careers but help others. Today, a well-publicized arrest and a (brief) stint in (a cushy) jail might actually seem like a smart career move. Here are just a few of the rich and famous who have had brushes with the law.

Ozzy Osbourne

In 1982, the Black Sabbath front man and reality TV superstar angered Texans everywhere by drunkenly urinating on a wall at the Alamo. Osbourne was banned from the city of San Antonio for a decade but later made amends by donating $20,000 to the Daughters of the Republic of Texas to help restore the fabled landmark.

Matthew McConaughey

In October 1999, following a noise complaint, McConaughey was found by police sitting naked in his home playing the bongos. The cops also found the actor's stash, which led to McConaughey being arrested for marijuana possession and resisting arrest. The drug charges were later dropped, and McConaughey was simply fined $50 for violating a municipal noise ordinance.

Winona Ryder

In December 2001, Ryder was nabbed for shoplifting merchandise at the ritzy Saks Fifth Avenue store in Beverly Hills. She was convicted of grand theft and vandalism but received a relatively light sentence: three years probation and 480 hours of community service and restitution.

Nicole Richie

In February 2003, the daughter of singer Lionel Richie was charged with heroin possession and driving with a suspended license. Three years later, she was arrested again for driving under the influence. Her sentence: four days in jail. Actual time served: 82 minutes.

Natasha Lyonne

Known for such films as *Slums of Beverly Hills* (1998) and *American Pie* (1999), Lyonne was arrested in December 2004 after verbally attacking her neighbor, breaking the neighbor's mirror, and threatening to harm the neighbor's dog. A warrant was issued against the troubled actress in April 2005 for failure to appear before a judge, and a second warrant was issued in January 2006. In December 2006, Lyonne was finally sentenced to a conditional discharge. She later went to rehab, and would go on to became known for her role in *Orange Is the New Black* and her lead role in Netflix's *Russian Doll*.

Paris Hilton

Over the years, media personality and socialite Paris Hilton has been charged with a variety of crimes, including driving under the influence of alcohol and driving with a suspended license (twice). In June 2007, the hard-partying hotel heiress finally received her due when she was sentenced to 45 days in jail, though she was quickly released because of an undisclosed medical condition. Instead of doing her time in the slammer, Hilton was given 40 days house arrest with a monitoring device. In 2010, she was arrested for cocaine possession. Her lawyers argued that the purse where the drugs were found was not hers—it simply wasn't up to the star's fashion standards! Ultimately she pled guilty to two misdemeanors, resulting in a fine, a year of probation, community service, and a drug-treatment program. Hilton has also been the victim of crime—she has dealt with multiple stalkers and a case of identity theft.

Lindsay Lohan

In July 2007, the former child star was found by police in a Santa Monica parking garage engaged in a heated argument with a former assistant. She failed a sobriety test, and police also found a small amount of cocaine on her person. Lohan pleaded guilty to cocaine possession and driving under the influence and was sentenced to one day in jail, community service, and three years probation. Actual time spent behind bars: 84 minutes.

Bill Murray

In 2007, during a trip to Sweden, the former *Ghostbusters* and *Saturday Night Live* funnyman was charged with driving under the influence—while driving a golf cart. He refused to take a breath test but signed a document saying he had been driving drunk. He was allowed to leave the country without punishment.

Lori Loughlin and Felicity Huffman

In 2019, a number of wealthy people were implicated in a conspiracy to get their children into the colleges of their choice by faking exam scores and outright bribery. Two of those people were well-known actresses Lori Loughlin, of *Full House* fame, and Felicity Huffman, known for her work on *Desperate Housewives* and other shows. Loughlin and her husband were accused of conspiracy to commit honest services mail fraud. She was fined and sentenced to two months in prison. Felicity Huffman ultimately served about ten days in prison and was fined; she was accused of trying to bribe someone to falsify her daughter's SAT results. Her husband, everyman actor William Macy, was never charged.

1924 Murder Mystery

Who's at the heart of the cloaked-in-secrets demise of Thomas Ince? Who, of the loads of lovelies and gallons of gents on the infamous Oneida yacht that night, was the killer? Curious minds demand to know.

The night is November 15, 1924. The setting is the *Oneida* yacht. The principal players are: Thomas H. Ince, Marion Davies, Charlie Chaplin, and William Randolph Hearst.

The Facts

- By 1924, William Randolph Hearst had built a huge newspaper empire; he dabbled in filmmaking and politics; he owned the *Oneida*. Thomas H. Ince was a prolific movie producer. Charlie Chaplin was a star comedian. Marion Davies was an actor. The web of connections went like this: Hearst and Davies were lovers; Davies and Chaplin were rumored to be lovers; Hearst and Ince were locked in tense business negotiations; Ince was celebrating a birthday.

- For Ince's birthday, Hearst planned a party on his yacht. It was a lavish one—champagne all around. In the era of Prohibition, this was not just extravagant, it was also illegal. But Hearst had ulterior motives: He'd heard rumors that his mistress, Davies, was secretly seeing Chaplin, and so he invited Chaplin to the party. The *Oneida* set sail from San Pedro, California, headed to San Diego on Saturday, November 15.

- An unfortunate but persistent fog settled over the events once the cast of characters were onboard the yacht. What is known definitively is that Ince arrived at the party late, due to business, and that he did not depart the yacht under his own power. Whether he was sick or dead depends on which version you believe, but it's a fact that Ince left the yacht on a stretcher on Sunday, November 16. What happened? Various scenarios have been put forward over the years.

- Possibility 1: Hearst shoots Ince. Hearst invites Chaplin to the party to observe his behavior around Davies and to verify their affair. After catching the two in a compromising position, he flies off the handle, runs to his stateroom, grabs his gun, and comes back shooting. In this scenario, Ince tries to break up the trouble but gets shot by mistake.

- Possibility 2: Hearst shoots Ince. It's the same end result as possibility 1, but in this scenario, Davies and Ince are alone in the galley after Ince comes in to look for something to settle the queasiness caused by his notorious ulcers. Entering and seeing the two people together, Hearst assumes Chaplin—not Ince—is with Davies. He pulls out his gun and shoots.

- Possibility 3: Chaplin shoots Ince. Chaplin, a week away from marrying a pregnant 16-year-old to avoid scandal and the law, is forlorn to the point where he considers suicide. While contemplating his gun, it accidentally goes off, and the bullet goes through the thin walls of the ship to hit Ince in the neighboring room.

- Possibility 4: An assassin shoots Ince. In this scenario, a hired assassin shoots Ince so Hearst can escape an unwanted business deal with the producer.

- Possibility 5: Ince dies of natural causes. Known for his shaky health, Ince succumbs to rabid indigestion and chronic heart problems. A development such as this would not surprise his friends and family.

Aftermath

Regardless of which of the various scenarios might actually be true, one fact is that Ince was wheeled off Hearst's yacht. But what happened next?

That's not so clear, either. The facts of the aftermath of Ince's death are as hazy as the facts of the death itself. All reports agree that Ince did, in fact, die. There was no autopsy, and his body was cremated. After the cremation, Ince's wife, Nell, moved to Europe. But beyond those matters of record, there are simply conflicting stories.

Self-protection Reigns

The individuals involved had various reasons for wanting to protect themselves from whatever might have happened on the yacht. If an unlawful death did indeed take place, the motivation speaks for itself. But even if nothing untoward happened, Hearst was breaking Prohibition laws. The damage an investigation could have caused was enough reason to make Hearst cover up any attention that could have come his way from Ince's death. As a result, he tried to hide all mention of any foul play. Although Hearst didn't own the *Los Angeles Times*, he was plenty powerful. Rumor has it that an early edition of the paper after Ince's death carried the screaming headline, "Movie Producer Shot on Hearst Yacht." By later in the day, the headline had disappeared.

For his part, Chaplin denied being on the *Oneida* in the first place. In his version of the story, he didn't attend the party for Ince at all. He did, however, claim to visit Ince—along with Hearst and Davies—later in the week. He also stated that Ince died two weeks after that visit. Most reports show that Ince was definitely dead within 48 hours of the yacht party.

Davies agreed that Chaplin was never aboard the *Oneida* that fateful night. In her version, Ince's wife called her the day after Ince left the yacht to inform her of Ince's death. Ince's doctor claimed that the producer didn't die until Tuesday, two days after the yacht party.

So, what really happened? Who knows? Most of the people on the yacht never commented on their experience. Louella Parsons certainly didn't. The famed gossip columnist was reportedly aboard the *Oneida* that night (although she denied it as well). She had experienced some success writing for a

Hearst newspaper, but shortly after this event, Hearst gave her a lifetime contract and wide syndication, allowing her to become a Hollywood power broker.

Coincidence? No one can say for certain.

Trouble for the Prince of Noir

Robert Mitchum was the original offscreen bad boy—before James Dean ever appeared on the scene. He defined cool before Hollywood knew the hip meaning of the word. He was rugged, handsome, and jaunty. A hobo turned actor, he was the antithesis of the typical movie hero—and he was on his way to becoming a star, primarily in film noir. Then it happened: A drug bust with a buxom blonde, and Mitchum was in the headlines in a way he never intended. Ironically, this incident accelerated his stardom.

In August 1948, Hollywood tabloids were emblazoned with headlines proclaiming the scandalous drug bust (for possession of marijuana) of actor Robert Mitchum, who was in the company of 20-year-old aspiring actress Lila Leeds. This was the era of the marijuana frenzy: The government was at war with cannabis users, and propaganda, entrapment, blatant lies, and excessive punishments were just a few of the weapons they used. Mitchum was the perfect whipping boy. The actor was no stranger to pot and hashish, having experimented with both as a teenage hobo riding the rails. He was also a fugitive from the law, having escaped from a Georgia chain gang after being arrested for vagrancy in Savannah at age 16. Despite hiring Jerry Giesler, Hollywood's hottest defense attorney, Mitchum was found guilty and was sentenced to 60 days on a prison farm. His "I don't give a damn" smirk when his sentence was pronounced would define the attitude of the drug culture that burst upon the scene as the '40s came to a close.

A Career Ruined?

When Mitchum was sentenced, he was earning $3,000 a week—a princely sum at the time. He was married to his childhood sweetheart, Dorothy Spence, and was in the midst of a seven-year contract with RKO studios. When the tabloids ran a picture of inmate 91234 swabbing the jail corridors in prison attire, Mitchum anticipated it would be "the bitter end" of his career and his marriage.

In reality, the publicity had the opposite effect. With the exception of causing a small embarrassment to the studio and causing the cancellation of a speech Mitchum was scheduled to deliver to a youth group, the actor's offscreen bad-boy persona had little negative effect on his career or personal life. If anything, it only added verisimilitude to his counterculture, tough-guy, antihero image.

Great PR

While Mitchum served his 60-day sentence on the honor farm (which he described as "Palm Springs without the riff-raff"), RKO released the already-completed film *Rachel and the Stranger* (1948). Not only did movie audiences stand and cheer when Mitchum appeared on the screen, the low-budget movie also became the studio's most successful film of the year.

In 1950, another judge reviewed Mitchum's conviction and reversed the earlier court decision because the arrest smelled of entrapment: Leeds's Laurel Canyon bungalow had been bugged by two overly ambitious narcotics agents. The judge changed Mitchum's plea to not guilty and expunged the conviction from his records—not that Mitchum appeared to care one way or the other. By then, he was a bona fide Hollywood star.

A Long and Successful Livelihood

Mitchum enjoyed an illustrious career, making more than 70 films, some to critical acclaim. He also enjoyed success as a songwriter and singer, with three songs hitting the best-seller charts. His marriage remained intact for 57 years, possibly a

Hollywood record. He earned a star on the Hollywood Walk of Fame along with several other prestigious industry awards. Not a bad lifetime of achievements for a pot-smoking vagabond fugitive from a chain gang. Often seen with a cigarette dangling from his sensual lips, Mitchum died of lung cancer and emphysema on July 1, 1997, at his home in Santa Barbara, California. He was 79 years old.

The Rise and Fall of Fatty Arbuckle

As the saying goes, "The bigger they are, the harder they fall." And when it comes to early Hollywood scandals, no star was bigger or fell harder than Roscoe "Fatty" Arbuckle.

The scurrilous affair that engulfed Roscoe "Fatty" Arbuckle (1887–1933) in 1921 remains one of the biggest Hollywood scandals of all time because of its repercussions on the film industry. (It was instrumental in the creation of organized film censorship in Hollywood.) The Fatty Arbuckle scandal rocked the world when it broke, and though few people today know the details, in 2007, *Time* magazine ranked it fourth on its list of the Top 25 crimes of the past 100 years.

As one of Hollywood's first headline-grabbing scandals, it contained all the elements that make a scandal juicy—drunkenness, debauchery, and death. But what made the tawdry tale big was Arbuckle, who himself was big in size (nearly 300 pounds), big in popularity, and, as Tinseltown's highest paid comedian, one of the biggest stars in the Hollywood galaxy at the time.

The Rise

Arbuckle began his career as a child, performing in minstrel shows and sing-alongs. The young entertainer already carried a noticeable girth, but his remarkable singing voice, acrobatic agility, and knack for comedy made him a rising star on the vaudeville circuit.

In 1913, Arbuckle got his big break in film when Mack Sennett hired him on at Keystone Film Company. Arbuckle initially rollicked as one of Sennett's Keystone Cops, but he was soon developing his unique comic persona as the lovable fat man and honing his own slapstick specialties based on the seeming contradiction between his size and graceful agility.

By 1914, Arbuckle was teamed with comedienne Mabel Normand for the extremely successful "Fatty and Mabel" shorts, in which the pair offered humorous interpretations of romantic rituals. Arbuckle's charming persona ensured that he always got the girl. He became so adept at working out the duo's physical gags for the camera that he soon took over direction of the films.

In 1917, Arbuckle formed Comique Film Corporation with Hollywood mogul Joseph Schenck, who offered Arbuckle creative control and an astounding paycheck. At Comique, Arbuckle launched the screen career of the great Buster Keaton, who played the rotund actor's sidekick in classic silent comedies such as *Coney Island* (1917), *Good Night, Nurse!* (1918), and *The Garage* (1920).

In 1919, Arbuckle reached unprecedented heights when Paramount Pictures handed him a monstrous three-year $3 million contract to make several feature-length films. But Hollywood's first million-dollar man would have to work like a dog to meet production schedules. So on Labor Day weekend in 1921, a worn out Arbuckle headed to San Francisco for some rest and relaxation.

The Scandal

For the large-living, heavy-drinking Arbuckle, R & R meant a weekend-long bash at the St. Francis Hotel. On September 5, several people joined Arbuckle for a party, including a 26-year-old actress named Virginia Rappe and her friend Maude Delmont. Much has been exaggerated about the sexual exploits of Rappe, but her bad reputation was largely the product of the sensationalized press of the day. However, Delmont was a convicted extortionist known for her penchant for blackmail.

Around 3:00 a.m., Arbuckle left the party for his suite. Shortly thereafter, screams emanated from his room. According to press accounts of the day, several guests rushed in to find Rappe's clothing torn. She hysterically shouted at Arbuckle to stay away from her, supposedly uttering, "Roscoe did this to me." Though very dramatic, Rappe's accusation was most likely untrue and was probably invented to sell newspapers.

The story goes that the shaken Rappe was placed in a cold bath to calm her down and was later put to bed when a doctor diagnosed her as intoxicated. The next day, the hotel doctor gave her morphine and catheterized her when Delmont mentioned that Rappe hadn't urinated in some time.

Delmont later called a doctor friend to examine Rappe, saying that Arbuckle had raped her. He found no evidence of rape but treated Rappe to help her urinate. Four days later Delmont took Rappe to the hospital, where she died of peritonitis caused by a ruptured bladder. Delmont called the police, and on September 11, Arbuckle was arrested for murder.

The Fall

Arbuckle told police—and would contend all along—that he entered his room and found Rappe lying on the bathroom floor. He said he picked her up, placed her on the bed, and rubbed ice on her stomach when she complained of abdominal pain.

Delmont told police that Arbuckle used the ice as a sexual stimulant, and years later, rumors circulated that Arbuckle had raped Rappe with a soda or champagne bottle. Yet, there was no mention of this in the press during the arrest and trial. Instead, police alleged that Arbuckle's immense weight caused Rappe's bladder to rupture as he raped her. But contemporary research speculates that Rappe was probably struck hard in the abdomen, not raped. Whatever the cause, the public—enraged by the extremely sensationalized reports in the newspapers—wanted Arbuckle hanged.

Over the next seven months, Arbuckle was tried three times for the death of Virginia Rappe. The first two ended with hung juries. In the final trial, the jury deliberated for six minutes before declaring Arbuckle not guilty and offering a written apology for the injustice placed upon him.

Arbuckle was exonerated, but the damage was done. In April 1922, the Hays Office, the motion picture industry's censorship organization, which was established in the wake of the scandal, banned Arbuckle's movies and barred him from filmmaking. Although the blacklisting was lifted in December 1922, it would be several years before Arbuckle resumed his Hollywood career. A few years after his acquittal, Arbuckle began directing under the name William Goodrich, and in the early 1930s, RKO hired him to direct a series of comic shorts. In 1933, Vitaphone—part of Warner Bros.— hired Arbuckle to appear in front of the camera again in a series of six sync-sound shorts shot in Brooklyn.

But his revitalized career was short-lived. On June 29, 1933, one day after finishing the sixth film and signing a long-term contract with Warner Bros., Arbuckle died of a heart attack at age 46. Nearly eight decades later, Arbuckle is sadly remembered more for a crime that he *didn't* commit than as the comedic genius he was.

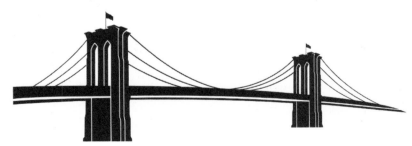

Albert Dekker's Gruesome Demise

When a veteran actor is found dead in his apartment, compromised circumstances unleash a wave of speculation.

Sex-O-Rama

If you enter "kinky Hollywood sex" into an Internet search engine (we don't recommend this idea, by the way), you probably won't find a reference to Albert Dekker. Yet, when Dekker, the star of Doctor Cyclops (1940) and The Killers (1946), died tragically more than 40 years ago, his body was found in a state that greatly pushed the envelope of accepted sexual mores of the time. When the seasoned thespian took his final bow at age 62, he left even the most jaded observers slack-jawed in disbelief.

Who Was Albert Dekker?

Born in Brooklyn, New York, in 1905, Albert Dekker was a highly respected character actor who had been trained for the stage. After a solid career on Broadway, in which he appeared in *Grand Hotel* and *Parnell* in the early 1930s, he moved to Hollywood. Interested in politics, Dekker held the Democratic seat in the California State Assembly from 1944 to 1946. However, his life was not without tragedy. In the early 1950s, Dekker was one of many victimized by the accusations of Joseph McCarthy, which resulted in the actor's return to the stage. Also, his son John died from an accidental gunshot wound. But by the 1960s, Dekker had returned to Hollywood.

Macabre Discovery

On May 5, 1968, when Dekker's fiancée Geraldine Saunders was unable to reach him by telephone, she drove to his Hollywood apartment and found a number of notes left on his door by concerned friends. After summoning the building's manager, Saunders entered the residence. What she saw sprawled before her was enough to make her lose consciousness. Dekker was dead, that was for certain, but the way that he had died was most disturbing. Kneeling nude in his bathtub, the actor wore a hangman's noose around his neck and sported a hypodermic needle in each arm. Suggestive words such as whip and slave were scrawled on his body in red lipstick, and a rubber-ball bit was stuffed in his mouth, with the metal chains from the bit tied behind his head. Blindfolded by a scarf, Dekker was attached to three leather straps that terminated in a hitch. These, in turn, were hooked to a strap that was held in Dekker's hand. Completing the bizarre picture were a pair of handcuffs around each wrist (with keys inserted) and obscene drawings on his abdomen.

All Choked Up

After a brief investigation, detectives concluded that Dekker had committed suicide. However, finding little evidence to support that theory, Los Angeles County Coroner Thomas Noguchi ruled the death an "accidental death, not a suicide." Some of Dekker's friends rejected both findings. They suspected murder even though the death scene showed no signs of forced entry or a struggle, although according to some reports, some camera equipment and cash were missing. Dekker's fiancée also insisted that the actor was murdered. She guessed that the killer was "someone he knew and let into the apartment." But coroner Noguchi rejected the idea of foul play in favor of accidental strangulation by "autoerotic asphyxia." The coroner explained that this solitary sexual act often features blindfolds, cross-dressing, and handcuffs. This appeared to be the case with Dekker.

A Sexual Pioneer

After his death, Albert Dekker became even more famous, but unfortunately, his heightened fame was for all the wrong reasons. Dekker's last film, *The Wild Bunch*, was released posthumously in 1969. The Western featured a group of desperados who had little use for conformity or rules. The film, directed by Sam Peckinpah, is now considered a masterpiece of editing and one of Hollywood's most provocative revisionist Westerns. It was a notable final film and a fitting epitaph considering the mode of Dekker's death.

In 2009, actor David Carradine was found dead in a similar embarrassing state. The circumstances surrounding Carradine's death invited speculation along the same lines as Dekker's demise. Sadly, both actors' deaths overshadowed their talents and accomplishments.

Little Rascals with Big Troubles

Our Gang *was a popular prepubescent posse of rogues, rascals, and scamps that appeared in more than 200 short films over the course of 20 years. During the 1950s, the series was sold to television and rechristened* The Little Rascals, *and it ran in syndication for decades. Most of the 41 actors who portrayed the troublesome tykes went on to live rich and resourceful lives. However, for some of the motley mites, tragedy, turmoil, and tribulation marked their adult years.*

Matthew "Stymie" Beard

Beard costarred in numerous *Our Gang* shorts in the 1930s, but he started using drugs in adulthood and eventually spent time in jail for possession and dealing. He finally kicked his heroin habit in the 1960s and enjoyed a minor comeback as an actor, appearing on television shows such as *Starsky and Hutch*, and in small roles in several critically acclaimed miniseries. He died in 1981.

Scott "Scotty" Beckett

A prodigious talent who joined the Rascals in 1934, Beckett became one of Hollywood's top child actors after leaving the *Our Gang* family in 1936. Beckett appeared in such notable films as *Dante's Inferno* (1935), *Charge of the Light Brigade* (1936), and *King's Row* (1942). But his childhood success didn't translate into adult employment, and he spent the last ten years of his life in a self-destructive spiral. He died of an apparent drug overdose in 1968 at age 38.

Robert Blake

One of the most famous and successful members of the *Our Gang* clan, Robert Blake appeared in 40 episodes of the series from 1939 to 1944 under the name Mickey Gubitosi. Later, he appeared as a regular in the Red Ryder film series. After serving in the U.S. Army, Blake became a noted movie actor, starring in such well-regarded films as *In Cold Blood* (1967) and *Tell Them Willie Boy Is Here* (1969). He also played the title character on the TV series *Baretta* from 1975 to 1978. But his career and personal integrity suffered a serious blow when he was arrested and charged with murdering his wife in 2001. Although he was acquitted of murder, he was found responsible for her death in a civil trial and was ordered to pay $30 million in damages to her children.

Jay R. "Freckle Face" Smith

Freckle Face was a steady contributor to the *Our Gang* series until 1929. At age 14, he retired from acting and later served in the U.S. Army and ran a retail paint business in Hawaii. In 2002, Smith was murdered by a transient that he'd befriended. His body was discovered in the desert near Las Vegas.

Carl "Alfalfa" Switzer

Carl Switzer was among the most popular and fondly regarded *Our Gang* alumni. A staple of the group from 1935 until 1940, he forged a fortuitous and formidable career as an adult character actor, appearing in such notable films as *It's a Wonderful Life* (1946), *Pat and Mike* (1952), and *The Defiant Ones* (1958). Despite that success, he also had difficulty dismantling his demons. In January 1959, he was shot and killed in a bizarre argument over an unpaid $50 debt and a missing hunting dog. He was just 31 years old.

Billie "Buckwheat" Thomas

Buckwheat, who was a member of *Our Gang* from 1934 until the series' demise in 1944, was one of the few African American members of the group. He appeared in 97 productions, including all 52 of the *Our Gang* films produced by MGM, the studio that assumed control of the series in 1938. After leaving the show, Thomas worked as a film technician until his death of a heart attack in 1980 at age 49. Ten years later, he was the subject of an odd controversy when the investigative program *20/20* aired an interview with an imposter—a grocery store clerk in Arizona—who claimed to be the "real" Buckwheat.

Thelma Todd: Suicide or Murder?

During her nine-year film career, Thelma Todd costarred in dozens of comedies with the likes of Harry Langdon, Laurel and Hardy, and the Marx Brothers. Today, however, the "Ice Cream Blonde," as she was known, is best remembered for her bizarre death, which remains one of Hollywood's most enduring mysteries. Let's explore what could have happened.

Sins Indulged

Todd was born in Lawrence, Massachusetts, in 1906 and arrived in Hollywood at age 20 via the beauty pageant circuit. Pretty and vivacious, she quickly became a hot commodity and fell headlong into Tinseltown's anything-goes party scene. In 1932, she married Pasquale "Pat" DiCicco, an agent of sorts who was also associated with gangster Charles "Lucky" Luciano. Their marriage was plagued by drunken fights, and they divorced two years later.

For solace, Todd turned to director Roland West, who didn't approve of her drinking and drug use, but he could not stop her. With his help, Todd opened a roadhouse called Thelma Todd's Sidewalk Café, located on the Pacific Coast Highway, and the actress moved into a spacious apartment above the restaurant. Shortly after, Todd began a romantic relationship with gangster "Lucky" Luciano, who tried to get her to let him use a room at the Sidewalk Café for illegal gambling. Todd repeatedly refused.

On the morning of December 16, 1935, Todd was found dead in the front seat of her 1934 Lincoln Phaeton convertible, which was parked in the two-car garage she shared with West. The apparent cause of death was carbon monoxide poisoning, though whether Todd was the victim of an accident, suicide, or murder remains a mystery.

Little evidence supports the suicide theory, outside the mode of death and the fact that Todd led a fast-paced lifestyle that sometimes got the better of her. Indeed, her career was going remarkably well, and she had purchased Christmas presents and was looking forward to a New Year's Eve party. So suicide does not seem a viable cause, though it is still mentioned as a probable one in many accounts.

The Accident Theory

However, an accidental death is also a possibility. The key to her car was in the "on" position, and the motor was dead when Todd was discovered by her maid. West suggested to investigators that the actress turned on the car to get warm, passed out because she was drunk, and then succumbed to carbon monoxide poisoning. Todd also had a heart condition, according to West, and this may have contributed to her death.

Nonetheless, the notion of foul play is suggested by several incongruities found at the scene. Spots of blood were discovered on and in Todd's car and on her mouth, and her nose was broken, leading some to believe she was knocked out then placed in the car to make it look like a suicide. (Police attributed the injuries to Todd falling unconscious and striking her head on the steering wheel.) In addition, Todd's blood-alcohol level was extremely high—high enough to stupefy her so that someone could carry her without her fighting back—and her high-heeled shoes were clean and unscuffed, even though she would have had to ascend a flight of outdoor, concrete stairs to reach the garage, which was a 271-step climb behind the restaurant. Investigators also found an unidentified smudged handprint on the left side of the vehicle.

Two with Motive

If Todd was murdered, as some have suggested, who had motive? Because of her wild lifestyle, there are several potential suspects, most notably Pasquale DiCicco, who was known to have a violent temper, and "Lucky" Luciano, who was angry at Todd for refusing to let him use her restaurant for his shady and illegal activities.

Despite the many questions raised by the evidence found at the scene, a grand jury ruled Todd's death accidental. The investigation had been hampered by altered and destroyed evidence, threats to witnesses, and cover-ups, making it impossible to ever learn what really happened. An open-casket service was held at Forest Lawn Memorial Park, where the public viewed the actress bedecked in yellow roses. After the service, Todd was cremated, eliminating the possibility of a second autopsy. Later, when her mother, Alice Todd, died, the actress's ashes were placed in her mother's casket so they could be buried together in Massachusetts.

The Sex-sational Trial of Errol Flynn

When a handsome leading man was charged with rape, his status in Hollywood was in doubt. But rather than signaling his end in the business, his popularity soared ever higher.

The saying "In like Flynn" means little these days, but during the 1940s, it was used to compliment one who was doing exceedingly well. More to the point, it usually referred to sexual conquests made by a lucky "man about town."

The saying originated with Hollywood heartthrob Errol Flynn (1909–1959), the swashbuckling star of *Captain Blood* (1935) and *The Adventures of Robin Hood* (1938). A "man's man" in the most cocksure sense, Flynn was known for his barroom brawls and trysts both on camera and off, which became part of his star image.

He wore this colorful mantle like a badge of honor, but he did suffer a hit to his reputation when he was charged with two counts of statutory rape.

Swashbuckling Seductor

The alleged crimes took place during the summer of 1942. In one instance, 17-year-old Betty Hansen claimed that Flynn had seduced her after she became ill from overimbibing at a Hollywood party. In the other, 15-year-old Peggy Satterlee insisted that Flynn took advantage of her on his yacht, *The Sirocco*, during a trip to Catalina Island. Both women claimed that he referred to them by the nicknames "S.Q.Q." (San Quentin Quail) and "J.B." (Jail Bait), thereby suggesting that Flynn knew that they were underage. Flynn was arrested that fall and charged with two counts of rape. Proclaiming his innocence, he hired high-powered attorney Jerry Giesler, who called the girl's motives and pasts into question and stacked the jury with nine women in the hopes that Flynn's considerable charm might win them over. The move would prove prophetic.

Questionable Character?

When the defense presented its case, Giesler went directly for the jugular. His cross-examination revealed that both girls had engaged in sexual relations *before* the alleged incidents with Flynn and that Satterlee had even had an abortion. More damning, Satterlee admitted to frequently lying about her age and was inconsistent in a number of her answers. Sadly, then and now, many girls and women who have been sexually active are no longer seen as worthy of protection or respect.

There was also Satterlee's claim that Flynn had taken her below deck to gaze at the moon through a porthole. Giesler challenged the expert testimony of an astronomer hired by the prosecution, getting the man to admit that, given the boat's apparent course, such a view was physically impossible through the porthole in Flynn's cabin.

The Verdict

By the time Flynn took the stand, the members of the all-female jury were half won over by his charm. By the time he finished arguing his innocence, their minds were made up. The effect was not at all surprising for a man whom actress and eight-time costar Olivia de Havilland once described as "...the handsomest, most charming, most magnetic, most virile young man in the entire world."

When a verdict of "not guilty" was read, women in the courtroom applauded and wept. Afterward, the jury forewoman noted: "We felt there had been other men in the girls' lives. Frankly, the cards were on the table and we couldn't believe the girls' stories."

Continued Fortune in a Man's World

Cleared of all charges, Errol Flynn continued to make movies, resumed his carousing ways, and grew even more popular in the public eye. Many felt that, despite the verdict, Flynn had indeed had sexual relations with the young women, but most were willing to forgive the transgression because the liaisons seemed consensual and the allegations of rape looked like a frame job.

Young men would regard the amorous actor as an ideal to emulate, and women would continue to swoon as always. But years of hard living eventually took their toll on Flynn. By the time he reached middle age, his looks had all but vanished. At the premature age of 50, Flynn suffered a massive heart attack and died. Death only served to cement Flynn's legendary status.

A Reckoning: Harvey Weinstein, #MeToo, and Time's Up

In Hollywood, everyone knew Harvey Weinstein's name. By the end of 2017, however, his reputation would wind up in tatters.

Admired—and feared—by much of the film industry, the movie producer's career took off in the late 1970s and early 1980s when Weinstein and his brother Bob created a film production company called Miramax.

By the late 1980s and early 1990s, Miramax produced a number of hits, including *The Thin Blue Line* (1988), *Sex, Lies, and Videotape* (1989), *Tie Me Up! Tie Me Down!* (1990), and *Pulp Fiction* (1994). The company won its first Academy Award for Best Picture in 1997 for *The English Patient*. Weinstein himself took home an Oscar for *Shakespeare in Love* in 1999.

As Weinstein's clout among the industry's best and brightest grew, the movie mogul developed a reputation as a notorious executive who called for his films to be fundamentally restructured or reedited prior to release. He earned and proudly wore the moniker "Harvey Scissorhands"; for example, fellow producer Scott Rudin infamously fought Weinstein over the music and final cut of *The Hours* (2002).

Weinstein and his brother left Miramax to form their own production company, The Weinstein Company, in 2005. He became increasingly active in politics and outspoken on issues like gun control and health care. And his colleagues continued to praise him: an analysis found that, between 1966 and 2016, Weinstein tied with God as the second-most thanked person during Academy Award acceptance speeches.

A Reckoning

Exposés by the *New York Times* and the *New Yorker*, each published days apart in early October 2017, painted a startling picture of the alleged harassment by the powerful producer.

The stories found that Weinstein harassed, assaulted, or raped more than a dozen women throughout his life and career. A number of prominent actresses, including Ashley Judd and Rose McGowan, described how Weinstein would appear in hotel rooms in nothing but a bathrobe and ask for a massage. A published audiotape from a 2015 New York Police Department sting found Weinstein pressuring model Ambra Battilana Gutierrez to come into his hotel room. In the tape, Weinstein admitted to groping Gutierrez.

Weinstein issued an apology and acknowledged "a lot of pain" but disputed the allegations. He said he was working with a therapist and was preparing to sue the *New York Times*. But Weinstein's leave of absence was short-lived: three days after the first story broke about his misconduct, his company's board announced his ouster.

The accusations against Weinstein piled up, and within months, more than 80 women came forward to accuse Weinstein of a host of inappropriate behavior. Police in Los Angeles, New York, and the United Kingdom separately confirmed investigations into allegations involving Weinstein. New York state prosecutors filed a lawsuit against the Weinstein Company in February 2018.

The Academy of Motion Picture Arts and Sciences voted overwhelmingly to expel Weinstein. Institutions across the United States and the United Kingdom took similar actions to revoke honors or memberships in Weinstein's name. Weinstein's legacy was eroding before his eyes, and the entertainment industry, alongside workplace culture across the nation, was undergoing rapid change.

#MeToo and Time's Up

Despite Weinstein's laundry list of allegations, the movie producer's behavior prompted a pair of wide-reaching campaigns. In 2006, activist Tarana Burke had created the phrase "Me Too" in an attempt to bring awareness to sexual assault victims.

After the explosive allegations, Burke's 12-year-old phrase was coopted by actress Alyssa Milano when she encouraged people to reply to a tweet about sexual harassment or assault with the words "me too." Immediately, Milano's call lit social media abuzz, and thousands of women—young, old, and from different backgrounds—shared their own stories.

"In many regards Me Too is about survivors talking to survivors," Burke told the *Boston Globe*. " … It was about survivors exchanging empathy with each other."

And on January 1, 2018, a group of 300 women in the film, television, and theater industries launched a complementary initiative called Time's Up, a manifesto and coalition aimed at providing a wealth of resources for victims of assault, harassment, and inequality in the workplace. A legal fund developed to assist victims amassed $21 million in two months.

Chaplin's Coffin Held for Ransom

In the silent era, he entertained millions without ever uttering a single word. During his career, he produced and starred in nearly 100 movies, making him a millionaire at an early age. Perhaps that's why after his death, two men thought Charlie Chaplin's casket was worth more than half a million dollars in ransom.

The Life and Death of a Silent Star

Born in London on April 16, 1889, Charles Spencer Chaplin had his first taste of show business at age five when his mother, a failing music hall entertainer, could not continue her act, and little Charlie stepped up and finished her show. After years of moving back and forth between his separated parents, workhouses, and school, he officially entered show business in 1898 (at age nine) when he became one of the Eight Lancashire Lads, a musical comedy act that worked the lower-class music halls in London. After a couple of years, he was seeking employment in various offices, factories, and households to support his mentally ill and sick mother. Finally, around age 12, he reentered the music hall scene, joining Fred Karno's London Comedians, a traveling music hall act.

Chaplin continued working with traveling shows until he signed his first contract with the legendary Keystone Studio, in late 1913, at age 24. In February 1914, Chaplin's first movie, *Making a Living*, premiered. It would be the first of more than 30 shorts that Chaplin made in 1914 alone. In fact, from 1915 until the end of his career, Chaplin was featured in nearly 100 movies, mostly shorts. No small feat considering that he wrote, starred in, directed, produced, and even scored all of his own movies. All of this not only made Charlie Chaplin a household name but also a very rich man.

Public Success, Private Mess

But not everything was wine and roses for Chaplin. After three failed marriages, the 54-year old actor caused quite a stir in 1943 when he married his fourth wife, Oona O'Neill, who was just 17 at the time. More scandal found Chaplin in the early 1950s when the U.S. government began to suspect that he and his family might be Communist sympathizers. There seemed to be very little to support their suspicions other than the fact that Chaplin had simply chosen to live in the United States while not declaring U.S. citizenship. Regardless, Chaplin soon tired of what he deemed harassment and moved to Switzerland, where he lived with his wife and their eight children until his death on Christmas Day 1977. Shortly thereafter, perhaps the strangest chapter in Charlie Chaplin's story began.

Grave Robbers

On March 2, 1978, visitors to Charlie Chaplin's grave were shocked to discover a massive hole where the actor's coffin had been. It soon became clear that sometime overnight, someone had dug up and stolen Chaplin's entire casket. But who would do such a thing? And why? It didn't take long to find the answer. Several days later, Oona began receiving phone calls from people claiming to have stolen the body and demanding a portion of Chaplin's millions in exchange for the casket. Oona dismissed most of the callers as crackpots, with the exception of one. This mysterious male caller seemed to know an awful lot about what Chaplin's coffin looked like. But because he was demanding the equivalent of $600,000 U.S. dollars in exchange for the coffin's safe return, Oona told the caller she needed more proof. Several days later, a photo of Chaplin's newly unearthed casket arrived in her mailbox, and Oona alerted Swiss police.

The Arrests

When Oona Chaplin first met with Swiss authorities, she could only show them the photo and tell them that the caller was male and that he spoke with a Slavic accent. She also told them that she had no intention of paying the ransom. But the police convinced Oona that the longer she pretended to be willing to pay the ransom, the better chance they had of catching the thief. Oona was emotionally unable to deal with the fiasco, so Chaplin's daughter Geraldine complied with the investigators' request.

During the next few weeks, Geraldine did such a convincing job that she talked the caller's ransom price down from $600,000 to $250,000, though the Chaplin family still did not plan to pay it. In the meantime, Swiss police were desperately trying to trace the calls. Their first big break came when they established that the calls were coming from a local Lausanne pay phone. However, there were more than 200 pay phones in the town. Undaunted, police began staking out all of them. Their hard work paid off when they arrested 24-year-old Roman Wardas, who admitted to stealing Chaplin's coffin, stating that he had gotten the idea after reading about a similar body "kidnapping" in an Italian newspaper. Based on information Wardas provided police, a second man, 38-year-old Gantcho Ganev, was also arrested. Like Wardas, Ganev admitted to helping take the casket but claimed that it was all Wardas's idea and that he just helped out.

So Where's the Body?

Of course, once the two suspects were in custody, the question on everyone's minds was the location of Chaplin's casket. Ganev and Wardas claimed that after stealing the casket from the cemetery, they drove it to a field and buried it in a shallow hole.

Following directions provided by both suspects, Swiss police descended upon a farm about 12 miles from the Chaplin estate. Spotting a mound of what appeared to be freshly moved dirt, they began digging, and on May 17, 1978, in the middle of a cornfield, Chaplin's unopened coffin was recovered.

Once word got out, people began flocking to the farm, so the farmer placed a small wooden cross, ornamented with a cane, over the hole where the casket had been buried. For several weeks, people brought flowers and paid their respects to the empty hole.

The Aftermath

After a short trial, both men were convicted of extortion and disturbing the peace of the dead. As the admitted mastermind of the crime, Wardas was sentenced to nearly five years of hard labor. Ganev received only an 18-month suspended sentence.

As for Chaplin's unopened casket, it was returned to Corsier- Sur-Vevey Cemetery and was reburied in the exact spot where it had originally been interred. Only this time, to deter any future grave robbers, Oona ordered it buried under six feet of solid concrete. And when she passed away 14 years later, her will stipulated that she also be buried under at least six feet of concrete. She was.

Anything but Splendor: Natalie Wood

The official account of Natalie Wood's tragic death is riddled with holes. For this reason, cover-up theorists continue to run hog-wild with conjecture. Here's a sampling of the questions, facts, and assertions surrounding the case.

A Life in Pictures

There are those who will forever recall Natalie Wood as the adorable child actress from *Miracle on 34th Street* (1947) and those who remember her as the sexy but wholesome grown-up star of movies such as *West Side Story* (1961), *Splendor in the Grass* (1961), and *Bob & Carol & Ted & Alice* (1969). Both groups generally agree that Wood had uncommon beauty and talent.

Wood appeared in her first film, *Happy Land* (1943), in a bit part alongside other people from her hometown of Santa Rosa, California, where the film was shot. She stood out to the director, who remembered her later when he needed to cast a child in another film. Wood was uncommonly mature and professional for a child actress, which helped her make a relatively smooth transition to ingenue roles.

Although Wood befriended James Dean and Sal Mineo—her troubled young costars from *Rebel Without a Cause* (1955)—and she briefly dated Elvis Presley, she preferred to move in established Hollywood circles. By the time she was 20, she was married to Robert Wagner and was costarring with Frank Sinatra in *Kings Go Forth* (1958), which firmly ensconced her in the Hollywood establishment. The early 1960s represent the high point of Wood's career, and she specialized in playing high-spirited characters with determination and spunk. She added two more Oscar nominations to the one she received for *Rebel* and racked up five Golden Globe nominations for Best Actress. This period also proved to be personally turbulent for

Wood, as she suffered through a failed marriage to Wagner and another to Richard Gregson. After taking time off to raise her children, Wood remarried Wagner and returned to her acting career.

Shocking News

And so, on November 29, 1981, the headline hit the newswires much like an out-of-control car hits a brick wall. Natalie Wood, the beautiful, vivacious 43-year-old star of stage and screen, had drowned after falling from her yacht, the *Splendour*, which was anchored off California's Santa Catalina Island. Wood had been on the boat during a break from her latest film, *Brainstorm,* and was accompanied by Wagner and *Brainstorm* costar Christopher Walken. Skipper Dennis Davern was at the helm. Foul play was not suspected.

In My Esteemed Opinion

After a short investigation, Chief Medical Examiner Dr. Thomas Noguchi listed Wood's death as an accidental drowning. Tests revealed that she had consumed "seven or eight" glasses of wine, and the coroner contended that in her intoxicated state Wood had probably stumbled and fallen overboard while attempting to untie the yacht's rubber dinghy. He also stated that cuts and bruises on her body could have occurred when she fell from the boat.

Doubting Thomases

To this day, many question Wood's mysterious demise and believe that the accidental drowning theory sounds a bit too convenient. Pointed questions have led to many rumors: Does someone know more about Wood's final moments than they're letting on? Was her drowning really an accident, or did someone intentionally or accidentally help her overboard? Could this be why she sustained substantial bruising on her face and the back of her legs? Why was Wagner so reluctant to publicly discuss the incident? Were Christopher Walken and Wood an item as had been rumored? With this possibility in mind, could a booze-fueled fight have erupted between the two men? Could Wood have then tried to intervene, only to be knocked overboard for her efforts? And why did authorities declare Wood's death accidental so quickly? Would such a hasty ruling have been issued had the principals involved not been famous, wealthy, and influential?

Ripples

At the time of Wood's death, she and Wagner were seven years into their second marriage to each other. Whether Wood was carrying on an affair with Walken, as was alleged, may be immaterial, even if it made for interesting tabloid fodder. But Wagner's perception of their relationship could certainly be a factor. If nothing else, it might better explain the argument that ensued between Wagner and Walken that fateful night.

Case Closed?

Further information about Wood's death is sparse because no eyewitnesses have come forward. However, a businesswoman whose boat was anchored nearby testified that she heard a woman shouting for help, and then a voice responding, "We'll be over to get you," so the woman went back to bed. Just after dawn, Wood's body was found floating a mile away from the *Splendour*, approximately 200 yards offshore. The dinghy was found nearby; its only cargo was a stack of lifejackets.

In 2008, after 27 years of silence, Robert Wagner recalled in his autobiography, *Pieces of My Heart: A Life*, that he and Walken had engaged in a heated argument during supper after Walken had suggested that Wood star in more films, effectively keeping her away from their children. Wagner and Walken then headed topside to cool down. Sometime around midnight, Wagner said he returned to his cabin and discovered that his wife was missing. He soon realized that the yacht's dinghy was gone as well. In his book, he surmised that Wood may have gone to secure the dinghy that had been noisily slapping against the boat. Then, tipsy from the wine, she probably fell into the ocean and drowned.

Walken notified the authorities.

Was Natalie Wood's demise the result of a deadly mix of wine and saltwater as the coroner's report suggests? This certainly could be the case. But why would she leave her warm cabin to tend to a loose rubber dinghy in the dark of night? Could an errant rubber boat really make such a commotion?

Perhaps we'll never know what happened that fateful night, but an interview conducted shortly before Wood's death proved prophetic: "I'm frightened to death of the water," said Wood about a long-held fear. "I can swim a little bit, but I'm afraid of water that is dark."

Lana Turner and the Death of a Gangster

On the evening of April 4, 1958, Beverly Hills police arrived at the home of actress Lana Turner to discover the dead body of her one-time boyfriend Johnny Stompanato, a violent gangster with underworld ties. He had been stabbed to death, but the exact circumstances of his demise were muddied by the sensational reporting of the tabloid press.

Sweater Girl

Lana Turner's first credited film role came in 1937 with *They Won't Forget*, which earned her the moniker "Sweater Girl," thanks to the tight-fitting sweater her character wore. Turner went on to star in hits such as *Honky Tonk* (1941), *The Postman Always Rings Twice* (1946), and *Peyton Place* (1957).

Hanging with the Wrong Crowd

Offscreen, Turner was renowned for her many love affairs. During her lifetime, she amassed eight marriages to seven different husbands. It was shortly after the breakup of her fifth marriage to actor Lex Barker in 1957 that Turner met Johnny Stompanato. When she discovered that his name was not John

Steele (as he had told her) and that he had ties to underworld figures such as Mickey Cohen, she realized the negative publicity that those ties could bring to her career, so she tried to end the relationship. But Stompanato incessantly pursued her, and the pair engaged in a number of violent incidents, which came to a head on the night of April 4.

Turner's 14-year-old daughter, Cheryl Crane, rushed to her mother's defense after hearing Stompanato threaten to "cut" Turner. Fearing for her mother's life, the girl grabbed a kitchen knife, then ran upstairs to Turner's bedroom. According to Crane's account, Turner opened the door and Cheryl saw Stompanato with his arms raised in the air in a fury. Cheryl then rushed past Turner and stabbed Stompanato, killing him. Turner called her mother, who brought their personal physician to the house, but it was too late. By the time the police were called, much time had passed and evidence had been moved around. According to the Beverly Hills police chief, who was the first officer to arrive, Turner immediately asked if she could take the rap for her daughter.

At the crime scene, the body appeared to have been moved and the fingerprints on the murder weapon were so smudged that they could not be identified. The case sparked a media sensation, especially among the tabloid press, which turned against Turner, essentially accusing her of killing Stompanato and asking her daughter to cover for her. Mickey Cohen, who paid for Stompanato's funeral, publicly called for the arrests of both Turner and Crane. For years, ugly rumors surrounding the case persisted.

"The Performance of a Lifetime"?

During the inquest, the press described Turner's testimony as "the performance of a lifetime." But police and authorities knew from the beginning that Turner did not do it. At the inquest, it took just 20 minutes for the jury to return a verdict of justifiable homicide, so the D.A. decided not to bring the case to trial. However, Turner was convicted of being an unfit mother, and Crane was remanded to her grandmother's care until she turned 18, further tainting Turner's image. There was an aura of "guilt" around Turner for years, though she was never seriously considered a suspect in the actual murder.

As fate would have it, Turner's film *Peyton Place*, which features a courtroom scene about a murder committed by a teenager, was still in theaters at the time of the inquest. Ticket sales skyrocketed as a result of the sensational publicity, and Turner parlayed the success of the film into better screen roles, including her part in a remake of *Imitation of Life* (1959), which would become one of her most successful films. She appeared in romantic melodramas until the mid-1960s, when age began to affect her career. In the '70s and '80s, she made the transition to television, appearing on shows such as *The Survivors, The Love Boat*, and *Falcon Crest*.

William Desmond Taylor

The murder of actor/director William Desmond Taylor was like something out of an Agatha Christie novel, complete with a handsome, debonair victim and multiple suspects, each with a motive. But unlike Christie's novels, in which the murderer was always unmasked, Taylor's death remains unsolved over 100 years later.

On the evening of February 1, 1922, Taylor was shot in the back by an unknown assailant; his body was discovered the next morning by a servant, Henry Peavey. News of Taylor's demise spread quickly, and several individuals, including officials from Paramount Studios, where Taylor was employed, raced to the dead man's home to clear it of anything incriminating, such as illegal liquor, evidence of drug use, illicit correspondence, and signs of sexual indiscretion. However, no one called the police until later in the morning.

Numerous Suspects

Soon an eclectic array of potential suspects came to light, including Taylor's criminally inclined former butler, Edward F. Sands, who had gone missing before the murder; popular movie comedienne Mabel Normand, whom Taylor had entertained the evening of his death; actress Mary Miles Minter, who had a passionate crush on the handsome director who was 28 years her senior; and Charlotte Shelby, Minter's mother, who often wielded a gun to protect her daughter's honor, tarnished though it might be in other people's views.

Taylor's murder was the last thing Hollywood needed at the time, coming as it did on the heels of rape allegations against popular film comedian Fatty Arbuckle. Scandals brought undue attention on Hollywood, and the Arbuckle story had taken its toll. Officials at Paramount tried to keep a lid on the Taylor story, but the tabloid press had a field day. A variety of personal foibles were made public in the weeks that followed, and both Normand and Minter saw their careers come to a screeching halt as a result. Taylor's own indiscretions were also revealed, such as the fact that he kept a special souvenir, usually lingerie, from every woman he bedded.

Little Evidence

Police interviewed many of Taylor's friends and colleagues, including all potential suspects. However, there was no evidence to incriminate anyone specifically, and no one was formally charged.

Investigators and amateur sleuths pursued the case for years. Sands was long a prime suspect, based on his criminal past and his estrangement from the victim. But it was later revealed that on the day of the murder, Sands had signed in for work at a lumberyard in Oakland, California—some 400 miles away—and thus could not have committed the crime. Coming in second was Shelby, whose temper and threats were legendary. Shelby's own acting career had fizzled out early, and all of her hopes for stardom were pinned on her daughter. She threatened many men who tried to woo Mary.

In the mid-1990s, another possible suspect surfaced—a long-forgotten silent-film actress named Margaret Gibson. According to Bruce Long, author of *William Desmond Taylor: A Dossier*, Gibson confessed to a friend on her deathbed in 1964 that years before she had killed a man named William Desmond Taylor. However, the woman to whom Gibson cleared her conscience didn't know who Taylor was and thought nothing more about it.

The Mystery Continues

Could Margaret Gibson (aka Pat Lewis) be Taylor's murderer? She had acted with Taylor in Hollywood in the early 1910s, and she may even have been one of his many sexual conquests. She also had a criminal past, including charges of blackmail, drug use, and prostitution, so it's entirely conceivable that she was a member of a group trying to extort money from the director, a popular theory among investigators. But according to an earlier book, *A Cast of Killers* by Sidney D. Kirkpatrick, veteran Hollywood director King Vidor had investigated the murder as material for a film script and through his research believed Shelby was the murderer. But out of respect for Minter, he never did anything about it.

Ultimately, however, we may never know for certain who killed William Desmond Taylor, or why. The case has long grown cold, and anyone with specific knowledge of the murder is likely dead. Unlike a Hollywood thriller, in which the killer is revealed at the end, Taylor's death is a macabre puzzle that likely will never be solved.

Long Live the Crime-Fighting King

If a chubby, jumpsuit-wearing Elvis came karate-kicking out of a limo, what would you do?

Back in 1977, shortly before Elvis ended his reign as the King of Rock and Roll, you would run, which is just what two trouble-making teens did when Presley gave them the scare of their lives.

Around midnight on June 23, The King arrived in Madison, Wisconsin, for a show. En route to his hotel from the airport, Presley's limousine, a 1964 Cadillac, hit a red light at the intersection of Stoughton Road and East Washington Avenue. Peering out the window to the right, Presley was watching a young man reading the gas meters at the corner Skyland Service Station, when two teenage misfits charged at the employee and began beating him up.

With a penchant for helping others, Presley, wearing his trademark aviator sunglasses and a dark blue Drug Enforcement Agency jumpsuit over his sequined outfit, busted out of the limousine, despite his bodyguards' requests. He ran toward the scene, kicking karate-style and saying, "I'll take you on."

The hoodlums ran off. As it turned out, the young attendant's father owned the service station and one of the attackers had recently been fired. Getting back in the limousine, Presley reportedly laughed and said, "Did you see the looks on their faces?"

With a caravan of fans in pursuit having just witnessed Presley's crime-prevention skills, the King's entourage continued on to the hotel. The next day, Presley gave a lackluster concert, prompting one local reviewer to write: "So, long live the King. His reign is over. But that is no reason for us not to remember him fondly."

Presley died 51 days later, on August 16, 1977, yet as the reviewer said, many remember his Madison exploits fondly. While Skyland closed years ago, the lot was most recently the site of a used car store, which paid homage to Elvis and Madison's famed gas station altercation with a marble plaque.

Bugsy Siegel's "Screen Test"

When mobster Bugsy Siegel acted out a scene at the behest of actor pal George Raft, the results proved eye-opening. Much to the surprise of all, the gangster could really act. Unfortunately, Siegel never pursued acting, choosing instead to remain on his murderous course. This begs the obvious question: "What if?"

In the annals of the underworld, there was perhaps no one more dapper, or more ruthless, than Benjamin "Bugsy" Siegel (1906–1947). Nearly six feet tall, with piercing blue eyes that melted the heart of many a woman, Siegel had movie-star looks and savoir faire that disguised a temperament that could easily be described as hair-triggered. During his hard-lived life, Siegel committed nearly every crime in the book and was implicated by the FBI for more than 30 murders.

Born Benjamin Hymen Siegelbaum, the up-and-coming mobster picked up the nickname "Bugsy" (the slang term *bugs* means "crazy") for his high level of viciousness. Siegel hated the tag, considering it a low-class connection to his hardscrabble youth, and threatened to kill anyone who used it in his presence. Still, the mobster was said to be a natural born charmer who never seemed at a loss for companionship, female or otherwise.

One of Siegel's closest friends was Hollywood actor George Raft, who was known for such memorable films as *Scarface* (1932), *I Stole a Million* (1939), and *They Drive by Night* (1940). The two had both grown up on the gritty streets of New York City's Lower East Side. Throughout their lives, the pair would engage in a form of mutual admiration. For example,

Raft's movie career featured many mob-related roles. So, when he needed the proper tough-guy "inspiration," the actor would mimic mannerisms and inflections that he picked up from his real-life mobster pals. Siegel, on the other hand, made no secret of the fact that he was starstruck by Hollywood and sometimes wished that he too had become an actor. He viewed Raft as the Real McCoy in this arena and gave him due respect. Hoping to get ever closer to the Hollywood action, while at the same time expanding his "operations," Siegel moved to California in 1937.

A Natural Born...Actor?

In no time, Siegel was hobnobbing with major celebrities even as his deadly business dealings escalated. In 1941, Raft was shooting *Manpower* with the legendary Marlene Dietrich, when Siegel showed up on the set to observe. After watching Raft go through a few takes before heading off to his dressing room, Siegel told his buddy that he could do the scene better. An amused Raft told his friend to go ahead and give it a shot. Over the course of the next few minutes, the smirk would leave Raft's face.

Siegel reenacted Raft's scene perfectly. He had not only memorized the dialogue line for line, but he interpreted Raft's nuanced gestures as well. This was no small feat given the fact that Siegel had absolutely no training as an actor. A stunned Raft told Siegel that he just might have what it takes to be an actor.

A Dream Unfulfilled

But such Tinseltown dreams were not to be. Despite his demonstrated talent, moviemakers probably wouldn't have used him. And who could blame them? What if Siegel decided to go "Bugsy" on them for not awarding him a role, for critiquing his performance, or for changing his lines? Temperamental actors are one thing; homicidal ones, quite another.

History shows that Siegel played it fast and loose from that point forward, putting most of his energies into creating the

Flamingo Hotel and, along with it, the gaming capital of the world—Las Vegas. Siegel's mob associates from the East Coast put him in charge of construction of the opulent hotel. Siegel envisioned an extravagent hotel and, at least for him, money was no object. But when costs soared to $6 million—four times the original budget—Siegel's associates became concerned.

On June 20, 1947, Siegel's dreams of a life on the silver screen came to an abrupt end when a number of well-placed rounds from an M-1 Carbine sent the Hollywood gangster into the afterlife at age 41. It is believed that Siegel was killed by his own mob associates who were convinced that he was pilfering money from the organization. Siegel's life and grisly end are grand pieces of mob drama that got their due on the silver screen in the 1991 flick *Bugsy*, which starred Warren Beatty as the doomed mobster.

More Stars Behind Bars!

Most actors have done their time working their way up the ladder through roles in B-movies, television, or theater. But a surprising number of actors have literally done time—as in prison time. Here's a sample:

Lillo Brancato

Brancato played Robert De Niro's son in *A Bronx Tale* (1993) and a bumbling mobster on *The Sopranos*. But drug addiction took its toll on his career. In December 2005, Brancato and a friend broke into an apartment looking for drugs. In the process, an off-duty policeman was shot and killed. Brancato was charged with second-degree murder and attempted burglary. He was acquitted on the murder charges in 2008 but served time for attempted burglary.

Rory Calhoun

A popular leading man who appeared in numerous Westerns, Calhoun was a petty criminal as a teenager and served three years in a federal reformatory for car theft. Reformed by a priest, he was a blue-collar worker until a chance meeting with star Alan Ladd led to a career in the movies, including two Marilyn Monroe films.

Stacy Keach

In the mid-1980s, the star of the acclaimed Western *The Long Riders* (1980) served six months in prison for smuggling cocaine into England.

Paul Kelly

Paul Kelly played lead roles in many B-films, mostly crime melodramas. In the late 1920s, he killed his best friend, actor Ray Raymond, in a fistfight over Raymond's wife, actress Dorothy MacKaye. He served two years for manslaughter, then went on to a successful film and stage career, receiving a Tony Award in 1948 for his role in *Command Decision*.

Tommy Rettig

As a child actor, Rettig gained lasting fame as Lassie's master in the popular 1950s TV series. But in 1972, he was arrested for growing marijuana, and in the mid-1970s, he was sentenced to five and a half years in prison for smuggling cocaine into the U.S. The charges were dropped after an appeal, as was another drug charge five years later.

Christian Slater

In 1989, Slater was involved in a drunken car chase that ended when he crashed into a telephone pole and kicked a policeman while trying to escape. He was charged with evading police, driving under the influence, assault with a deadly weapon (his boots), and driving with a suspended license. In 1994, Slater was arrested for trying to bring a gun onto a plane. In 1997, he was sentenced to 90 days in jail for cocaine abuse, battery, and assault with a deadly weapon.

Mae West

In 1926, Mae West, one of Hollywood's most iconic sex symbols, was sentenced to ten days in jail when her Broadway show, *Sex*, was declared obscene.

Chapter 6

Organized Crime: Gangsters, Mobsters, and the Mafia

Who Founded the Mafia?

To be honest, we really didn't want to answer this question. But then our editors made us an offer we couldn't refuse.

This is like asking, "Who founded England?" or "Who founded capitalism?" The Mafia is more of a phenomenon than an organization—it's a movement that rose from a complicated interaction of multiple factors, including history, economics, geography, and politics. Hundreds of thousands of pages have been written by historians, sociologists, novelists, screenwriters, and criminologists who have attempted to chart the history and origins of the Mafia, so it's doubtful that we'll be able to provide any real revelations in five hundred words. But we're a hardy bunch, and we'll do our best.

By all accounts, the Mafia came to prominence in Sicily during the mid-nineteenth century. Given Sicily's history, this makes sense—the island has repeatedly been invaded and occupied, and has generally been mired in poverty for thousands of years. By the mid-nineteenth century, Italy was in total chaos due to the abolition of feudalism, and the lack of a central government or semblance of a legitimate legal system.

As sociologists will confirm, people who live in areas that fall victim to such upheaval tend to rely on various forms of self-government. In Sicily, this took the form of what has become known as the Mafia. The fellowship, which originated in the rural areas of the Mediterranean island, is based on a complicated system of respect, violence, distrust of government, and the code of *omertà*—a word that is synonymous with the group's code of silence and refers to an unspoken agreement to never cooperate with authorities, under penalty of death. Just as there is no one person who founded the Mafia, there is no one person who runs it. The term "Mafia" refers to any group of organized criminals that follows the traditional Sicilian system of bosses, *capos* ("chiefs"), and soldiers. These groups are referred to as "families."

In the United States

Although the Mafia evolved in Sicily during the 19th century, most Americans equate it to the crime families that dominated the headlines in Chicago and New York for much of the 20th century. The American Mafia developed as a result of the huge wave of Sicilian immigrants that arrived in the United States in the late nineteenth and early twentieth centuries. These newcomers brought with them the Mafia structure and the code of *omertà*.

These Sicilian immigrants often clustered together in poor urban areas, such as Park Slope in Brooklyn and the south side of Chicago. There, far from the eyes of authorities, disputes were handled by locals. By the 1920s, crime families had sprung up all over the United States and gang wars were prevalent. In the 1930s, Lucky Luciano—who is sometimes called the father of the American Mafia—organized "The Commission," a faux-judiciary system that oversaw the activities of the Mafia in the United States.

Though Mafia families have been involved in murder, kidnapping, extortion, racketeering, gambling, prostitution, drug dealing, weapons dealing, and other crimes over the years, the phenomenon still maintains the romantic appeal that it had when gangsters like Al Capone captivated the nation. Part of it, of course, is the result of the enormous success of the Godfather films, but it is also due, one presumes, to the allure of the principles that the Mafia supposedly was founded upon: self-reliance, loyalty, and *omertà*.

So there you have it: a summary of the founding of the Mafia. Of course, we could tell you more, but then we'd have to...well, you know.

Spin Mobsters

In times past, the Mafia's PR machine went into overdrive during the holidays.

Members of the Mafia always claimed to outsiders that "the Mafia" didn't even exist, but they weren't dumb enough to believe that anyone was buying that line. They knew that the general public was aware that La Cosa Nostra controlled everything from gambling to prostitution to garbage pickup in some cities across America. Throughout the 20th century, New York, Chicago, Las Vegas, and every major metropolitan area in the United States had an active mob presence, and the leaders of these criminal gangs were eager to pacify the "little people" in the communities they controlled. What better time to present a kinder, gentler face of the Mafia than during the Christmas season?

A Turkey You Can't Refuse

New York gangster Joe Colombo tried denying the Mafia's existence by founding such groups as the Italian-American Civil Rights League (first called the Italian American Defamation League), which fought the stereotyping of Italians as mobsters and even sent members to picket the offices of the FBI. But Chicago mob boss Al Capone took a more practical approach to community relations. When the holidays rolled around, he'd roll his troops into the poor Italian, Irish, and Jewish neighborhoods he controlled. Their trucks were piled high with booze, turkeys, and toys. Compared to the money they were making on their nefarious dealings, what they spent on these Christmas handouts was just a drop in the bucket, but to the poverty-stricken residents of the ghettos, it looked like a fortune.

Why wasn't the mob prevented from manipulating the poor in this deceitful manner? The truth is, many in law enforcement turned a blind eye because they, too, were being paid off. It would be many years before the Mafia was pressured to end such public displays during the Christmas season.

The Real Gangs of New York

New York's gang history reflects the city's global diversity.

- Amberg Gang (Jewish, Brooklyn, ca. 1920–35). Run by Joseph, Hyman, and Louis "Pretty" Amberg. Was mostly involved in labor/protection racketeering in Brooklyn.

- Bonanno Family (Italian, all boroughs, 1931–present). Born from the post-Castellammarese War truce of 1931. The only Family still bearing its original name. Diverse criminal activity.

- Bowery Boys (Anglo-Saxon, Manhattan, ca. 1850–63). Mostly political in nature, specifically anti-Irish Catholic, plus other ethnic violence and petty crime.

- Broadway Mob (Sicilian, Manhattan and Brooklyn, ca. 1921–33). A Joe "Adonis" Doto, "Lucky" Luciano, and Frank Costello operation, precursor to the Five Families. Created to violate Prohibition.

- Brownsville Boys (Italian/Jewish, Brooklyn, ca. 1927–57). Tagged by media as "Murder, Inc." Mainly enforcement and murder for hire.

- Bug & Meyer Mob (Jewish, various boroughs, ca. 1920–35). Benjamin "Bugsy" Siegel and Meyer Lansky, sometimes called the "La Kosher Nostra;" gambling, bootlegging, and murder for hire.

- Colombo Family (Italian, mainly Brooklyn, 1931–present— in diluted form). They began as the Profaci Family after the Castellammarese War truce; diverse criminal activity.

- Dead Rabbits (Irish, Manhattan, 1850s). Partly political in focus, they were the Bowery Boys' rivals (especially during the famed 1857 riot). Mostly petty crime.

- East Harlem Purple Gang (Mostly Italian, Manhattan, 1970s). Including some very famous names, later amalgamated into the Mafia families. Drugs and murder for hire.

- Five Percenters (African American, Manhattan/ Brooklyn, 1963–present). An offshoot of the Nation of Islam that smokes and drinks. On the cusp between street gang and church.

- Five Points Gang (Italian, Manhattan, ca. 1890–1910s). Prep school for Johnny Torrio and Al Capone centered on the famously poor Victorian district. Diverse petty crime: strong-arming, loansharking, and robbery.

- Gambino Family (Italian, all boroughs, 1920s–present). Began as the Mangano Family after the Castellammarese War truce. Led by Albert Anastasia, later John Gotti. Diverse criminal activity.

- Genovese Family (Italian, all boroughs, ca. 1900–present). Started as the Luciano Family under "Lucky" Luciano after the Castellammarese War truce. Perhaps the most powerful Family today; diverse criminal activity.

- Hip Sing Tong (Chinese, Manhattan, 1890s–present). Fought the On Leong for control of Chinatown in the early 1900s. Some legit activities plus gambling, loansharking, and drugs.

- Jolly Stompers (African American, Bronx/Brooklyn, ca. 1960s–1970s). Recruited a young Mike Tyson into their ranks. Very violent, mostly into robbery.

- Latin Kings (Hispanic, various boroughs, 1986–present). Came from Chicago. Strong in hierarchy and philosophy but also strong in arson, theft, drugs, and murder.

- Lucchese Family (Italian, various boroughs, ca. 1917–present). Grew out of the Reina gang after the Castellammarese truce. Diverse criminal activity.

- Mau Maus (Mostly Puerto Rican, Brooklyn, 1954–62). A particularly ruthless gang, they engaged in some petty crime and drug dealing but mostly violence for its own sake.

- Monk Eastman Gang (Mainly Jewish, Manhattan, ca. 1890s–1917). Fierce rival to the Five Points Gang. Pimping, political violence at Tammany's behest, petty crime.

- On Leong Tong (Chinese, Manhattan, 1893–present). Fought the early 1900s Tong Wars. Many legitimate endeavors; have also dealt in racketeering, drugs, gambling, and human trafficking.

- Whyos (Irish, Manhattan, 1860s–90s). Dominated Manhattan underworld until crushed by the Monk Eastman Gang. Extortion, prostitution, intimidation for hire.

Bloody Angle: The Most Violent Place in New York?

If you're looking for some NYC history but don't feel like hitting a museum, take a trip over to Chinatown and check out Bloody Angle. This infamous area at the bend in Doyers Street was the site of untold bloodshed for years.

Lower Manhattan today is quite the place to be. The East Village is full of restaurants and boutiques; SoHo offers high-end shopping and crowds of tourists; the Lower East Side is hipster central, and, of course, the crocodiles that inhabit Wall Street keep that area bustling. But not so long ago, the southern end of the island was rife with gangs, prostitution rings, corruption, and general debauchery.

Chinatown, a neighborhood that became "official" (and ghettoized) around 1882 with ratification of the Chinese Exclusion Act, was particularly active in terms of violence and chaos. Secret societies called "tongs" were formed to protect and support Chinese American residents, but before long the groups were simply gangs that spent their time dealing in criminal activity—and they weren't afraid to use violence against anyone who didn't like it. Many different tong gangs existed, and they didn't all get along. Unrest grew, and by the end of the 19th century and beginning of the 20th, the Tong Wars were on. Few participants made it through alive.

Doyers Street: A Bad Part of Town

Running more or less north and south between Pell Street and the Bowery, Doyers Street is just one block long. Halfway down the block, Doyers turns sharply—hence the "angle" part of Bloody Angle's name. This turn provided a great spot for ambush, and the battling gangs knew it. In 1909, the bloodiest tong war in Chinatown history began when a gang that called themselves the Hip Sings killed an On Leong comedian for being disrespectful. The ensuing war was ruthless, and its locus was the bend in Doyers Street. From then on, the spot would be known as the Bloody Angle.

Herbert Asbury, whose book *The Gangs of New York* was later made into a hit movie by Martin Scorsese, wrote, "The police believe, and can prove it as far as such proof is possible, that more men have been murdered at the Bloody Angle than at any other place of like area in the world." The tongs were vicious and showed no mercy: If you got in their way, you were a goner.

Adding to the danger of the area was a warren of underground tunnels. Connecting buildings and adjacent streets, the tunnels were frequented by gang members who used them to facilitate their dastardly deeds. An assassin would ambush and kill a victim and then disappear down into the tunnels. Several minutes later the killer would emerge, far from the scene of the crime.

Plenty of places near Bloody Angle offered killers opportunities to calm their nerves with a drink—and nail down an alibi. Gang hangouts included The Dump, The Plague, The Hell Hole, and McGuirck's Suicide Hall.

New Violence, and a Cleanup

Eventually, the Tong Wars quieted down, at least for protracted periods of time. By 1930, it was mostly safe to take Doyers if you were passing through Chinatown. But then in the late 1980s, crack cocaine gripped New York, and as a result, gangs grew once again. Bloody Angle returned to being the most dangerous block in the city as the Chinese Flying Dragon gang launched a turf war against the Vietnamese Born to Kill (or BTK) gang.

Anticrime crusades in the 1990s and 2000s cleaned up much of New York. Today, Bloody Angle is more likely to be called "Hair Alley" because of the multitude of salons and barbershops located there.

As for the hidden tunnels, most have either been closed up or repurposed by locals. A tunnel once used by criminals to escape capture in the 1900s is now a belowground shopping arcade—and don't worry, it's safe to shop there.

All about Al

If you took three pushpins and stuck them into a map of the United States in the three places Al Capone spent most of his time, you'd have a triangle spanning New York, Chicago, and Florida. Considering the size of the globe, this triangle wouldn't look like much. And yet, Capone is one of the world's most notorious criminals.

He's the racket guy everyone's heard of, and most people associate him with Chicago. But Al Capone was a native Brooklynite. Alphonse Gabriel Capone entered the world January 17, 1899, in Brooklyn. Papa Capone came from a town just south of Naples, while Mama hailed from a smaller town farther south, near Salerno. Alphonse was the fourth child (and fourth son) for Gabriele and Teresina Capone; three more boys and two girls (one survived infancy) would follow. Gabriele was a barber, while Teresina made dresses.

They initially lived near the Navy Yard and then moved to Park Slope. By all accounts, Capone's childhood was a normal, if rather harsh, one. The neighborhood by the Brooklyn Navy Yard was tough. But soon, Capone's father moved the family to an apartment over his barbershop. The new neighborhood had a greater diversity of nationalities than the one in which they had previously lived. Capone was a typical child, hanging out with friends.

Fourteen-year-old Alphonse was a promising student, but he was naturally foul tempered. One day, after his sixth-grade teacher hit him, he swiftly retaliated against her with a punch. Not surprisingly, such behavior was frowned upon. The principal whaled the daylights out of Alphonse, who had had enough and quit school.

Street Education

Shortly after these events, the family moved again, and the new neighborhood would have quite an effect on the young Capone. He met the people who would have the most influence on him throughout his life. Because Alphonse was drawn to the action, he began hanging out near the John Torrio Association. Torrio's Five Points Gang had begun in Manhattan's notorious neighborhood of that name and expanded into Brooklyn. Now, Torrio was a prominent local racketeer and pimp, and he'd occasionally hire Alphonse to carry out errands.

The "gentleman gangster" taught him how to have what seemed like an outwardly respectable life while simultaneously conducting business in the numbers racket and brothels. Torrio came to trust Alphonse immensely over time, and he and Frankie Yale, another notorious Brooklyn thug and loan shark, mentored young Alphonse in crime. Frankie was a muscle guy who used aggression and strong-arm tactics to build a successful criminal business. Another early Brooklyn associate was Salvatore Lucania, who, after a slight name change, became world famous as "Lucky" Luciano.

In the midst of all this lawless learning, Capone met Mae Coughlin, a middle-class Irishwoman. They had a son in 1918 and married shortly after. Capone made an attempt to earn a legitimate living—moving to Baltimore after he was married and doing well as a bookkeeper. But when his father died in 1920, Capone followed Torrio to Chicago to start the career that would make him infamous.

Torrio had taken over the underworld business in Chicago, and with the coming of Prohibition in 1920, he ended up controlling an empire that included brothels, speakeasies, and gambling clubs. Torrio brought Capone on board as partner. Capone moved his family into a house on Chicago's Far South Side. But after a reform-minded mayor was elected in the city, Torrio and Capone moved their base of operations southwest to suburban Cicero, where the pair essentially took over the town. Frank Capone, Al's brother, was installed as the front man of the Cicero city government and was fatally shot by Chicago police in 1924.

Rivalries and Threats

By this point, Capone had made a name for himself as a wealthy and powerful man. He was also a target. When gangland rival Dion O'Bannon was killed, Capone and Torrio easily took over O'Bannon's bootlegging territory—but they also set themselves up for a lifelong war with the remaining loyalists in O'Bannon's gang.

Capone and Torrio survived many assassination attempts. In 1925, when Hymie Weiss and Bugs Moran attempted to kill Torrio outside the crime boss's own home, Capone's partner finally decided to retire. He handed the empire over to Capone. Capone adapted to his role as the head honcho very easily. He actively cultivated a public persona, showing up at the opera, Chicago White Sox games, and charity events. He played politics with the smoothest politicians. And he dressed impeccably.

From 1925 to '29, Capone simultaneously polished his public persona and meted out violence to retain his superior gangland status. In New York in 1925, he orchestrated the Adonis Club Massacre, killing a rival gang leader and establishing his influence outside of Chicago. In 1926, he is believed to have had Billy McSwiggin, a public prosecutor, killed. When public perception turned against him, Capone stepped up his community involvement. He frequently told the press that his motto was "public service." In fact, because he provided jobs for hundreds of Italian immigrants through his bootlegging business, he genuinely considered himself a public servant.

When it came to his employees, Capone could be generous to a fault. He also cultivated relationships with jazz musicians who appeared in his Cicero nightspot, The Cotton Club. In 1926, Capone even organized a peace conference to try to stop the violence among gangs.

The crime boss was wildly successful in creating his public image—so successful, in fact, that he caught the attention of the president of the United States. After the St. Valentine's Day Massacre in Chicago (see the next page for details) in February 1929, in which seven members or associates of a rival gang were killed, the government initiated a focused attempt to put Capone behind bars. In 1930, Capone was listed as Public Enemy Number One. Knowing PR is everything, he was also running a soup kitchen that provided free meals. In 1931, he was convicted on multiple counts of tax evasion and was sentenced to 11 years behind bars. He was ultimately transferred to Alcatraz, where he was unable to use money or personal influence to carve out the kind of pampered life he expected to live while in prison.

Florida

Because of intense media scrutiny in Chicago, Capone bought an estate in Palm Island, Florida, in 1928. Though the residents of the town were chilly to his family's arrival, the Capones established a home and a retreat in this small community. It was to this estate that Capone would return when looking to avoid the glare of his public profile in Chicago, and it was at this estate that he eventually died. While in prison, Capone suffered from neurosyphilis and was confused and disoriented. He was released from prison in 1939 and had a brief stay in a Baltimore hospital, but he returned to Palm Island, where he slowly deteriorated until his death on January 25, 1947. The man who took the world by storm with his organized and brutal approach to crime was survived by his wife, son, and four grandchildren. Though he occupied only a small corner of the world, Al Capone left a huge mark on it.

My Bloody Valentine

The episode is infamous in American history. Almost no one dared to stand up to Capone and his men, including the police, because that meant possibly winding up on the wrong end of a gun. Still, one man was determined to dethrone Capone—George "Bugs" Moran. For a few years, Moran and his North Side Gang had been slowly muscling their way into Chicago in an attempt to force Capone and his men out. As 1929 began, rumors started to fly that Capone was fed up and was planning his revenge. As the days turned into weeks and nothing happened, Moran and his men began to relax and let their guard down. That would prove to be a fatal mistake.

Gathering for the Slaughter

On the morning of February 14, 1929, six members of the North Side Gang—James Clark, Frank Gusenberg, Peter Gusenberg, Adam Heyer, Reinhart Schwimmer, and Al Weinshank—were gathered inside the SMC Cartage Company at 2122 North Clark Street in the Lincoln Park neighborhood on Chicago's north side. With them was mechanic John May, who was not a member of the gang but had been hired to work on one of their cars. May had brought along his dog, Highball, and had tied him to the bumper of the car while he worked. Supposedly, the men were gathered at the warehouse to accept a load of bootleg whiskey. Whether that is true or not remains unclear. What is known for certain is that at approximately 10:30 a.m., two cars parked in front of the Clark Street entrance of the building. Four men—two dressed as police officers and two in street clothes—got out and walked into the warehouse.

Murderers in Disguise

Once the men were inside, it is believed they announced that the warehouse was being raided and ordered everyone to line up facing the back wall. Believing the armed men were indeed police officers, all of Moran's men, along with John May, did as they were told. Suddenly, the four men began shooting, and, in a hail of shotgun fire and more than 70 submachine-gun rounds, the seven men were brutally gunned down.

When it was over, the two men in street clothes calmly walked out of the building with their hands up, followed by the two men dressed as police officers. To everyone nearby, it appeared as though there had been a shootout and that the police had arrived and were now arresting two men.

"Nobody Shot Me"

Minutes later, neighbors called police after reportedly hearing strange howls coming from inside the building. When the real police arrived, they found all seven men mortally wounded. One of the men, Frank Gusenberg, lingered long enough to respond to one question. When authorities asked who shot him, Gusenberg responded, "Nobody shot me." The only survivor of the massacre was Highball the dog, whose howls first alerted people that something was wrong.

When word of the massacre hit the newswire, everyone suspected Al Capone had something to do with it. Capone stood strong, though, and swore he wasn't involved. Most people, however, felt that Capone had orchestrated the whole thing as a way to get rid of Moran and several of his key men. There was only one problem—Bugs Moran wasn't in the warehouse at the time of the shooting. Some believe that Moran may have driven up, seen the cars out front, and, thinking it was a raid, driven away. One thing is for certain: February 14, 1929, was Moran's lucky day.

Police launched a massive investigation but were unable to pin anything on Capone, although they did arrest two of his gunmen, John Scalise and Jack "Machine Gun" McGurn, and charged them with the murders. Scalise never saw the inside of the courthouse—he was murdered before the trial began. Charges against McGurn were eventually dropped, although he was murdered seven years later, on Valentine's Day, in what appeared to be retaliation for the 1929 massacre.

Al Capone Haunted by the Truth

Publicly, Al Capone may have denied any wrongdoing, but it appears that the truth literally haunted him until his dying day. In May 1929, Capone was incarcerated at Philadelphia's Eastern State Penitentiary, serving a one-year stint for weapons possession. Such a span was considered "easy time" by gangster standards, but Capone's time inside would be anything but. Haunted by the ghost of James Clark—who was killed in the St. Valentine's Day Massacre—Capone was often heard begging "Jimmy" to leave him alone.

The torment continued even after Capone was released. One day, Capone's valet, Hymie Cornish, saw an unfamiliar man in Capone's apartment. When he ordered the man to identify himself, the mysterious figure slipped behind a curtain and vanished. Capone insisted that Cornish, like himself, had seen the ghost of Clark. Some say that Clark didn't rest until Capone passed away on January 25, 1947.

Ghosts Still Linger

The warehouse at 2122 North Clark Street, where the bloody massacre took place, was demolished in 1967. The wall against which the seven doomed men stood, complete with bullet holes, was dismantled brick by brick and sold at auction. A businessman bought the wall and reassembled it in the men's room of his restaurant. However, the business failed and the owner, believing the wall was cursed, tried getting rid of it to recoup his losses.

He sold the individual bricks and was successful in getting rid of many of them, but they always seemed to find their way back to him. Sometimes they would show up on his doorstep along with a note describing all the misfortune the new owner had encountered after buying the brick.

At the former site of the warehouse, some people report hearing the sounds of gunfire and screams coming from the lot. People walking their dogs near the lot claim that their furry friends suddenly pull on their leashes and try to get away from the area as quickly as possible. Perhaps they sense the ghostly remnants of the bloody massacre that happened nearly 100 years ago.

Gangster's Paradise

Throughout the 1920s and '30s, Wisconsin's Northwoods were the place for bad guys looking to escape the heat—literally and figuratively—of Chicago. After the Chicago & North Western Railroad expanded due north into Wisconsin's wooden hinterlands, Chicagoland's elite came to vacation on the crystal-clear lakes. But they didn't come alone. For gangsters and their henchmen, the Northwoods were both a summer playground and a year-round hideout. Today, numerous communities have their own stories of gangster legend and lore. Here's a lineup of the most memorable.

The Capones

Big Al Capone turned 21 the day after the Volstead Act, the legislation that made alcohol illegal, went into effect. This seems like an ironic twist for someone who would go down in history known as a bootlegger, gangster, and criminal mastermind.

The Northwoods wasn't a temporary escape for Big Al, as it served as his permanent getaway. He didn't even try to cover up this fact, dubbing his Couderay retreat "The Hideout." His home on the shores of Cranberry Lake came complete with a gun turret alongside the driveway, openings in the stone walls for machine guns, and a personal jail. Booze runners from Canada would land their planes on the lake, and Capone's gang then took care of the distribution.

Al's older brother, Ralph "Bottles" Capone, was the director of liquor sales for the mob and covered his tracks by operating Waukesha Waters, a distribution company for Waukesha Springs mineral water. But Ralph had another passion: bookmaking. Ralph was less vicious than his brother, but bookmaking got him into trouble. He landed in prison in the early 1930s for tax evasion, coincidentally the same charge that sent Al to Alcatraz, where he was imprisoned for seven-and-a-half years. When Big Al was released in November 1939, he was so stricken with syphilis that he was unseated as leader of the criminal underworld. He died seven years later.

Later, Ralph lived in Mercer, from 1943 until his death on November 22, 1974. He managed the Rex Hotel and Billy's Bar and owned a house that had previously belonged to his brother. Ralph sponsored community Christmas parties, donated food and gifts to the needy, contributed to churches, and financed high school class trips. Despite his criminal history, locals remember him mostly for his kindness and charity. He also earned at least $20,000 a year from an Illinois cigarette vending machine business and was repeatedly investigated by the Internal Revenue Service. After 1951, Ralph Capone didn't even bother to file tax returns. At the time of his death he owed $210,715 in back taxes.

The Most Vicious

Few gangster aficionados know the story of John Henry Seadlund, dubbed "The World's Most Vicious Criminal" by FBI director J. Edgar Hoover. A loafer from Minnesota, Seadlund turned to crime after a chance meeting with Tommy Carroll, a veteran of John Dillinger's gang. To make fast cash as a new criminal, Seadlund considered kidnapping wealthy Chicagoans vacationing in the Northwoods and demanding ransom. But after joining with a new lowlife, James Atwood Gray, Seadlund's kidnapping plot expanded to include a professional baseball player. The plan was to kidnap the St. Louis Cardinals' star pitcher Dizzy Dean, but Seadlund gave up when he realized how exactly hard it might be to get ransom from Dean's ballclub.

Kidnapping ballplayers didn't pan out, so Seadlund abducted a retired greeting card company executive while heading out of Illinois in September 1937. After getting ransom, he exacted a kidnapping and murder scheme on the retiree, leaving him and accomplice Gray dead in a dugout near Spooner. He was caught when marked bills from the ransom were used at a racetrack the following January.

Beyond Bigwigs

Northwoods legend and lore extends beyond the mob's biggest names. During Prohibition, federal agents found and confiscated major gang-run stills in towns across Wisconsin's northern third. Elcho was the purported home to a mob doctor who traded bullet removal for booze, and Hurley was a gangster hot spot, as it was a "wide-open" town that flouted Prohibition and laws against prostitution. Wisconsin's Northwoods mob stories are as big as its fish tales.

Public Enemy No. 1

After serving eight-and-a-half years for robbery and assault, John Dillinger took off on a ten-month crime spree that earned him the title "Public Enemy No. 1." He and his gang rampaged across the Upper Midwest, busting cronies out of the slammer, robbing banks, murdering lawmen, and escaping from the FBI each time. Possibly needing a quiet vacation, Dillinger and accomplices headed to northern Wisconsin in 1934. For that story, read on...

Shoot-out at Little Bohemia

Infamous gangster John Dillinger was something of a media darling during his long, terrorizing reign. He was also the force behind one of the most embarrassing federal mishaps of all time.

Born June 22, 1903, John Dillinger was in his early thirties when he first caught the FBI's eye. They thought they were through with him in January 1934, when he was arrested after shooting a police officer during a bank robbery in East Chicago, Indiana. However, Dillinger managed to stage a daring escape from his Indiana jail cell using a wooden gun painted with black shoe polish.

In an era known for its long list of public enemies, John Dillinger and his crew stood out more like endeared celebrities than the convicted killers and robbers they were known to be. Historians attribute this strange awe to the gang's Robin Hood–like appeal during a stressful time for the public.

Robbing the Rich

The public, demoralized by the ongoing Depression, lacked financial and bureaucratic faith after suffering devastating losses at what they saw to be the hands of irresponsible government and financial institutions. When the dashing, physically graceful Dillinger and his equally charismatic crew began tearing through banks, they not only provided an exciting and dramatic media distraction, they also destroyed banks' potentially devastating mortgage paperwork in their wake. The masses seemed eager to clasp onto the real-life drama and connect it to their own plight. The public was more than willing to forgive the sins of outlaws such as Dillinger's crew in favor of the payback they provided to financial institutions.

Law officials, however, weren't so keen on the criminals. J. Edgar Hoover and his newly formed Federal Bureau of Investigation were weary of gangsters' soft public perception and crafted a series of hard-hitting laws meant to immobilize them. Those found guilty of crimes such as robbing banks would now face stiffer penalties. Dillinger, one of the most prominent, popular, and evasive of the lot, was at the top of Hoover's hit list. However, keeping the gangster in jail and strapped with a sufficient sentence seemed like more work than Hoover could handle.

Hiding Out

Dillinger, always hard to contain, had fled the supposedly escape-proof county jail in Crown Point, Indiana, in March 1934. A month and a few bank robberies later, Dillinger and company ended up hiding out in a woodsy Wisconsin lodge called Little Bohemia, so named because of the owner's Bohemian ethnic roots. Tipped off by the lodge owner's wife, Hoover and a team of federal investigators from Chicago responded with an ill-fated ambush that would go down in history as one of the greatest federal fiascoes of all time.

The Dillinger gang, including well-known characters such as Harry Pierpont and "Baby Face" Nelson, plus gang members' wives and girlfriends, had planned only a short layover at the wilderness retreat. Although owner Emil Wanatka and wife Nan had befriended an outlaw or two during the days of Prohibition, the Dillinger crew was a notch or two above the types they had known. The couple didn't share the public's glorified view of these men.

So, upon discovering that their new slew of guests were members of the notorious gang, Wanatka made a bold move and confronted them. Dillinger assured him that they would be of no inconvenience and would not stay long. Apparently bank robbers are not the most trustworthy folks, because in the several days of their stay the bunch proved to be much more than an inconvenience. Wanatka and his wife were basically held hostage at their humble hostel for the entire length of the Dillinger gang's stay. Telephone calls were monitored, lodge visitors were subject to scrutiny at both arrival and departure, and anyone, including Emil and Nan themselves, who went into town for supplies was forced to travel with a Dillinger escort. Even beside that, the sheer fear of housing sought-after sociopaths was too much for the Wanatka couple and their young son to handle. A plan for relief was soon hatched.

Knowing that any lodge departure would be surveyed closely, the Wanatkas decided to plant a note on Nan to pass to police. They would convince the gangsters that she and their ten-year-old son were merely departing for a nephew's birthday party and then would find a way to transmit their cry for help.

Although Dillinger gave permission for the pair's trip, the frightened mother soon discovered "Baby Face" Nelson hot on their trail and ready to jump at the first sight of suspicious activity. Still, Nan managed to pass word to her family, who then contacted the authorities. At the birthday party for her nephew, Nan provided details that were ultimately shared with law enforcement. Officials planned a siege.

The Heat Is On

Seizing the opportunity to make an example of Dillinger and his exploits, FBI agents Hugh Clegg and Melvin Purvis plotted an ambush at the lodge under Hoover's guidance. Unfortunately for the agents and innocent bystanders, Dillinger and company were not so easily taken.

As the agents approached, the lodge's watchdogs indeed barked at the strangers, but only after a series of miscalculated gunshots did the Dillinger gang stir. Clegg and Purvis had mistakenly fired at three patrons leaving the lodge's bar. This was the first tragedy of Little Bohemia that day: one of the patrons was killed instantly, and the other two were brutally wounded.

The Dillinger gang had long grown weary of the watchdogs' random yelps, but when they heard these unfortunate shots they knew their hideout had been discovered. They made a

hasty escape. Nelson, in a nearby cabin, escaped along the shoreline of Star Lake. Both parties forced nearby neighbors to provide getaway cars.

The agents didn't have the same knowledge of the land's lay and fell victim to a nearby ditch and a wall of barbed wire. Wounded and entangled, the agents were sitting ducks. Their suspects were free to flee and take their turn at gunfire now that they had the upper hand.

Unhappy Ending

A premature and somewhat pompous notion had Hoover pledging a significant story to the press in anticipation of the planned attack. Unluckily for him, with the unintentional victims and their families involved, the story would be a hellish one. The ambush resulted in not a single loss for the Dillinger gang. On the other side were two injured law officers, two wounded bystanders, and the death of a complete innocent.

Both Dillinger and Nelson were killed within the year. But Little Bohemia Lodge remains on Highway 51, the main thoroughfare to and through the Northwoods. It still serves breakfast, lunch, and dinner, with a heaping helping of history.

The Death of John Dillinger... or Someone Who Looked Like Him

After the botched trap at Little Bohemia, the public was in an uproar and the FBI was under close scrutiny. To everyone at the FBI, the message was clear: Hoover wanted Dillinger, and he wanted him ASAP.

On July 22, 1934, outside the Biograph Theater on Chicago's north side, John Dillinger passed from this world into the next in a hail of bullets. Or did he? Conspiracy theorists believe that FBI agents shot and killed the wrong man and covered it all up when they realized their mistake. So what really happened that fateful night?

The Woman in Red

The FBI's big break came in July 1934 with a phone call from a woman named Anna Sage. Sage was a Romanian immigrant who ran a Chicago-area brothel. Fearing that she might be deported, Sage wanted to strike a bargain with the feds. Her proposal was simple: In exchange for not being deported, Sage was willing to give the FBI John Dillinger. According to Sage, Dillinger was dating Polly Hamilton, one of her former employees. Melvin Purvis personally met with Sage and told her he couldn't make any promises but he would do what he could about her pending deportation.

Several days later, on July 22, Sage called the FBI office in Chicago and said that she was going to the movies that night with Dillinger and Hamilton. Sage quickly hung up but not before saying she would wear something bright so that agents could pick out the threesome in a crowd. Not knowing which movie theater they were planning to go to, Purvis dispatched several agents to the Marbro Theater, while he and another group of agents went to the Biograph. At approximately

8:30 p.m., Purvis believed he saw Dillinger, Sage, and Hamilton enter the Biograph. As she had promised, Sage indeed wore something bright—an orange blouse. However, under the marquee lights, the blouse's color appeared to be red, which is why Sage was forever dubbed "The Woman in Red."

Purvis tried to apprehend Dillinger right after he purchased tickets, but he slipped past Purvis and into the darkened theater. Purvis went into the theater but was unable to locate Dillinger in the dark. At that point, Purvis left the theater, gathered his men, and made the decision to apprehend Dillinger as he was exiting the theater. Purvis positioned himself in the theater's vestibule, instructed his men to hide outside, and told them that he would signal them by lighting a cigar when he spotted Dillinger. That was their cue to move in and arrest Dillinger.

"Stick 'em up, Johnny!"

At approximately 10:30 p.m., the doors to the Biograph opened and people started to exit. All of the agents' eyes were on Purvis. When a man wearing a straw hat, accompanied by two women, walked past Purvis, the agent quickly placed a cigar in his mouth and lit a match. Perhaps sensing something was wrong, the man turned and looked at Purvis, at which point Purvis drew his pistol and said, "Stick 'em up, Johnny!" In response, the man turned as if he was going to run away, while at the same time reaching for what appeared to be a gun. Seeing the movement, the other agents opened fire. As the man ran away, attempting to flee down the alleyway alongside the theater, he was shot four times on his left side and once in the back of the neck before crumpling on the pavement. When Purvis reached him and checked for vitals, there were none. Minutes later, after being driven to a local hospital, John Dillinger was pronounced DOA. But as soon as it was announced that Dillinger was dead, the controversy began.

Dillinger Disputed

Much of the basis for the conspiracy stems from the fact that Hoover, both publicly and privately, made it clear that no matter what, he wanted Dillinger caught. On top of that, Agent Purvis was under a lot of pressure to capture Dillinger, especially since he'd failed with a previous attempt. Keeping that in mind, it would be easy to conclude that Purvis, in his haste to capture Dillinger, might have overlooked a few things. First, it was Purvis alone who pointed out the man he thought to be Dillinger to the waiting agents. Conspiracy theorists contend that Purvis fingered the wrong man that night, and an innocent man ended up getting killed as a result. As evidence, they point to Purvis's own statement: While they were standing at close range, the man tried to pull a gun, which is why the agents had to open fire. But even though agents stated they recovered a .38-caliber Colt automatic from the victim's body (and even had it on display for many years), author Jay Robert Nash discovered that that particular model was not even available until a good five months after Dillinger's alleged death! Theorists believe that when agents realized they had not only shot the wrong man, but an unarmed one at that, they planted the gun as part of a cover-up.

Another interesting fact that could have resulted in Purvis's misidentification was that Dillinger had recently undergone plastic surgery in an attempt to disguise himself. In addition to work on his face, Dillinger had attempted to obliterate his fingerprints by dipping his fingers into an acid solution. On top of that, the man who Purvis said was Dillinger was wearing a straw hat the entire time Purvis saw him. It is certainly possible that Purvis did not actually recognize Dillinger but instead picked out someone who merely looked like him. If you remember, the only tip Purvis had was Sage telling him that she was going to the movies with Dillinger and his girlfriend. Did Purvis see Sage leaving the theater in her orange blouse and finger the wrong man simply because he was standing next to

Sage and resembled Dillinger? Or was the whole thing a setup orchestrated by Sage and Dillinger to trick the FBI into executing an innocent man?

So Who Was It?

If the man shot and killed outside the theater wasn't John Dillinger, who was it? There are conflicting accounts, but one speculation is that it was a man named Jimmy Lawrence, who was dating Polly Hamilton. If you believe in the conspiracy, Lawrence was simply in the wrong place at the wrong time. Or possibly, Dillinger purposely sent Lawrence to the theater hoping FBI agents would shoot him, allowing Dillinger to fade into obscurity. Of course, those who don't believe in the conspiracy say the reason Lawrence looked so much like Dillinger is because he was Dillinger using an alias. Further, Dillinger's sister, Audrey Hancock, identified his body. Finally, they say it all boils down to the FBI losing or misplacing the gun Dillinger had the night he was killed and inadvertently replacing it with the wrong one. Case closed.

Not really, though. It seems that whenever someone comes up with a piece of evidence to fuel the conspiracy theory, someone else has something to refute it. Some have asked that Dillinger's body be exhumed and DNA tests be performed, but nothing has come of it yet. Until that happens, we'll probably never know for sure what really happened on that hot July night back in 1934. But that's okay, because everyone loves a good mystery.

Entrepreneurs of Death: The Story of the Brownsville Boys

Following the rise of the National Crime Syndicate, or what people now call the Mafia, a group of enterprising killers formed an enforcement arm that the press dubbed "Murder, Incorporated." Officially, they were known as "The Combination" or "The Brownsville Boys," since many of them came from Brooklyn's Brownsville area.

The Combination began their mayhem-for-money operation around 1930 following the formation of the National Crime Syndicate. Until their demise in the mid-1940s, they enforced the rules of organized crime through fear, intimidation, and murder. Most of the group's members were Jewish and Italian gangsters from Brooklyn; remorseless and bloodthirsty, murder for money was their stock-in-trade. The number of murders committed during their bloody reign is unknown even today, but estimates put the total at more than a thousand from coast to coast. The title "Murder, Incorporated" was the invention of a fearless *New York World-Telegram* police reporter named Harry Feeney; the name stuck.

Filling a Need

The formation of the group was the brainchild of mob overlords Johnny Torrio and "Lucky" Luciano. The most high-profile assassination credited to the enterprise was the murder of gang lord Dutch Schultz, who defied the syndicate's orders to abandon a plan to assassinate New York crime-buster Thomas Dewey. The job went to one of the Combination's top-echelon gunsels, Charles "Charlie the Bug" Workman, whose bloody prowess ranked alongside such Murder, Inc., elite as Louis "Lepke" Buchalter, the man who issued the orders; Albert Anastasia, the lord high executioner; Abe "Kid Twist" Reles, whose eventual capitulation led to the group's downfall; Louis Capone (no relation to Al); Frank Abbandando; Harry "Pittsburg Phil" Strauss, an expert with an ice pick; Martin

"Buggsy" Goldstein; Harry "Happy" Maione, leader of the Italian faction; Emanuel "Mendy" Weiss, who is rumored to have never committed murder on the Sabbath; Johnny Dio; Albert "Allie" Tannenbaum; Irving "Knadles" Nitzberg, who twice beat a death sentence when his convictions were overturned; Vito "Socko" Gurino; Jacob Drucker; Philip "Little Farvel" Cohen; and Sholom Bernstein, who like many of his cohorts turned against his mentors to save his own life. It was an era of infamy unequaled in mob lore.

Loose Lips

Though many of the rank and file of Murder, Inc., appeared to enjoy killing, Reles, a former soda jerk, killed only as a matter of business. Known as "Kid Twist," Reles may not have been as bloodthirsty as some of his contemporaries, but he was cursed with a huge ego and a big mouth, and he wasn't shy about doing his bragging in front of cops, judges, the press, or the public at large. The little man with the big mouth would eventually lead to the unraveling of the Combination and greatly weaken the power of the National Crime Syndicate. When an informant fingered Reles and "Buggsy" Goldstein for the murder of a small-time hood, both men turned themselves in, believing they could beat the rap just as they had a dozen times before, but this one was ironclad. Reles sang loud and clear, implicating his peers and bosses in more than 80 murders and sending several of them to the electric chair, including the untouchable Buchalter. He also revealed the internal secret structure of the National Syndicate. Reles was in protective custody when he "fell" to his death from a hotel room on November 12, 1941, while surrounded by police. By the mid-1940s, Murder, Inc., was a thing of the past, and the National Crime Syndicate was in decline.

When it came to singing like a canary, only Joe Valachi would surpass the performance of Reles, once the most trusted member of the Brownsville Boys.

Albert Anastasia

A gun; an ice pick; a rope; these were some of the favorite tools of Albert Anastasia, notorious mob assassin. When he wasn't pulling the trigger himself, this head of Murder, Inc. was giving the orders to kill, beat, extort, and rob on the mob-controlled waterfronts of Brooklyn and Manhattan.

Born in Italy in 1902 as Umberto Anastasio, Anastasia worked as a deck hand before jumping ship in New York, where he built a power base in the longshoremen's union. Murder was his tool to consolidate power. Arrested several times in the 1920s, his trials were often dismissed when witnesses would go missing. It wasn't long before he attracted the attention of mob "brain" Lucky Luciano and subsequently helped whack Joe "the Boss" Masseria in 1931, an act that opened the way for Luciano to achieve national prominence within the organization.

Luciano put Anastasia, Bugsy Siegel, and Meyer Lanksy in charge of what became known as Murder, Inc. With his quick temper and brutal disposition, Anastasia earned the nickname "Lord High Executioner."

A History of Violence

After Reles began singing like a canary and had his mysterious "fall," Anastasia climbed the next rung in the mob ladder by ordering the violent 1951 deaths of the Mangano brothers and ultimately taking over the Mangano family. Eventually, however, he alienated two powerful rivals, Vito Genovese and Meyer Lansky. On October 25, 1957, as Albert Anastasia dozed in a barber's chair at New York's Park Sheraton Hotel, he was riddled by two masked gunmen (possibly Larry and Joe Gallo), who acted on orders from Genovese.

Anastasia had evaded justice for decades, but he couldn't escape the violence he himself cultivated in organized crime.

The Mayfield Road Mob

Cleveland's most notorious criminal gang kept the streets of Little Italy safe while turning the city into one of America's most notorious Mafia towns.

On July 5, 1930, the two biggest players in the Cleveland criminal underworld met to negotiate a new power-sharing arrangement. One was Joe Porrello, head of the Porrello family gang and reigning Cleveland mob boss. The other was Frank Milano, leader of the Mayfield Road Mob, which ran most of Cleveland's illegal rackets from the city's Little Italy district.

The meeting was held at Milano's Venetian Restaurant at the corner of Mayfield and Murray Hill roads in the heart of Little Italy. The mood was friendly until the upstart Milano demanded a piece of the Porrello clan's lucrative corn sugar business (corn sugar was a key ingredient for making bootleg whiskey). When Porrello balked, Milano's henchman gunned him down—leaving the Mayfield Road Mob to take over the corn sugar business and Milano to step in as the new Cleveland don.

The Reign of Quiet

Once in control, Milano moved the Mayfield Road Mob into gambling, loan sharking, and labor union racketeering—its main operation once Prohibition had ended—and eventually molded the Cleveland crime syndicate into one of the top Mafia organizations in the United States. Ironically, Milano's boys kept Mayfield Road and surrounding neighborhood streets crime-free. Burglars, muggers, and punks knew that misbehaving in Little Italy meant swift and severe retribution from Milano's crew. Milano's run as boss ended in 1934 after he fled to Mexico to avoid charges of tax evasion, and his lieutenant that succeeded him, Alfred Polizzi, retired from the racket in 1944. Leadership of the Cleveland Mafia passed to a faction headed by John Scalish, thus ending the Mayfield Road Mob's magnanimous reign.

Cold and Clammy

Gangster "Crazy" Joe Gallo went about his underworld business with style and panache. If there was limelight to be sampled, chances are Gallo would be standing directly beneath it. Unfortunately for the crime boss, such flamboyance would trigger his early demise.

Wise Guy of Note

In some ways, Joe Gallo was a gangster ahead of his time. He certainly viewed himself that way. Here was a dutiful, workaday mobster who, for all of his limitations, saw opportunity in areas of criminal activity where others saw only strife. Before long, Gallo pioneered alliances with non-Mafia gangs that proved profitable all around. These unlikely but shrewd couplings of rival groups were masterful strokes.

But there was another side to Gallo that wasn't nearly as good for business: his public side. Much like Benjamin "Bugsy" Siegel before him, Gallo had a sense of flair, a taste for the good life, and plenty of celebrity friends.

Gallo and his boys were well-known for their keen sense of style. The wise guys looked like they had come straight from central casting in their black suits, narrow black ties, and darker-than-pitch sunglasses. Tabloids often ran covers of the boys done up in such "gangster chic." The public seemed to love it. The mob, not so much.

Gallo simply couldn't resist being the center of attention. And he liked to talk. In an enterprise that conducts its business well beneath the radar, this was *not* the preferred path.

Wild Child

Born on April 7, 1929, in the tough Red Hook section of Brooklyn, Gallo quickly rose from street criminal to key enforcer in the Profaci Crime Family. With help from brothers Albert and Larry—as well as mobsters Frank Illiano, Nicholas

Bianco, and Vic Amuso—no tactic seemed too ruthless or too bloody. In 1957, after allegedly rubbing out gangster Albert Anastasia in a barber chair at New York's Park Sheraton Hotel, Gallo (perhaps not unreasonably) asked mob boss Joseph Profaci for a bigger slice of the pie. The don's refusal sparked a turf war between the Gallo gang and the Profacis. The bloody feud continued into the 1960s, ultimately working to the favor of the Profacis.

Can't Win for Trying

After Joe Profaci died of cancer in 1962, power was transferred to his underboss, Joseph Magliocco, then later to Joseph Colombo. Due to Gallo's inability to achieve the exalted seat—as well as his ten-year incarceration for extortion—the mobster's leadership skills were placed in question. It wasn't that the Gallo boys didn't try. They had even gone so far as kidnapping Magliocco (during the Profaci-Gallo wars) in hopes that a human bargaining chip would bring them better profits. It didn't. In the long run nothing seemed to work out for the gang. The huge cash tributes that Profaci demanded of the Gallos prior to the kidnapping were suspended—but only for a brief period. After Magliocco was returned, the fees were reinstated. In the bloody dream of big-time money, Gallo and his crew had been effectively squeezed out of the action.

The Gang That Couldn't Shoot Straight

The gang's big ideas and general ineptitude caught the eye of *New York Post* columnist Jimmy Breslin, who lampooned them in his bestselling 1969 novel, *The Gang That Couldn't Shoot Straight*. A movie would follow with the buffoonish lead role (loosely based on Gallo's life) given to actor Jerry Orbach.

Things got interesting after the movie's release when Gallo, fresh out of prison, approached Orbach to set history straight. Oddly, the two men took to each other and became friends. Orbach was astonished by Gallo's grasp of art and literature and introduced him to his circle of friends. Soon, Gallo was hobnobbing with

Hollywood figures and members of the literary set. Everybody, it seemed, wanted to meet this real-life *Mafioso* with the cultural dexterity to quote from such figures as Camus and Sartre. After rotting for ten long years behind bars and suffering countless indignities as Profaci's underpaid soldier, could Gallo's star finally be on the rise?

Stars in His Eyes

Although suspected in the recent assassination of boss Joe Colombo, Gallo announced that he was "turning legit" in 1972. The purportedly reformed mobster planned to write a book about his life and perhaps even try his hand at acting. This might explain why Gallo found himself in the company of Jerry Orbach, comedian David Steinberg, and columnist Earl Wilson at New York's Copacabana one night before his 43rd birthday. It may also explain why the mob no longer wanted Gallo around. In the eyes of syndicate members, they didn't come much riskier than a starstruck, publicity-mad mobster who invited the scrutiny of federal agents bent on destroying La Cosa Nostra. In fact, the only thing that might trump such an actionable offense would be a gangster who had taken the oath of *omertà*, only to go straight and announce plans to write a tell-all book.

Bad Clams

During the wee hours of April 7, 1972, the unlikely group disbanded. Gallo, his bodyguard Pete Diapoulas, and four women made their way to Umberto's Clam House on Mulberry Street. While mobsters regarded this popular Little Italy location as Mafia holy ground, a hit was nevertheless in the making. As Gallo and his bodyguard pondered menu choices with their backs to the door, one or two gunmen barged in. Hearing the danger, Gallo and Diapoulas instinctively rose and made a run for it. Despite their maneuvers, both men were hit. Diapoulas took a bullet to his hip (he would later recover) and Gallo caught no less than five slugs. The mortally wounded mobster wobbled out the front door, making it as far as his Cadillac before collapsing in a lifeless heap.

While it wasn't quite the Hollywood ending that the mobster had hoped for, it was a Hollywood ending of sorts. The death of "Crazy" Joe Gallo had been every bit as flamboyant as his existence. To live in the limelight, to die in the limelight—maybe it was all somehow equal.

Bombs Away

A modern-day Robin Hood and a calculated killer, Danny Greene's dual roles made him the most notorious celebrity in Cleveland, Ohio—or, as it was called during Greene's time, Bomb City, U.S.A.

Northeast Ohio has a history of colorful locals, and Cleveland is no exception. During the 1960s and 1970s, one legendary gangster made his mark as a modern-day Robin Hood, befriending poor families and blowing up his competition.

Cleveland's Other Nickname

Irish American gangster Danny Greene was part of a headline-making underworld fueled by bullets and bombs. In fact, Greene's penchant for homemade incendiaries helped earn Cleveland's nickname: Bomb City, U.S.A. In 1976 alone, 36 bombs ripped through the cityscape. Most of them were either made by—or aimed at—Greene.

Greene's hard-knocks childhood in Cleveland ended when he left school to join the Marines in 1951. When his years in the service ended, Greene circled back to Cleveland where he worked the docks and became president of the local International Association of Longshoremen. He reportedly used green ink to write union bylaws, but his tactics were anything but whimsical. Greene issued a 25-percent dues increase and expected members to "voluntarily" work extra hours and donate the proceeds—or suffer the consequences.

Unwanted Attention

It wasn't long before Greene's dealings with other union leaders captured the attention of the FBI. Greene became an informant but only shared information about his competition. In 1964, his heavy-handed management style fueled an old-fashioned exposé by the *Cleveland Plain Dealer*. Greene laughed off the story, but the IRS didn't find it funny. Neither did the U.S. attorney's office, local prosecutors, or the U.S. Department of Labor. The verdict: Greene had emptied the union's coffers and lined his pockets with the money.

Although Greene escaped jail time, his days as a union boss were over. He found work offering "protection" to area businesses. He enforced his own bomb- or bullet-ridden version of the law and became a modern-day Robin Hood. He paid Catholic school tuition for children from poor families and had more than two dozen turkeys delivered to neighborhood homes for Thanksgiving.

Unsavory Connections

Greene also teamed with local mobster Alex "Shondor" Birns. The partnership soured when more than $60,000 of Birns's money went missing on Greene's watch. The feud between Greene and Birns ended only when both players were blown to bits. In 1975, Birns was fatally sent through the roof of his own car. Even after Birns's death, Greene's life was still on the line. Reportedly, the dead man had left a $25,000 reward on Greene's head.

Next, Greene's home exploded, but he survived with only minor injuries. In the ensuing months, Greene was shot at, returned fire, lost his "assistant" (who blew up in a car bombing), and detected a bomb in his car that failed to detonate. He also found a bomb that wasn't wired effectively and another that would have worked—had the hit men been within range to detonate it. When Greene traveled out of state, assassins followed but got lost before they could kill him. Shots were fired at Greene as he strolled down a sidewalk, but he wasn't hit.

The Bombs Catch Up

When Greene went to the dentist on October 6, 1977, however, his charmed life was soon to be over. Rival mobsters stuffed a vehicle with explosives, parked next to Greene's vehicle, and waited for him to return. This time it was a successful hit. The bomb blew Greene's left arm 100 feet from his body, but his emerald-encrusted ring stayed on his finger. His back was ripped open during the fatal attack, and his clothing was torn away, except for his ankle-high boots and socks. Next to Greene, untouched, was a gym bag containing a loaded gun and a printed prayer to the Virgin Mary.

What Happened to Jimmy Hoffa?

James Riddle Hoffa was born on February 14, 1913, in Brazil, Indiana, but his family moved to Detroit in 1924. It was here that a teenaged Hoffa became active in unions, after working for a grocery chain that paid poorly and offered substandard conditions for its employees. Hoffa eventually became a powerful figure in the Teamsters union, and he spent the rest of his life working with unions in Detroit. At least, that's the assumption. In truth, no one knows where Hoffa spent the end of his life, because in 1975, he simply disappeared.

A Poor Career Choice

In a 2004 episode of the popular Discovery Channel show *MythBusters*, the show's hosts, Adam Savage and Jamie Hyneman, traveled to Giants Stadium in East Rutherford, New Jersey, for a reason that had nothing to do with football. The curious television hosts were exploring an oft-told urban legend claiming that the body of Jimmy Hoffa had been encased in concrete and buried in the end zone of the stadium. Using ground-penetrating radar, Savage and Hyneman searched the field for anything unusual beneath the surface, but ultimately found nothing. Their findings were later confirmed when Giants Stadium was demolished to make way for a new sports complex in 2010.

The *MythBusters* search was just one of many investigations into Hoffa's disappearance, which is rife with unknowns. But here's what we do know: Hoffa began to rise to power in the International Brotherhood of Teamsters (IBT) union in the 1940s, eventually becoming president of the IBT in 1957. While it seems like a respectable career path, the union was heavily influenced by organized crime, and Hoffa spent much of his time with the IBT making deals and arrangements with gangsters to strengthen and expand its power in the region.

By the 1960s, Hoffa's corrupt dealings began to catch up with him, and in 1967, he was sentenced to 13 years in prison for bribery and fraud.

A Struggle to Regain Power

Hoffa's sentence was commuted by President Richard Nixon in 1971, under the condition that he not seek "direct or indirect management of any labor organization" until 1980. But, with newfound freedom and a thirst for the power he once had, Hoffa ignored this term. Within two years, he was once again vying for presidency of the IBT. But if Hoffa thought he'd be welcomed back with open arms, he was wrong. His attempts to regain power were met with strong resistance, not only by IBT members, but also many of the gangsters he had once worked with. On July 30, 1975, Hoffa was invited to attend a "peace meeting" between him and two of his organized crime contacts, Anthony Provenzano and Anthony Giacalone, presumably to smooth out tensions between the groups.

The Meeting, the Mob, and the Mystery

Several witnesses saw Hoffa at the location of the meeting, which was set for 2:00 p.m. in the afternoon. At 2:15 p.m., he called his wife from a pay phone to impatiently say that Provenzano and Giacalone hadn't shown up yet. What happened next has been the subject of countless speculation. Hoffa simply vanished, leaving behind his unlocked car and very few other clues. Provenzano and Giacalone denied ever setting up a meeting, and both had alibis that placed them away from the meeting location that afternoon.

Many theories have circulated about Hoffa's fate, but he was officially declared legally dead in 1982. Over the years, various Teamsters and mobsters have alleged to "know the truth" about what happened to him, but none of these claims have panned out. The FBI has investigated scores of tips, searching for traces of Hoffa in the homes of gangsters, backyard sheds, horse farms, landfills, and even the Florida Everglades.

A particularly creative theory posits that Hoffa's body was dismembered and the pieces were added to steel in a Detroit auto factory, which were then exported to Japan. The real story is probably much more mundane. But until we know for sure, the mysterious fate of Jimmy Hoffa will no doubt continue to inspire macabre tales.

Crime and Punishment: When Mobsters Screw Up

Not everything goes off without a hitch. In fact, it rarely does. Here are some examples of some of the most-botched crime jobs in history.

Organized crime is serious business. After all, it usually involves violence, weapons, other people's money, the law, and prison. With those pieces loose on the chessboard, it's really easy to mess up. Take the two New York mobsters who agreed to do a little job: hit Al Capone. They had a nice trip on the Twentieth Century Limited, but in Chicago they were met at the train, taken someplace quiet, and beaten to death. Pieces of them were sent back with a note: "Don't send boys to do a man's job."

Don't Mess with the Wrong Guy

There's also the mistake of not knowing who you're dealing with. Faced with debts in his electrical business, Florida businessperson George Bynum borrowed $50,000 from a mob loan shark. He was able to make $2,500 payments on the interest, but he couldn't pay off the principal, so he decided to go into the crime business himself. He tipped off a burglary gang about a house that he had wired, in exchange for a cut of the take. The burglars broke in, but the home owner was there, and they beat him up. The owner was Anthony "Nino" Gaggi, a Gambino family mobster. Gaggi found out that Bynum had planned the burglary. On July 13, 1976, John Holland called Bynum from the Ocean Shore Motel and pitched a lucrative wiring contract. When Bynum arrived at the motel, Gaggi and some friends were waiting, and that was the last anyone heard from Bynum.

If You're Laying Low, Lay Low!

Often the bungling of criminals is much more humorous. Enrico "Kiko" Frigerio was a Swiss citizen, and when the famed Pizza Connection—a scheme to push heroin through pizza parlors in New York—was broken by the FBI in 1984, he fled to Switzerland. Frigerio stayed there for years, until a documentary film crew decided to do a movie about his life. As technical advisor, he decided to give them a tour of his old New York haunts, but when he stepped off a plane onto U.S. soil, he was immediately arrested. Frigerio hadn't realized that he was still under indictment. Oops!

A Continuing Comedy of Errors

Jimmy Breslin once wrote a comic novel called *The Gang That Couldn't Shoot Straight*. He must have been thinking about New Jersey's DeCavalcante crime family, the only one never given a seat on the Mafia's ruling commission. Vincent "Vinnie Ocean" Palermo ruled the DeCavalcante family like a bad Marx Brothers movie. Once, Palermo's men were given a supply of free cell phones—supplied by the FBI to tap their conversations. Another time, Palermo put a .357 Magnum to the head of a boat mechanic to force him to admit that he'd ruined the motor on Palermo's speedboat. "I was so mad, I bit his nose," Palermo said.

Then there was the time that Palermo and the missus went on vacation, and he decided to hide the family jewelry—$700,000 worth—in the bottom of a trash bag. "My wife took the garbage out for the first time in 20 years, and that was the end of the jewelry."

Finally, in 1999, Palermo was arrested and agreed to turn informant in exchange for leniency in sentencing. He helped to put away such stalwarts as Frankie the Beast, Anthony Soft-Shoes, and Frank the Painter. Palermo himself admitted to four murders, including that of newspaper editor Frank Weiss. He said that it was a good career move: "I shot him twice in the head. They made me a captain." He will not be missed.

Valachi Speaks

On June 22, 1962, in the federal penitentiary in Atlanta, Georgia, a man serving a sentence of 15 to 20 years for heroin trafficking picked up a steel pipe and murdered another convict. The killer was Joseph "Joe Cargo" Valachi; the intended victim was Joseph DiPalermo—but Valachi got the wrong man and killed another inmate, Joe Saupp. This mistake touched off one of the greatest criminal revelations in history.

Joe Valachi, a 59-year-old Mafia "soldier," was the first member of the Mafia to publicly acknowledge the reality of that criminal organization—making La Cosa Nostra (which means "this thing of ours") a household name. He opened the doors to expose an all-pervasive, wide-ranging conglomerate of crime families, the existence of which was repeatedly denied by J. Edgar Hoover and the FBI. By testifying against his own organization, Valachi violated *omertà*, the code of silence.

The Boss's Orders

Vito Genovese was the boss of New York's powerful Genovese crime family. Valachi had worked for the family for much of his life—primarily as a driver, but also as a hit man, enforcer, numbers runner, and drug pusher. When Valachi was on his way to prison after having been found guilty of some of these activities, Genovese believed the small-time operator had betrayed him to obtain a lighter sentence for himself. So Genovese put a $100,000 bounty on Valachi's head. He and Valachi were actually serving sentences in the same prison when Valachi killed Joe Saupp—mistaking him for Joseph DiPalermo, whom he thought had been assigned by Genovese to murder him. Whether or not Valachi had broken the code of silence and betrayed Genovese before the bounty was placed on his head, he certainly did it with a vengeance afterward.

But why did Valachi turn informer? The answer to that question isn't entirely clear. Most speculate that Valachi was afraid of a death sentence for killing Saupp and agreed to talk to the Feds in exchange for a lighter sentence.

The Cat Is Out of the Bag

Valachi was a barely literate, street-level miscreant whose knowledge of the workings of the organization was limited. However, when he was brought before John L. McClellan's Senate Permanent Investigations Subcommittee in October 1963, he began talking beyond his personal experience, relaying urban legends as truth, and painting a picture of the Mafia that was both fascinating and chilling.

All in all, Joe Valachi helped identify 317 members of the Mafia. His assistance gave Attorney General Robert Kennedy "a significant addition to the broad picture of organized crime." Unlike Hoover, Bobby Kennedy had no problem acknowledging the Mafia. (One theory about Hoover's denials is that they were a result of long-term Mafia blackmail regarding his homosexuality.)

Valachi's revelations ran the gamut from minor accuracies to babbling exaggerations, as well as from true to false, but the cat was out of the bag. Americans became fascinated with crime families, codes of honor, gang wars, hit killings, and how widely the Mafia calamari had stretched its tentacles. Very private criminals suddenly found their names splashed across headlines and blaring from televisions. During the next three years in the New York–New Jersey–Connecticut metropolitan area, more organized criminals were arrested and jailed than in the previous 30 years. Whatever safe conduct pass the Mafia may have held had expired.

On-screen and in Print

When journalist Peter Maas interviewed Valachi and came out with *The Valachi Papers*, the U.S. Department of Justice first encouraged but then tried to block its publication. Regardless, the book was released in 1968. This work soon became the basis of a movie that starred Charles Bronson as Joe Valachi. The novel *The Godfather* was published in 1969, and in the film, *The Godfather: Part II*, the characters of Willie Cicci and Frank Pentangeli were reportedly inspired by Valachi.

The $100,000 bounty on the life of Joseph Valachi was never claimed. In 1966, Valachi unsuccessfully attempted to hang himself in his prison cell using an electrical cord. Five years later, he died of a heart attack at La Tuna Federal Correctional Institution in Texas. He had outlived his chief nemesis, Genovese, by two years.

Chapter 7

An Unlawful Payday: Robberies and Heists

Mailing It In

It was the world's most valuable necklace, said to be worth twice as much as the Hope Diamond. Yet surprisingly, this precious string of pearls was remarkably easy to steal.

Stealing for Sport

Joseph Grizzard had a reputation for being a debonair gentleman. The wealthy man often threw lavish parties at his home in Hatton Garden, the neighborhood in London where he claimed to be a jeweler. In reality, Grizzard acquired his wealth through criminal means, although by 1913 he was so well-off that he easily could have retired from his life of heists and thefts.

But money wasn't the only reason Grizzard stole. To him, pulling off a heist was a bit of a game; he enjoyed showing off his winnings. One story credits him with stealing the Ascot Cup, a trophy given to the winner of the Gold Cup horse race. The cup, made of 68 ounces of gold, was stolen in 1907 and never found. But according to those who attended Grizzard's parties, he would serve cocktails from the famous cup for his guests. Another story recounts how Grizzard graciously allowed the police to search his home for stolen diamonds, even though he was hosting dinner guests. The police found nothing and left, at which time Grizzard sat down at the dinner table with his guests and pulled a string of diamonds from the bottom of his soup bowl.

So when Max Mayer, a legitimate jeweler in Hatton Garden, bought a strand of perfect pink pearls, Grizzard took note. The process of culturing pearls was not yet widespread, which meant that all 61 of the blush-pink pearls in the necklace had been plucked from rare oysters. Assembling the entire necklace took ten years, and it was insured by Lloyd's of London for £135,000—an amount that would be equal to around $20 million today.

Postal Pearls

One of the prospective buyers for Mayer's rare necklace was a Parisian jeweler, who wanted to inspect the piece before buying. Amazingly, in the early 20th century it was common practice for jewelers to send expensive jewels through the mail. Mayer simply sent the necklace to Paris and, when the deal fell through, the Parisian jeweler sent it back the same way. This was where Grizzard saw an opportunity.

Grizzard and several accomplices spent weeks eavesdropping on Mayer to find out exactly when the pearls would be in the mail. They also paid close attention to the comings and goings of the mailman on Mayer's mail route. They befriended the unsuspecting man and discovered that he was a heavy drinker who only made a few pounds a week. Seeing an easy target, Grizzard offered him £200, more than his entire year's salary, if he would simply allow Grizzard quick access to a package in his mailbag one day.

When the package arrived, the mailman delivered it to Grizzard, who sliced it open, removed the necklace, and replaced it with a page from a French newspaper and eleven sugar cubes, which weighed the same as the necklace. He then resealed the package and returned it to the mailman. When Mayer received the package that day, he was shocked to find the sugar cubes in place of his priceless necklace.

Cat and Mouse

At first, police believed the necklace must have been stolen in France, as the sugar cubes had been wrapped in a French newspaper. But Alfred Ward, chief inspector of Scotland Yard, wasn't so sure. He suspected the charming Grizzard might have something to do with it, so he assembled a team of undercover operatives to keep an eye on the thief. But Grizzard was just as suspicious of Ward, and had his own team of observers, keeping an eye on the police. The ensuing game of cat and mouse was almost comical.

Eventually, it came down to one weak link within the circle of Grizzard's accomplices, a man named Lesir Gutwirth who just couldn't help but brag about stealing the necklace. Grizzard and his gang were arrested, but even Ward admitted that he liked the affable thief. He frequently visited him in prison, and even advocated for Grizzard's early release. Once Grizzard was out of prison, he acted as a consultant for Ward, helping him out on cases. The two remained unlikely friends until Ward's untimely death in 1916, when a zeppelin bomb hit his home. Grizzard, it is believed, returned to his life of crime; but he surely never accomplished a bigger heist than the Mayer pearls.

The Real Bonnie and Clyde

Bonnie and Clyde, Texas's most notorious outlaws, rose to fame during the Great Depression of the 1930s. The pair gained a mythical, Robin Hood–like status, but the real Bonnie and Clyde were different from the figures portrayed by the popular media.

The early 1930s was a time when businesses folded at an unprecedented rate and plummeting crop prices forced farmers from their lands in record numbers. Men desperate for work trawled city streets looking for jobs, soup kitchens were swamped, and the value of a dollar plunged. When Bonnie and Clyde began their crime spree, the public viewed them as outsiders fighting back against an uncaring system that had failed the working man.

Where They Started

Bonnie Parker was born on October 1, 1910, in Rowena. When she met Clyde Barrow in 1930, she was already married to a man used to being on the wrong side of the law. However, Bonnie was not a typical gangster's moll. She had been an honor-roll student in high school who excelled in creative writing and even won a spelling championship. After her husband was sentenced to the penitentiary, Bonnie scraped together a living by working as a waitress in West Dallas. Then Clyde Barrow entered her life.

Clyde Barrow was born on March 24, 1909, in Telico, just south of Dallas, and spent more of his poverty-stricken youth in trouble with the law than he did in school. He was arrested for stealing turkeys, auto theft, and safecracking. Soon after his romance with Bonnie began, he was sentenced to two years for a number of burglaries and car thefts. Bonnie managed to smuggle a Colt revolver to him, and Clyde was able to escape with his cell mate, William Turner.

A Life on the Run

Clyde and Turner were soon recaptured and sentenced to 14 years at the Texas State Penitentiary. But Clyde was pardoned in February 1932 after his mother intervened and Clyde had had a fellow inmate chop off two of his toes in order to garner sympathy.

After two months of attempting to go straight, Clyde started a crime spree with Bonnie that stretched from Texas to Oklahoma, Missouri, Iowa, New Mexico, and Louisiana. They robbed gas stations, liquor stores, banks, and jewelry stores. They also captured the public imagination by frequently taking hostages as they made their daring escapes and then releasing them unharmed when they were out of danger. Other outlaws came and went from the Barrow Gang, but it was only after several of the robberies culminated in murder that public opinion turned against Bonnie and Clyde.

In total, the Barrow Gang is believed to have murdered at least nine police officers and several civilians during their robberies. While Bonnie posed alongside Clyde clutching a machine gun for photos, many argue that at no time did she ever fire a weapon, let alone kill or injure anyone. Another popular misconception had her dubbed as the cigar-smoking moll of the Barrow Gang. Again, Bonnie was known to smoke only cigarettes, but she once posed with a cigar in what later became a famous photograph.

The Final Showdown

But in January 1934, Clyde made a fatal mistake while carrying out what he called the Eastham Breakout. The plan was to help two Barrow Gang members, Raymond Hamilton and Henry Methvin, break out of jail. The plan worked, but during the escape, a police officer was shot and killed. As a result, an official posse, headed by Frank Hamer, was formed with the sole intent of tracking down Bonnie and Clyde.

Wanted: Dead or Alive

In the month after the Eastham Breakout, Hamer studied Bonnie and Clyde's movements. He discovered that the pair kept to a fairly regular pattern that involved traveling back and forth across the Midwest. Hamer also learned that Bonnie and Clyde used specific locations to meet in the event they were ever separated from the rest of the Barrow Gang. Upon hearing that the pair had recently split off from other gang members during a chase, Hamer checked his maps for the couple's nearest rendezvous point, which turned out to be the Louisiana home of Methvin's father, Ivy. Hamer quickly held a meeting and told the posse they were heading south.

By mid-May, the posse had arrived in the tiny town of Gibsland, Louisiana. Finding that Bonnie and Clyde hadn't arrived yet, Hamer decided to set up an ambush along Highway 154, the only road into Gibsland. The posse picked a wooded location along the road and began unpacking the dozens of guns and hundreds of rounds of ammunition they had brought with them, which included armor-piercing bullets. The only thing left to figure out was how to get Bonnie and Clyde to stop their car so arrests could be made (or a clear shot could be had if they attempted to run).

Setting the Trap

Hamer came up with a solution: Ivy Methvin's truck was placed on one side of the road as if it had broken down, directly opposite from where the posse was hiding in the trees. Hamer hoped that Bonnie and Clyde would recognize the truck and stop to help Ivy. This would put the pair only a few feet away from the posse's hiding place. As for Methvin's role in all this, some say he willingly helped the posse in exchange for his son getting a pardon. Others claim the posse tied Methvin to a tree and gagged him before stealing his truck. Either way, the truck was put in place, and the posse took its position in the trees along the road on the evening of May 21.

Working in shifts, the posse waited all night and the following day with no sign of Bonnie and Clyde. They were about ready to leave on the morning of May 23 when, at approximately 9:00 a.m., they heard Clyde's stolen car approaching. At that point, Hamer and the other five men present—Texas ranger Manny Gault, Dallas deputy sheriffs Bob Alcorn and Ted Hinton, and Louisiana officers Henderson Jordan and Prentiss Oakley—took cover in the trees.

So Much for a Peaceful Surrender

The official report said that Clyde, with Bonnie in the passenger seat, slowed the car as it neared Methvin's truck. At that point, standard procedure would have been for the posse to make an announcement and give the couple a chance to surrender peacefully. Hamer, however, gave the order to simply fire at will.

The first shot was fired by Oakley, which, by all accounts, fatally wounded Clyde in the head. The rest of the posse members weren't taking any chances, though, and they all fired at the car with their automatic rifles, using up all their rounds before the car even came to a complete stop. The posse members then emptied their shotguns into the car, which had rolled past them and had come to a stop in a ditch. Finally, all of the men fired their pistols at the car until all weapons were empty. In all, approximately 130 rounds were fired.

When it was all over, Bonnie and Clyde were both dead at the respective ages of 23 and 24. Upon examination, it was reported that the bodies each contained 25 bullet wounds, though some reports put that number as high as 50. Unlike Clyde, who died almost instantly, it is believed that Bonnie endured an excruciating amount of pain, and several members of the posse reported hearing her scream as the bullets ripped into her. For this reason, many people to this day question the actions of the posse members and wonder why they never gave the pair a chance to surrender.

The Aftermath

Afterward, members of the posse removed most of the items from Bonnie and Clyde's car, including guns, clothing, and even a saxophone. Later, they supposedly allowed bystanders to go up to the car and take everything from shell casings and broken glass to bloody pieces of Bonnie and Clyde's clothing and locks of their hair. There are even reports that two different people had to be stopped when they attempted to remove parts of Clyde's body (his ear and his finger) as grisly souvenirs.

Despite Bonnie and Clyde's wish to be buried alongside each other, Bonnie's parents chose to bury her alone in the Crown Hill Memorial Park in Dallas. Clyde Barrow is interred at another Dallas cemetery, Western Heights.

Even though it's been more than 80 years since Bonnie and Clyde left this earth, they are still as popular as ever. Every May, the town of Gibsland, Lousiana holds its annual Bonnie and Clyde Festival, the highlight of which is a reenactment of the shootout, complete with fake blood. You can visit the Bonnie and Clyde Ambush Museum any time of the year.

Brazen Armored Car Heists

From Butch Cassidy to John Dillinger, bank robbers have captured the imagination of the American public. Here are some of the most brazen heists of armored cars in American history.

The Great Vault Robbery, Jacksonville, Florida: $22 million

In March 1997, 33-year-old Philip Johnson, who made $7 an hour as a driver for armored-car company Loomis Fargo, took off with one of the cars he was supposed to be guarding. Johnson pulled off the caper by waiting until the end of the night, when the armored cars returned to the Loomis Fargo vaults. Johnson tied up the two vault employees, loaded an armored car with about $22 million in cash, and took off.

He remained on the lam for more than four months, despite a half-million-dollar reward for his arrest. He was finally arrested crossing into the United States from Mexico in August 1997.

The majority of the money—which had been stashed in a rental storage unit in rural North Carolina—was recovered shortly afterward.

Dunbar Armored, Los Angeles, California: $18.9 million

Though not technically an armored-car robbery, the 1997 heist of $18.9 million dollars from the Dunbar Armored vaults in Los Angeles, is noteworthy for its meticulous planning and the fact that it is considered the largest armed cash robbery in American history.

The mastermind behind the theft was Dunbar Armored employee Allen Pace III, who used his knowledge of the vault's security system, along with his company keys, to gain access to the loot. Pace and his gang were eventually brought down when one of his cohorts, Eugene Hill, paid for something with a stack of bills banded in a Dunbar wrapper. That, plus a shard of taillight that had been the only piece of evidence left at the scene, was enough for investigators to crack the case. Despite the arrest of Pace and several coconspirators, nearly $10 million of the haul still remains unaccounted for.

Armored Motor Service of America, Rochester, New York: $10.8 million

In June 1990, a driver for the Armored Motor Service of America (AMSA) and his female partner stopped for breakfast at a convenience store near Rochester. While the female guard went into the store, a band of armed thieves attacked the driver, waited for the female guard to return, then ordered them to drive the truck to an unnamed location, where the thieves transferred the money to a waiting van, tied up the two guards, and escaped with the money. The total haul of $10.8 million ranked as one the largest heists in history. The robbery was also noteworthy for the fact that it remained unsolved for more than a decade. In 2002, though, the driver of the robbed AMSA truck, Albert Ranieri, admitted to masterminding the whole scheme.

Express Teller Services, Columbia, South Carolina: $9.8 million

In 2007, two young men overpowered an Express Teller Services armored car driver when he and his partners stopped to fuel up. They drove the car to a remote area, where two accomplices waited with another vehicle to transfer the cash. The theft of $9.8 million was one of the biggest in American history, but it wasn't particularly well executed. First, the thieves didn't bring a large enough vehicle or enough bags to take the nearly $20 million that was in the truck. Next, the bandits savagely beat one of the guards, while leaving the other one—who was later arrested as the mastermind—untouched. But the gang really did themselves in by going on a weeklong spending spree involving strippers, tattoos, and Mother's Day gifts. Not surprisingly, just about the entire gang was arrested less than a week later.

The Outlaws

Legends have often portrayed them as romantic, and even heroic, figures, but do Jesse and Frank James deserve such accolades, or have their exploits been exaggerated for dramatic effect?

A Famous Pair

For almost as long as there have been films, there have been films about Jesse and Frank James. In fact, the first two movies to feature stories about Jesse James— *Jesse James Under the Black Flag* and *Jesse James as the Outlaw*, both released in 1921—starred the famous bandit's son, Jesse James Jr. And the flattering fiction doesn't stop at movies; depictions of the brothers have been included in novels, comic books, video games, and songs, including the folk song "Jesse James," which has been recorded by Woody Guthrie, Van Morrison, Bob Seger, Johnny Cash, and Bruce Springsteen, among others.

One thing that many of these cultural depictions have in common is their portrayal of the brothers as almost "Robin Hood-like" figures. The song "Jesse James" even includes the line, "He stole from the rich and he gave to the poor." But history doesn't necessarily agree with this narrative.

War and Crime

Alexander Franklin James and Jesse Woodson James were born, respectively, on January 10, 1843, and September 5, 1847, in Clay County, Missouri. Their family, who were farmers and slaveholders, were sympathetic to the Southern cause when the Civil War broke out in 1861. Young Jesse and Frank each joined bands of Confederate guerrillas during the war, reportedly participating in the murders of dozens of civilians who were loyal to the Union.

After the war, the brothers began their soon-to-be infamous outlaw career. They are believed to be part of a group that robbed the Clay County Savings Association in Liberty, Missouri, on February 13, 1866, the first daylight armed robbery of a bank in the United States during peacetime. This began a years-long string of bank robberies for the brothers, who gradually recruited other criminals to join "the James gang." The James gang robbed banks from Missouri to Iowa to Texas, and in 1873 they branched out their criminal activity to include train robberies, stagecoaches, and stores.

For a decade, as the James gang roamed the South and West, preying upon victims, writers romanticized their exploits for readers in the Northern and Eastern parts of the country, who knew little about the West except for these tales of daring bravery they read in books and magazines. Jesse and Frank James became folk heroes, seemingly forced into their lives of crime by authorities who persecuted them for their loyalties to the South. But although they attained a reputation for being like Robin Hood, there is no evidence that Jesse and Frank ever shared any of their stolen goods with anyone outside their gang. What's more, many of their robberies ended in injured or murdered bank workers, sheriffs, or civilians.

An Ending and a Second Chance

September 7, 1876, was the beginning of the end for the James brothers. After a horribly botched robbery attempt at the First National Bank of Northfield, Minnesota, in which their entire gang was either killed or captured and only Jesse and Frank escaped, the brothers decided to keep a low profile. Jesse moved back to Missouri, while Frank headed east to Virginia. Jesse began the work of building a new gang, by recruiting brothers Charley and Robert Ford. But unbeknownst to Jesse, Robert had been secretly working with Missouri Governor Thomas T. Crittenden to bring down the outlaw.

On the morning of April 3, 1882, Jesse and the Ford brothers were at the James home preparing to leave for a robbery. In his living room, Jesse turned to rearrange a picture on the wall, and Robert Ford shot the unarmed man in the back of the head, killing him instantly. Although the Ford brothers were charged with first-degree murder, they were immediately pardoned by the governor.

Six months later, Frank James surrendered to Governor Crittenden. He was tried for only two train robberies and one murder, and found not guilty on all charges. He retired from his life of crime and lived the rest of his life a free man. He eventually returned to his family's farm, where he died on February 18, 1915, in the very room where he had been born.

Machine Gun Molly

It's not unusual for single mothers to work odd jobs in order to take care of their children. But single Montreal mom Monica Proietti found a much more lucrative way to provide for her family: robbing banks.

A Lost Childhood

Monica Proietti was born on February 25, 1940, in a poor area of Montreal, Quebec, in Canada. With eight siblings, there were few luxuries to go around, and at a young age Proietti began turning to petty crime. Not that it was entirely her own idea; her grandmother, who had spent time in jail for receiving stolen goods, taught her and other neighborhood children the tricks of the trade.

With such an awful role model, it's no wonder Proietti continued down a path of lawlessness. By 13 years old, she had dropped out of school and was arrested for prostitution, which she saw as the only way to make enough money to help her mother support her siblings. But a few years later, she settled down at the age of 17, marrying a 33-year-old Scottish gangster named Anthony Smith. Proietti and Smith had two children together, and for a short time, she relished in her new role as stay-at-home mother.

Loss and Larceny

Her simple life soon turned tragic, however, when a gas leak explosion killed her pregnant mother and three of her siblings in 1958. Proietti was dealt another blow in 1962 when Smith was caught robbing a café and deported to Scotland. With her mother dead and her husband gone, Proietti was left alone to raise her children. She struggled to find work, having no job experience and little education.

But the lonely single mother soon met a new man named Viateur Tessier, who happened to be a proficient bank robber. Like her grandmother years earlier, Tessier became Proietti's teacher in the art of bank robberies. The two began planning robberies together, carrying out heists until 1966, when Tessier was caught and sentenced to 15 years in prison. Proietti was once again a single mother.

This time, however, she knew exactly how she would support her children. In 1967, Proietti began robbing banks with several male accomplices. She started off in minor roles, acting as a lookout and getaway driver, but the men she worked with were so impressed with her calm nerves and the way she handled a gun that soon she was "promoted." Over the next two years Proietti and her crew robbed 20 different banks in Montreal, stealing a total of $100,000.

A Legend Is Born

The public wasn't used to seeing a woman bank robber, so Proietti became a hit in the media. The newspapers dubbed her "Machine Gun Molly," although she never used a machine gun. She did, however, always carry a gold-plated, semi-automatic M-1 rifle, which she often fired into the ceiling of the banks she robbed. To her credit, she never once shot or injured a person, but she loved to appear intimidating.

Even with her fame, Proietti managed to outwit the authorities for two years. She always dressed as a man when robbing a bank, using wigs and other accessories as disguises, and then dressed in very feminine outfits in her everyday life. But she couldn't hide forever, and her luck would soon run out.

According to some accounts, the robbery that Proietti planned on September 19, 1967, was always meant to be her last. She had finally grown tired of her life of crime and wanted to pull off one last heist before retiring and moving with her children to Florida. That morning, she and two accomplices robbed the Caisse Populaire, stealing around $3,000.

But their getaway didn't go as smoothly as planned. The trio ended up stealing a car and speeding away, but the police quickly found them and chased them down. Proietti lost control of the car and crashed into a bus, and her two accomplices fled the scene. But Proietti, injured in the crash, stayed in the car with her gun, firing at approaching police. They fired back, hitting her in the chest and killing her.

Proietti's death was not the end of her legend. Over the years, "Machine Gun Molly" has been featured in magazine articles, documentaries, books, a musical, and the French-Canadian film *Monica la mitraille*, released in 2004.

Out in 90 Seconds: The Story of the Stopwatch Gang

In the 1970s and '80s, Canada and the United States experienced a whirlwind of unforgettable bank heists pulled by debonair "celebrity" robbers. Even today, their story isn't over.

In October 2005, FBI agents arrested Stephen Duffy, a successful Florida real estate agent, during a security investigation involving passport fraud. They weren't actually looking for the man they found. A fingerprint check showed that Duffy was, in reality, Christopher Clarkson, a fugitive from justice who was once a member of a daring group of bank robbers known as the Stopwatch Gang. As Stephen Duffy, he'd eluded Canadian and American authorities for three decades. Time had finally run out for the last member of the most notorious and resourceful group of bank robbers since the feared Jesse James Gang of the 19th century.

Speed Demons

Speed was the essential ingredient of the Stopwatch Gang. Precision timing and painstaking planning made the thieves so successful. No heist ever exceeded 2 minutes; in most cases the robbers were in and out in 90 seconds. Becoming living legends, they held up more than 100 banks through-out Canada and the United States with panache, precision, and politeness.

The leader of the band was Patrick "Paddy" Michael Mitchell, a Canadian Irishman who, together with his partners Stephen Reid and Lionel Wright, netted somewhere between $8 and $15 million in all. Reid wore a stopwatch around his neck to time the robberies so they wouldn't exceed two minutes in dura-tion—that's how the gang earned its colorful sobriquet. Reid's favorite comment to his intended victims was, "This won't take long, folks."

If they'd stuck to robbing banks, the criminals might still be enjoying the luxury of their posh Arizona hideaway; unfortu-nately, they decided to branch out into drug smuggling. That's when Clarkson, who had some expertise as a drug runner, joined the gang. Their first attempt at smuggling cocaine into Canada, however, was a disaster, and the group was busted. Clarkson made bail and disappeared. Though he was tried in absentia and found guilty, he would remain free all those years by stealing the identity of a four-year-old California boy, Stephen Duffy, who drowned in the family swimming pool. The fate of the other gang members during those 30 years is the stuff of which legends are made.

Creative Convicts
After they were captured, Mitchell, Reid, and Wright received heavy jail sentences. All three escaped, or as it's known in urban slang, enacted "jackrabbit parole." After recapture, Reid and Wright were sent to Canadian prisons on an inmate exchange.

Mitchell engineered two daring jackrabbit paroles and is believed to be the first fugitive ever to appear on the FBI's Ten Most Wanted List twice. He was arrested for the final time in 1994 after a solo bank heist in Mississippi and sent to Leavenworth Prison. Mitchell's requests for an exchange to Canada so that he could be near his family (he married while on the lam and had a son and two grandchildren) were continually denied by U.S. authorities, who, as Mitchell expressed it, "wanted their pound of flesh."

Mitchell, known as "the gentleman bandit" due to his nonviolent approach to robbery, became a successful author and Internet blogger while incarcerated. Mitchell's blog posts were sent via snail mail to a third party who posted them in Mitchell's name on a Canadian website, where they became quite popular. As a result, his autobiography, *This Bank Robber's Life*, became a brisk seller online. Because he achieved all this while in custody since 1994, Mitchell never even knew what the Internet was like. He died from lung and brain cancer on January 14, 2007, in a North Carolina prison hospital at age 64. On January 25, his remains returned to his hometown of Ottawa, where hundreds of friends, family members, and admirers turned out for a good old-fashioned Irish wake in honor of this "gentle" bandit who loved robbing banks but never harmed a soul.

Stephen Reid, who was serving a 14-year sentence, also made good use of his time behind bars, writing a semi-fictional novel entitled *Jackrabbit Parole*. A copy of Reid's manuscript was sent to critically acclaimed Canadian poet and editor Susan Musgrave, writer-in-residence at the University of Waterloo. Susan agreed to edit Reid's novel, leading to a string of correspondence that resulted in her proposal of marriage to him. They were married in 1986, the same year that Reid's best-selling novel was published. It was Musgrave's third marriage, yet her first in the confines of a penitentiary, where the couple also spent their honeymoon. In 1987, Reid was paroled, and the couple settled down in a seaside tree house near Victoria, British Columbia, with Susan's daughter from a previous marriage, Charlotte. In 1989, the couple's daughter, Sophie, was born. It seemed like a modern fairy tale, if a little rough around the edges.

For quite some time, Stephen trod the straight and narrow. Life appeared blissful. However, as Susan's literary career continued to blossom, Reid's began to flounder. Struggling with the stress of trying to complete his second novel, Reid turned to the overriding demon in his life—heroin. He'd been addicted to the drug since his early teens

and hadn't kicked the habit. This time his addiction would have dire consequences, shattering the near-idyllic family life of the ex-con and the writer.

During the process of building a new home, Reid met Allan McCallum, a recovering drug addict. On June 9, 1999, while doing heroin and cocaine, the two men became fairly strung out and decided to rob a bank—a bad idea that ended in a worse fate. A total disaster, the heist was a careless, sloppy, ill-planned attempt and very uncharacteristic for a former member of the Stopwatch Gang. The men were captured after a chase and five-hour standoff. Reid was charged with ten counts, including attempted murder for shooting at pursuing police officers. On December 22, 1999, the 49-year-old was sentenced to 18 years in prison. After serving more than eight years, Reid was granted day parole in January 2008. This allowed him freedom during the day but required him to spend his nights at a halfway house.

Speeding Along the Straight and Narrow
It seems the only member of the Stopwatch Gang to remain outside of prison and really go straight was Lionel Wright, who cut off all contact with his former cohorts. Wright is said to be working as an accountant for Correctional Service of Canada, a division of the criminal justice system. A richer irony may be hard to find.

D. B. Cooper: Man of Mystery

D. B. Cooper is perhaps the most famous criminal alias since Jack the Ripper. Although the fate of the infamous hijacker remains a mystery, the origins of the nom de crime "D. B. Cooper" is a matter that's easier to solve.

The Crime

At Portland (Oregon) International Airport the night before Thanksgiving in 1971, a man in a business suit, reportedly in his mid-40s, boarded Northwest Orient Airlines flight 305 bound for Seattle, Washington. He had booked his seat under the name Dan Cooper. Once the flight was airborne, Cooper informed a flight attendant that his briefcase contained an explosive device. In the days before thorough baggage inspection was standard procedure at airports, this was a viable threat. The flight attendant relayed the information to the pilots, who immediately put the plane into a holding pattern so that Cooper could communicate his demands to FBI agents on the ground.

When the Boeing 727 landed at Seattle–Tacoma Airport, the other passengers were released in exchange for $200,000 in unmarked $20 bills and two sets of parachutes. FBI agents photographed each bill before handing over the ransom and then scrambled a fighter plane to follow the passenger craft when Cooper demanded that it take off for Mexico City via Reno, Nevada. At 10,000 feet, Cooper lowered the aft stairs of the aircraft and, with the ransom money strapped to his chest, parachuted into the night, still dressed in his business suit. The pilot noted the area as being near the Lewis River, 25 miles north of Portland, somewhere over the Cascade Mountains.

The mysterious hijacker was never seen again. The FBI found a number of fingerprints on the plane that didn't match those of the other passengers or members of the crew, but the only real clue that Cooper left behind was his necktie. On February 10, 1980, an eight-year-old boy found $5,800 in decaying $20 bills along the Columbia River, just a few miles northwest of Vancouver, Washington. The serial numbers matched those included in the ransom. Other than that, not a single note of the ransom money has turned up in circulation.

Origins of the Name

The FBI launched a massive hunt for the man who had hijacked Flight 305. This included checking the rap sheets of every known felon with the name Dan Cooper, just in case the hijacker had been stupid enough to use his real name. When Portland agents interviewed a man by the name of D. B. Cooper, the story was picked up by a local reporter. This D. B. Cooper was cleared of any involvement in the case, but the alias stuck and was adopted by the national media.

Who was Dan Cooper?

Countless books, TV shows, and even a movie have attempted to answer this question. The FBI has investigated some 10,000 people, dozens of whom had at some point confessed to family or friends that they were the real D. B. Cooper. In October 2007, the FBI announced that it had finally obtained a partial DNA profile of Cooper with evidence lifted from the tie he left on the plane. This has helped rule out many of those suspected of (or who have confessed to) the hijacking.

The author of one book about the case, a retired FBI agent, offered a $100,000 reward for just one of the bills from the ransom money. He's never had to pay out. Officially, the FBI does not believe that Cooper survived the jump. However, no evidence of his body or the bright yellow and red parachute he used to make the jump has ever been found. On December 31, 2007, more than 36 years after the man forever known as D. B. Cooper disappeared into the night sky, the FBI revived the case by publishing never-before-seen sketches of the hijacker and appealing for new witnesses.

Masks Only a Robber Could Love

Do bank robbers actually wear Richard Nixon masks? Or is that just something we see in the movies? You might be surprised.

Laughing on the Inside

Hollywood gave us *Quick Change* in 1990, in which Bill Murray dresses as a clown to rob a bank. In 2008's *Batman* movie *The Dark Knight*, the Joker and his gang dress in clown masks to rob a bank of their own.

In real life, a gang of six thieves, some of whom dressed in clown costumes, robbed a jewelry store in the Mexican city of Guadalajara in July 2009. They got away with at least 1.2 million pesos worth—about $900,000 USD—of stolen goods. Police, though, got the last laugh: In October, prosecutors filed robbery charges against two alleged members of the gang.

I'm Not a Crook. Well...

Patrick Swayze and company robbed a bank while wearing the masks of former presidents in *Point Break* (1991). One of the robbers wore a Richard Nixon mask, while the others wore masks of Jimmy Carter, Lyndon Johnson, and Ronald Reagan.

In October 2009, a robber wearing his own Richard Nixon mask held up a Dunn County, Wisconsin, bank at gunpoint. No word on whether he declared "I am not a crook," before he fled the scene.

He's Not Really Going Skiing

Countless bank robbers in movies and television shows have worn ski masks. In January 2009, a robber in Stow, Ohio, followed suit. Obviously having been taught the value of good manners, Feliks Goldshtein waited in line at the National City Bank branch behind several other customers. When he finally reached a teller, though, his good manners disappeared. He refused to take off his mask when asked and instead pointed a gun at the teller. The police caught Goldshtein after a chase.

Restaurant Heists

Some go to a fast food or fast casual restaurant for a quick, easy meal. Other people go for other purposes.

Macaroni Salad for Three

Even though you break into a restaurant to steal its cash register and surveillance system, it doesn't mean that there is no evidence leading back to you. Mt. Morris, New York, restaurant Build-A-Burger received justice when three burglars—who stole various electronics, cash, and a big bowl of macaroni salad—were arrested after their trail of evidence led the cops straight to them.

The cops arrived on the scene of the restaurant to begin their investigation when they discovered a trail of cash register parts, rubber gloves, and macaroni salad along the pedestrian trail behind the restaurant. After following the evidence for a short time, the trail of evidence led to the hungry burglars' hideout.

Arrested for the offense was M. Sapetko, thirty-four, J. Marullo, thirty-five, and T. Walker, twenty-three, who were later charged with fourth-degree grand larceny, third-degree burglary, and third-degree criminal mischief. According to the police report, the three men passed around the bowl of macaroni salad to eat as they escaped, leaving a mess of evidence behind them.

Although all of the other merchandise was returned to the restaurant, the macaroni salad had to be thrown away. That night, the three men were able to fall asleep in jail with their bellies full of their last meal as free men for many years to come.

Miami Ice

Miami Police arrested a man who held up a local Checkers restaurant for cash and customers' jewelry. Early that morning as the restaurant was opening, the Florida man jumped out of the storage freezer and began his heist. The customers ran outside to safety, calling 911 in hopes that the police would get there in time. They did, and the man was arrested for third-degree burglary.

The puzzling thing for the cops working the case is how long the man waited in the freezer before he began his heist. It could have been an hour or a few, but it certainly wasn't all night because it is likely the man would have frozen to death before he had a chance to make his move.

Hamburglars Foiled by the King

Two men from Stockton, California, attempted to rob a Burger King but had trouble finding their get-away car afterwards. The two criminals, J. Lovitt and G. Gonzales, entered the burger joint with their guns out and loaded at 9:45 p.m. The two men focused on one crew member and the manager to get their loot as— unbeknownst to them—the third employee snuck out the back entrance of the restaurant.

Lovitt and Gonzales packed their sacks with cash as quickly as possible in order to get back to their running getaway car parked out back, but what they didn't realize was that their car wouldn't be waiting for them. As the third employee snuck out back to call the cops, he noticed a running car that he figured belonged to the burglars. The quick-thinking employee jumped in the car and drove it around the corner, leaving the hamburglars without a fast-food escape route.

The two came running outside only to realize that their plan had been foiled. They ran around the parking lot frantically, looking for their car, but to no avail. Lovitt and Gonzales fled on foot but were soon apprehended by the Stockton Police and taken to San Joaquin County Jail. Maybe they'll be smart enough to use Grimace as a getaway driver the next time they decide to mess with the king of burgers.

Chapter 8

White-Collar Crimes

It's Probably a Con If...

From shell games to e-mail scams, nearly all con games are played the same way: The "mark" gives up something of value to get a reward that never comes. Here are a few surefire signs that you're being conned.

- You trade money for something with questionable value. "The swap" is the heart of most cons. For example, a con artist might pose as a bank examiner, standing outside a bank. He flashes a badge, "inspects" a customer's withdrawn cash, and seizes the bills, claiming they are evidence in an embezzling case. He gives the customer a receipt and sends him or her back into the bank for replacement bills. When the mark goes back in, the con artist escapes.

- You pay for future money. This basic recipe is a con staple: You hand over your own money to access much more money. For example, in one scam, an e-mail asks you to put up thousands of dollars to pay administrative fees that will unlock millions of dollars held overseas. Of course, after you wire your money, it disappears.

- You're running out of time. Con artists fog a mark's decision making by saying time is limited. The mark doesn't want to miss the opportunity and so throws caution to the wind.

- A stranger trusts you. One way to earn someone's trust is to trust them first. For example, a con man might trust you to hold onto a diamond necklace he "found," if you put up a small fraction of what the necklace is worth (say, $200). A great deal...except the necklace is really a $5 knockoff.

- Someone else trusts the stranger. Many con games involve a "shill," a co-conspirator who pretends to be like the mark. Seeing that someone else believes the con artist, the mark follows suit.

- You're misbehaving. When the mark breaks societal rules, like taking found valuables rather than turning them in, he's less likely to go to the police after figuring out the scam.

True Tales of the Counterfeit House

On a hill overlooking the Ohio River in Monroe Township, Adams County, sits a house that isn't what it seems. Its modest size and quiet exterior hide countless architectural and historical secrets— secrets that have earned it the nickname "The Counterfeit House."

In 1850, Oliver Ezra Tompkins and his sister, Ann E. Lovejoy, purchased 118 acres and built a rather peculiar house to suit the needs of their successful home-based business. Tompkins and Lovejoy were counterfeiters who specialized in making fake 50-cent coins and $500 bills. They needed a house that could keep their secrets. Although passersby could see smoke escaping from the house's seven chimneys, only two of those chimneys were connected to working fireplaces; the others were fed by ductwork and filled with secret compartments. The front door featured a trick lock and a hidden slot for the exchange of money and products, and the gabled attic window housed a signal light.

The counterfeiting room was a windowless, doorless room in the rear of the house, accessible only through a series of trap-doors. A trapdoor in the floor led to a sizeable tunnel (big enough to fit a horse) that provided an escape route through the bedrock of the surrounding hills to a cliff. Although no records exist to support the imagined use of these features, local historians believe the reports to be true.

Visitors Not Welcome

While Lovejoy was in Cincinnati spending some of her counterfeit money, she was noticed by the police. A Pinkerton agent followed her home and watched as she opened the trick lock on the front door. He waited until she was inside, then followed her in.

Immediately past the door, in a 10-foot by 45-foot hallway, Tompkins was waiting—he beat the agent to death. To this day, bloodstains are still visible on the walls and floor. Tompkins and Lovejoy buried the agent's body in one of the nearby hills, and Tompkins used the hidden tunnel to escape to a friendly riverboat, collapsing the tunnel with explosives as he went. Lovejoy held a mock funeral for Tompkins and inherited his estate, although shortly after the incident she went into debt and moved away.

Keeping Up the Counterfeit House

Although Tompkins never returned to the house, both his ghost and that of the agent are said to haunt it. Tourists have reported seeing a man's shape in the front doorway and have complained of unexplained cold spots and an unfamiliar spooky "presence."

In 1896, a great-great uncle of Jo Lynn Spires, the later long-time owner, purchased the property. It passed to Spires's grandparents in the 1930s, and Spires and her parents lived in the house with her grandfather. Although privately owned, the house was a tourist attraction, and Spires regularly kept the house clean, repaired, and ready for the stream of visitors that would trickle in each weekend. Unable to keep up with the repairs on the house, however, Spires moved into a trailer on the property in 1986. She continued to welcome approximately 1,000 tourists each summer.

In February 2008, windstorms caused severe damage to the house. One of the false chimneys blew apart, and the roof ripped off. Although Spires was able to prevent damage to the antiques and furnishings within the house, she was not able to prevent future dilapidation. After Spires passed and the house was inherited by her daughter, the attraction was closed, and the house drifted further towards ruin. Perhaps someone will find the money to someday restore—or, in keeping with the history of the house, they'll print some!

Did You Know?

Creative bookkeeping has not gone out of fashion—it's just gone corporate. In a 2005 scandal nicknamed "Coingate" by the Toledo Blade, a rare coin investment fund reported missing two coins worth more than $300,000. Coin dealer and GOP fundraiser Thomas Noe was trusted with investing Ohio taxpayer dollars in coins— $50 million worth—and made most of it disappear, covering his crime with a second set of books. Lacking any secret passageways, Noe was convicted in 2006 and sentenced to 18 years in prison.

The Franklin Syndicate

What does it take to fleece the public? Confidence, a believable lie, and something everybody wants: money. Take a closer look at the first big American pyramid scheme.

In 1898, a low-wage clerk named William F. Miller was working at a New York brokerage firm, desperately trying to support his family on meager earnings. At only 19 years old, Miller was tantalizingly close to the world of financial success but lacked the funds to participate. One evening while leading his Bible study class, Miller hit upon the idea of inviting the men in his group to invest $10 each in return for a 10 percent return every week. Though skeptical at first, the men eventually agreed, knowing that their friend had some sort of job on Wall Street.

Robbing Peter to Pay Paul

Although Miller originally conceived his scheme as a means to raise quick money to speculate in the stock market, he quickly realized that it was far easier to simply find new investors and pocket the profits. These investors, convinced by the returns being paid to the current investors, gladly contributed money and most often chose to reinvest their dividends. Miller named his new enterprise "The Franklin Syndicate" and set up a Brooklyn office. Because he promised a 10 percent return every week (520 percent per year), he quickly became known as "520% Miller."

144 Floyd Street

All of the syndicate's advertising featured the visage of Benjamin Franklin and his quotation: "The way to wealth is as plain as the road to the market." Indeed, many were beguiled into believing that the road to wealth lay in Miller's office located in a house at 144 Floyd Street. Miller soon began hiring clerks to accommodate the crush of eager investors.

At the peak of the syndicate's popularity, the house was a beehive of financial activity with 50 clerks working into the night. Miller, sitting at the top of the front porch stoop, received the cash, distributed receipts, and seemed to hardly notice as the money piled up behind him. His clerks opened correspondence, distributed dividends, and mailed advertisements. It was reputed that investors could receive or drop off money in any of the rooms, including the kitchen, parlor, or laundry.

People from as far away as Louisiana and Manitoba, Canada, sent money. The activity and evidence of so much money easily enticed even the delivery men and postal carriers to deposit their cash as well. The press of people eager to hand over their hard-earned wages was so great on one particular Friday that the stoop collapsed. At the end of each day, Miller and his clerks literally waded through knee-high mounds of cash.

Overwhelmed, Miller added Edward Schlessinger as a partner. Schlessinger helped open the Franklin Syndicate's second office in Boston. In return, he took a third of the profits away in a money-filled bag every evening.

Enter the Colonel

When the newspapers, particularly the *Boston Post* and a New York financial paper edited by E. L. Blake, began to cast doubts about the syndicate's legitimacy, Miller's advertising agent introduced him to an attorney named Colonel Robert A. Ammon. Charismatic, compelling, and utterly corrupt, Ammon incorporated the company, did battle with the press, and increasingly became the syndicate's chief behind-the-scenes operator.

When the *Post* alleged that the Franklin Syndicate was a swindle, Ammon and Miller took $50,000 in a bag to the paper's office to prove their liquidity. When a police chief referred to the Franklin Syndicate as a "green goods business" the two men repeated the display, whereupon the police chief apologized.

The Swindler Is Swindled

Miller, Ammon, and Schlessinger knew that the end was near, but only Ammon knew just how close it really was. Having fully duped Miller into believing he was acting in his best interest, Ammon prodded the young man to squeeze every last dollar from the enterprise before it collapsed.

On November 21, 1899, Miller placed $30,500 in a satchel and went to Ammon's office. Ammon advised his client to give him the money to protect it from the investors. Ammon also convinced Miller to surrender securities, bonds, and a certificate of deposit, all of which totaled more than $250,000. On Ammon's advice, Miller opened the Floyd Street office the following day, a Friday and the last best chance to gather additional funds. After work, Miller was pursued by a detective, but eluded his pursuer by ducking through a laundry and fleeing to Ammon's office. Upon learning that Miller had been indicted in Kings County for conspiracy to defraud, the lawyer convinced his client to flee to Canada.

Die in Prison or Let Your Family Suffer?

It's unclear whether Miller returned two weeks later because he missed his wife and baby or because Ammon, nervous about scrutiny being cast on his own role in the syndicate, convinced him to come back. What is certain is that, with Ammon acting as his counsel, Miller was sentenced to the maximum ten years in Sing Sing prison. Knowing that Miller was the only man capable of implicating him, Ammon gave his client's family $5 a week and reminded Miller that without the allowance his family would starve. After three years, the District Attorney finally convinced Miller, sick from his years in prison and tempted by the possibility of a pardon, to turn evidence against Ammon.

Just Desserts?

Ammon served five years—the maximum penalty for receiving stolen goods.

Schlessinger fled with $175,000 in cash to Europe where he gambled and lived well until his premature death in 1903.

Miller was released after five years in prison. He moved his family to Long Island where he operated a grocery until his death. When a man named Charles Ponzi was being tried for running a pyramid scheme 20 years later (read on for that story), a reporter from the *Boston Post* located Miller and asked him to compare his scheme to Ponzi's. Though there is no record that Ponzi knew of "520% Miller," the reporter concluded that the two men's schemes were remarkably similar.

Ponzi: The Man and The Scam

Do you want to get rich quick? Are you charming and persuasive? Do you lack scruples? Do you have a relaxed attitude toward the law? If so, the Ponzi Scheme may be for you!

Yes, there was a real Mr. Ponzi, and here's how his scam works. First, come up with a phony investment—it could be a parcel of (worthless) land that you're sure is going to rise in value in a few months or stock in a (nonexistent) company that you're certain is going to go through the roof soon.

Then recruit a small group of investors, promising to, say, double their money in 90 days. Ninety days later, send these initial investors (or at least some of them) a check for double their investment. They'll be so pleased, they'll tell their friends, relatives, neighbors, and coworkers about this surefire way to make a fast buck.

You use the influx of cash from these new investors to pay your initial investors—those who ask for a payout, that is. The beauty part is that most of your initial investors will be so enchanted with those first checks that they'll beg to reinvest their money with you.

Eventually, of course, your new investors will start to wonder why they aren't getting any checks, and/or some government agency or nosy reporter might come snooping around... but by then (if you've timed it right) you'll have transferred yourself and your ill-gotten gains out of the country and out of reach of the authorities.

Like related scams that include the Pyramid Scheme and the Stock Bubble, financial frauds like this one have been around for centuries, but only the Ponzi Scheme bears the name of a particular individual—Charles Ponzi.

Mr. Ambition Learns His Trade

As you might imagine—given that he was a legendary con man—Ponzi gave differing accounts of his background, so it's hard to establish facts about his early life. He was likely born Carlos Ponzi in Italy in 1882. He came to America in 1903 and lived the hardscrabble existence of a newly arrived immigrant. While working as a waiter, he slept on the floor of the restaurant because he couldn't afford a place of his own. But the handsome, suave Ponzi was determined to rise in the world—by fair means or foul. The foul means included bank fraud and immigrant smuggling, and Ponzi wound up doing time in jails in both the United States and Canada.

The Check is (Not) in the Mail

While living in Boston in 1919, the newly freed Ponzi more or less stumbled across the scheme that would earn him notoriety. It involved an easily obtained item called an International Postal Reply Coupon. In simple terms, the scam involved using foreign currencies to purchase quantities of a kind of international postal stamp, then redeeming the stamps for U.S. dollars.

This brought a big profit because of the favorable exchange rate of the time, and it actually wasn't illegal. The illegal part was Ponzi's determination to bring ever-growing numbers of investors into the scheme...and just keep their money. Until the roof fell in, Ponzi became a celebrity. Before long, people across New England and beyond were withdrawing their life savings and mortgaging their homes to get in on the action.

The end came in the summer of 1920, when a series of investigative reports in a Boston newspaper revealed that the House of Ponzi had no foundations. By that time, he'd taken some 40,000 people for a total of about $15 million. In 21st-century terms, that's roughly $150 million. Ponzi spent a dozen years in prison on mail fraud charges. Upon release, he was deported and continued his scamming ways abroad before dying, penniless, in Brazil in 1948.

French Assurance

A break-and-enter scene in Calgary, Alberta, had all the signs of a real crime scene—missing electronics and jewelry, a hysterical victim, smashed windows, and dirty footprints leading away from the scene. Everything seemed to add up to a robbery that left the victims with nothing, but as the case unraveled, the victims turned out to be the criminals.

Everything at the scene started to make sense as Constable Charanjit Meharu arrived and began interviewing one of the victims. The victim's phone rang, and she asked the constable to excuse her while she answered a call from her father.

The victim spoke Quebecois French to her father, explaining everything that had happened, but what she was telling her father was not what she had told the constable. Const. Meharu spoke seven different languages, and that day, his French lessons were paying off.

The victim—not knowing the constable was a polyglot and well-versed in French—began explaining her and her boyfriend's plot to make a fraud insurance claim for some extra cash. She explained over the phone how they had hid all of their jewelry and electronics, smashed their windows, and even planted fake footprints leading away from the home. She reassured him that law enforcement was buying it.

Slowly, the victims' machinations unraveled, revealing the couple not as victims but as perpetrators. As the phone call ended, Const. Meharu put away his ten pages of notes he had just taken from the phone call and said, "Merci beaucoup," startling the woman with the fact that he understood every word she said.

The couple was charged with mischief.

Con Artists, Fake Stocks, and Federal Agents: ABSCAM

What do a convicted con artist, fake Arab sheikhs, U.S. politicians, and the FBI have in common? They were all a part of a sting operation called ABSCAM in the late 1970s and 1980s.

An Elaborate Setup

In July 1978, the FBI set up an undercover operation in order to catch thieves dealing in stolen art. To help with the logistics, they brought a convicted con artist and swindler, Melvin Weinberg, and his girlfriend, Evelyn Knight, in on the plan. In exchange for their help, Weinberg and Knight—who were both facing prison sentences—were let out on probation. Weinberg helped the FBI create a fake company called Abdul Enterprises – the "AB" in ABSCAM. To make it look legitimate, Weinberg told the FBI to set up a million-dollar account under the name of Abdul Enterprises at the Chase Manhattan Bank.

Next, FBI employees posed as fictional Arab sheikhs named Kambir Abdul Rahman and Yassir Habib. The "sheikhs" were said to have millions of dollars to invest in the United States and were looking for profitable oil companies and rare art.

Weinberg suggested art thieves who might be willing to do business with Abdul Enterprises, and within a few weeks, the FBI had recovered two paintings worth $1 million. The operation then switched focus to criminals who were dealing in fake stocks and bonds: thanks to the FBI's efforts, they halted the sale of approximately $600 million worth of fraudulent securities.

Political Targets

At this point, ABSCAM began taking aim at political corruption. A forger who was under investigation approached the fake sheikhs with the idea that they invest in New Jersey casinos, saying they could obtain licensing for the "right price." So for the first time in American history, the FBI began videotaping government officials as they were approached by the sheikhs' representatives and offered money in exchange for building permits, licenses, and "private immigration bills": proposed laws that would allow foreigners working for Abdul Enterprises into the country.

Thirty-one political officials were targeted during ABSCAM, and when it was all over, one senator and six congressmen were found guilty of bribery and conspiracy. Also convicted were three Philadelphia city councilmen, and Angelo Errichetti, the mayor of Camden, New Jersey.

Errichetti was the first to be caught during the ABSCAM sting, when he accepted money in exchange for a casino license for Abdul Enterprises. Errichetti then introduced the "sheikhs" to Senator Harrison Williams and Congressmen Michael Myers, Raymond Lederer, and Frank Thompson. All would later be convicted.

Entrapment?

In February 1980, ABSCAM was made public. Some had an ethical issue with the secretive videotaping employed by the FBI, as well as the fact that Weinberg was paid $150,000 and avoided prison thanks to his part.

Many felt that the FBI was overzealous in its tactics and ABSCAM amounted to nothing short of entrapment. Still, all of the convictions due to ABSCAM were upheld in court.

Following the controversy, however, Attorney General Benjamin Civiletti issued "The Attorney General's Guidelines for FBI Undercover Operations," which formalized procedures to be used during sting operations, in an effort to avoid future debates about FBI tactics.

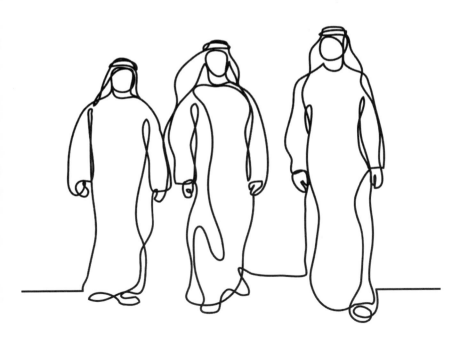

Coupon Schemes Similar to Drug Cartels

These criminals took "extreme couponing" very seriously. A little too seriously.

Phoenix police arrested 40-year-old Robin Ramirez, 42-year-old Amiko Fountain, and 54-year-old Marilyn Johnson after the trio took extreme couponing too far. The three were running a counterfeit coupon scheme, the Associated Press reported. Police recovered $40 million dollars of fake coupons from the women's homes, according to a local TV station.

Yahoo Finance reported that up to 40 major manufacturers, including Proctor & Gamble, were affected by the illegal operation. The manufacturers joined the Phoenix Police Department and the FBI to investigate and ultimately stop the illegal ring.

The fake coupons were allegedly sold through sites that eventually helped coordinate the investigation.

Police also seized $2 million in assets from the three homes, which included vehicles worth $240,000, 22 guns, and a 40-foot speed boat, according to reports. Sgt. David Lake of the Phoenix Police Department described the women's lavish lifestyles as the "equivalent of drug cartel-type stuff," according to reports.

The three suspects were charged with illegal control of an enterprise, forgery, counterfeiting, fraudulent schemes, and artifices and trafficking in stolen property.

A Charlatan of Epic Proportions

"Greed is good," said Gordon Gekko in Oliver Stone's 1987 hit movie Wall Street. *Greed resides at the center of the financial industry. For the powerful real-life stockbroker Bernie Madoff, greed knew no boundaries.*

Madoff, a well-respected broker who became chairman of the Nasdaq in 1990 and served in the position in 1991 and 1993, orchestrated the largest Ponzi scheme in history: an estimated $65 billion fraud. He conned thousands of investors and would later pled guilty to 11 felony charges—including money laundering, perjury, and fraud—and earn a prison sentence of 150 years.

Bernie Madoff was, according to the New York Times, *a "charlatan of epic proportions, a greedy manipulator so hungry to accumulate wealth that he did not care whom he hurt to get what he wanted."*

Small Beginnings

Madoff founded Bernard L. Madoff Securities in 1960. He started his firm with a paltry $5,000 he saved from lifeguarding. His wife's father allowed Madoff to work out of his Manhattan accounting firm. A market maker, Madoff dealt in over-the-counter penny stocks. He was also, Madoff would later recall in an interview, a "little Jewish guy from Brooklyn" who felt like he was on the outside looking in.

Madoff steadily grew his business—and reputation—as he embraced new trading technology and crafted friendships with industry regulators. While traders described him as obsessive, paranoid, secretive, and manipulative, Madoff earned the trust of employees, investors, and Wall Street. At the same time, Madoff was overseeing a massive con involving fraudulent transactions on an epic scale.

He later claimed that a handful of powerful clients known as the "Big Four" forced him into a Ponzi scheme beginning in the early 1990s.

A Confession

In the late 1990s, Frank Casey, an investment firm executive, asked a colleague to look into Madoff's trades. The colleague, Harry Markopolos, quickly became suspicious and suspected a Ponzi scheme. Casey told *PBS FRONTLINE* that Markopolos compared Madoff's returns to a baseball player "hitting .925 straight for 10 years in a row." Markopolos sent an eight-page memo to the SEC, but the agency did not follow up with an investigation. He wrote additional memos to the SEC, and in January 2006, the SEC launched an investigation. Finally, at the height of the 2008 financial crisis, Madoff's jig was up.

On December 10, 2008, Madoff allegedly confessed to his sons that his business was a massive Ponzi scheme. The next day, authorities arrested Madoff on one count of securities fraud, and he was released on $10 million bail. In June 2009, a federal judge sentenced Madoff to 150 years in prison. He did not appeal the sentence.

Taking Responsibility?

The Department of Justice announced in December 2017 that it had begun to return money to Madoff's many thousands of victims, such as thousands of respected individuals and institutions. The initial distribution included $772.5 million, a fraction of the more than $4 billion in assets recovered for the victims. An additional $504 million was announced in April 2018.

In a 2011 interview with Barbara Walters, Madoff said he has no fear because, "I'm no longer in control of my own life." He told Walters that he took full responsibility for his crimes, but he said, "Nobody put a gun to my head. I never planned to do anything wrong. Things just got out of hand."

Even prison hasn't keep Madoff's profit-motivating instincts at bay, however. At one point, the aging criminal reportedly purchased hot chocolate packets from the commissary and sold them for a profit in the prison yard.

Just Don't Stick Those Bills in the Washing Machine

If only the black art of money laundering were as simple as putting your cash through a spin cycle or two.

Hiding the Loot

You knock over an armored car and suddenly your mattress is overflowing with cash. But if you enjoy your ill-gotten gains by treating yourself to something big—a solid-gold yacht, say—the Feds will want to know where the money came from. And if you can't point to a legitimate source, it's off to the big house with you.

When faced with this dilemma, criminals turn to money laundering, the process of making "dirty" money look "clean"—in other words, making it appear that the money is legitimate income. For relatively small amounts of dirty cash, the go-to trick is to set up a front: a business that can record the cash as profit. For example, Al Capone owned laundromats all over Chicago so that he could disguise the income from his illegal liquor business as laundry profits (how appropriate). There wasn't any way to know how much money people really spent at the laundromat, so all the profit appeared to be legitimate.

On a larger scale—like when drug traffickers take in millions— the laundromat scheme doesn't really work, and things get more complicated. But no matter how elaborate the scheme, you can usually break it down into three basic steps: placement, layering, and integration.

Step One: Placement

In the placement stage, the goal is to get the hard cash into the financial system, which usually means depositing it into accounts of some kind. In the U.S., banks report any transaction greater than $10,000 to the authorities, so one placement strategy is to deposit money gradually, in smaller increments, across multiple bank accounts. Another option is to use a bank in a country with lax financial monitoring laws.

Step Two: Layering

The goal of the next stage—layering—is to shift the money through the financial system in such a complicated way that nobody can follow a paper trail back to the crime. In other words, the criminals are trying to disguise the fact that they are the ones who put the money into the financial system in the first place. Every time launderers move money between accounts, convert it into a different currency, or buy or sell anything—particularly in a country with lax laws—the transaction adds a layer of confusion to the trail.

Step Three: Integration

Finally, in the integration stage, the criminals get the money back by some means that looks legitimate. For example, they might arrange to have an offshore company hire them as generously paid consultants; this way, the money that they earned from their crimes enters their bank accounts as legitimate personal income.

Money laundering is big business, and it's a key foundation for drug trafficking, embezzling, and even terrorism. Many nations have enacted stricter laws and boosted enforcement in order to crack down on money laundering, but they can't put a stop to it unless everyone is vigilant. As long as there are countries with lax financial regulations that trade in the world economy, criminals will have a way to launder their funds. So, if you've been scrubbing your ill-gotten cash in the sink and hanging it on the line to dry, stop it now. You're doing it wrong.

The Fall of the Crooked E: Who Killed Enron?

For a company that seemed to have everything going its way, the end sure came quickly.

In the 1990s, the U.S. Congress passed legislation deregulating the sale of electricity, as it had done for natural gas some years earlier. The result made it possible for energy trading companies, including Enron, to thrive. In effect, the law allowed a highly profitable market to develop between energy producers and those local governments that buy electricity—a system kept in place because of aggressive lobbying by Enron and other such firms. By the turn of the 21st century, Enron stock was trading for $80 to $90 a share.

Trouble in the Waters

All was not smooth sailing, however, for the energy giant. Its new broadband communications trading division was running into difficulties, its power project in India was behind schedule and over budget, and its role in the California power crisis of 2000–2001 was being scrutinized.

Then, on August 14, 2001, CEO Jeffrey Skilling announced he was resigning after only six months in his position. He also sold off 450,000 shares of Enron stock for $33 million.

Ken Lay, the chairman at Enron, affirmed that there was "absolutely no accounting issue, no trading issue, no reserve issue, no previously unknown problem" that prompted Skilling's departure. He further asserted that there would be "no change or outlook in the performance of the company going forward." Though he did admit that falling stock prices were a factor behind Skilling's departure, Lay decided he would assume the CEO position.

Don't Worry, Everything's Under Control

Enron's financial statements were so confusing because of the company's tax strategies and position-hedging, as well as its use of "related-party transactions," that Enron's leadership assumed no one would be able to analyze its finances. A particularly troubling aspect was that several of the "related-party" entities were, or had been, controlled by Enron CFO Andrew Fastow (who may or may not have realized that he was being groomed as a scapegoat).

Sound confusing? Good, then the plan worked. And if all this could confuse government regulatory agencies, think of how investors must have felt. Stock prices slowly started sliding from their highs at the beginning of 2001, but as the year went on, the tumble picked up speed. On October 22, for instance, the share price of Enron dropped $5.40 in one day to $20.65. After Enron officials started talking about such things as "share settled costless collar arrangements" and "derivative instruments which eliminated the contingent nature of restricted forward contracts," the Securities and Exchange Commission (SEC) had a quote of its own: "There is the appearance that you are hiding something."

Things Fall Apart

The landslide had begun. On October 24, Lay removed Fastow as CFO. Stock was trading at $16.41. On October 27, Enron began buying back all of its shares (valued around $3.3 billion). It financed this purchase by emptying its lines of credit at several banks.

On October 30, in response to concerns that Enron might try a further $1–2 billion refinancing due to having insufficient cash on hand, Enron's credit rating was dropped to near junk-bond status. Enron did secure an additional billion dollars, but it had to sell its valuable natural gas pipeline to do so.

Enron desperately needed either new investment or an outright buyout. On the night of November 7, Houston-based energy trader Dynegy voted to acquire Enron at a fire-sale price of $8 billion in stock. It wasn't enough.

The sale lagged, and Standard & Poor's index determined that if it didn't go through, Enron's bonds would be rated as junk. The word was out that Lay and other officials had sold off hundreds of millions of dollars of their own stock before the crisis and that Lay stood to receive $60 million dollars if the Dynegy sale went through. But the last, worst straw was that Enron employees saw their retirement accounts—largely based on Enron stock—wiped out.

By November 7, after the company announced that all the money it had borrowed (about $5 billion) had been exhausted in 50 days, Enron stock was down to $7.00 a share. The SEC filed civil fraud complaints against Arthur Andersen, Enron's auditor. And on November 28, the sky fell in: Dynegy backed out of the deal to acquire Enron, and Enron's stock hit junk-bond status. On December 2, 2001, Enron sought Chapter 11 protection as it filed for the biggest bankruptcy in U.S. history. Around 4,000 employees lost their jobs.

So Who Killed Enron?

There was blame aplenty.

- Ken Lay and Jeffrey Skilling were indicted for securities and wire fraud. Lay was convicted on 6 of 6 counts, and Skilling on 19 of 28. Skilling was sentenced to 24 years and 4 months in prison. Lay avoided prison time by dying of a heart attack before he was sentenced.

- Arthur Andersen accountants signed off on this fraud. Why? They were getting a million dollars a week for their accounting services. The firm was convicted of obstruction of justice for shredding documents related to the Enron audit and surrendered its licenses and right to practice. From a high of more than 100,000 employees, Arthur Andersen went down to 200, before eventually dissolving.

- Investors bought stock in a company they didn't understand for the greedy promise of quick money.

- Stock ratings companies said it was a great investment, even though they had no idea what shape Enron was in.

- Investment bankers who knew that Enron was shaky bought in for a shot at quick and easy profits. They, too, are being sued by investors.

- And we can't forget the Enron employees, some of whom knew that something was fishy yet stayed silent because they were getting paid. There were a few whistleblowers, but the ones who knew and said nothing earned their places at the unemployment office.